A Jacob Family
Tramore in the 1900s

Compiled
by
Philip R. Jacob

A Jacob Family
Tramore in the 1900s

Charles, Dorothy, and Bernard B. Jacob, 1912.

Table of Contents

Chapter		Written by	Page
	Acknowledgements		5
	Introduction		7
1	Edwin and Jessie Jacob.	Philip Jacob	9
2	Charles, Kathleen & Stella Jacob, Weston and Philip – Early years.	ditto	31
3	The Cottage in the Comeraghs.	ditto	63
4	Tramore in the Thirties and Forties.	ditto	69
5	1939 – A Watershed Year.	ditto	87
6	Along the Coast.	ditto	93
7	Newtown School.	ditto	99
8	Caragh Lake.	ditto	109
9	Harvey & Son, 12 Gladstone Street, Waterford.	ditto	111
10	Dunmore East 1944-1950.	ditto	117
11	Sailing for Most of a Lifetime.	ditto	125
12	Memories of Edwin & Jessie Jacob.	Jenny (Jacob) O'Sullivan	137
13	EBJ, JEJ, BBJ & SJ	Ann Jacob	139
14	Dorothy (Jacob) Clay and Family.	Rosemary (Clay) Lawson	149
15	Clay Family Memories.	Elizabeth (Clay) Davies	173
16	Marguerite (Jacob) Skelton.	Janet (Skelton) Jerram	181
17	Memories of Tramore.	Peter Skelton	187
18	Jack Skelton.	Jack and Peter Skelton	199
19	Memories of Midvale.	Bernard A. Skelton	217
20	Our time in Ireland 1940-41.	Susan (Maguire) Hill	221
21	Ireland 1940-41.	Timothy Maguire	225
22	Reminiscences of Ireland 1948-9.	Marianne (Fischer) Johannsen	227

A Jacob Family
Tramore in the 1900s

Edwin and Jessie Jacob with family c. 1915.
Edwin, Bernard, Marguerite, Jessie, Charles, and Dorothy.

Acknowledgments

I am very grateful to the various members of the family and friends that have written their memories for inclusion, some of which were completed some years ago when I started the project. Sally Walker was highly efficient and good-natured, turning my dictation into the printed word in electronic form. David Lowe, attached to the Central Remedial Clinic's Desktop Publishing Training Unit in Dublin, deserves the greatest thanks of all. David's generous efforts and guidance in the design and production of this book, allied to his restoration expertise and treatment of the illustrations, were quite outstanding. Thanks also to David Bolger print production co-ordinator. Indeed, my thanks are also due to the many people who have given help and assistance along the way, and who have contributed to my own enjoyment in the creation of this book.

Philip Jacob

Copyright: © 2008 Philip R. Jacob and contributing relations and friends.

Published by Jacobooks,
Dublin, Ireland.
ISBN 09561167-0-3

Illustrations drawn by Philip Jacob.

Graphic Design and Print Reproduction, David Lowe,
in association with the Central Remedial Clinic DTP Training Unit,
Clontarf, Dublin 3, Ireland.

Printed by Santry Printing Dublin.

Front Cover
Photo Collage - Jacob Generations.

A Jacob Family
Tramore in the 1900s

Edwin B and Jessie E Jacob's, Golden Wedding in 1952.

Left to Right

Back row:- Weston Jacob, Hilda Shaw (later Jacob), Charles Jacob, Marguerite Skelton, Peter Skelton, Kenneth Clay, Sally Jacob.

Middle row:- Ann Jacob, Stella Jacob, Bernard Jacob, Jessie Jacob, Edwin Jacob, Elizabeth Clay, Dorothy Clay, Rosemary Clay, Lynne Jacob.

Front row:- Lesley Jacob, Jenny Jacob, Bernard Skelton, Janet Skelton.

(Jack Skelton and Philip Jacob were not present).

Introduction

Various relations have said to me in recent years that they would like to know a bit more about Edwin and Jessie Jacob, and about the family background in Tramore in the first half of the 20th Century. I started to gather reminiscences from members of the family, and also from others with whom we were closely involved, in 2003, and I have written some of my own. If there are any inaccuracies in what I have written myself, I am to blame.

This book is the result. As it has progressed one memory of mine has often sparked off another, so there is much more about my own life than I had intended. I hope it all will succeed in building up a picture of how things were in "those days". Most of what I myself have written is about the period of my childhood and adolescence. Some other chapters extend right up to the present day. Readers will notice a number of inconsistencies in dates, or particular episodes, between chapters written by different people. It is not surprising when much of it depends on memory after 50 or 60 years. I have not altered these discrepancies, or the style in which these chapters were written.

In due course I hope to write more about the period from 1950 onwards.

Philip Jacob

A Jacob Family

Tramore in the 1900s

Charles Henry, Edwin Binyon, and Charles Shuttleworth Jacob, 1904.

Chapter 1

Edwin B. Jacob and Jessie E. Jacob

Edwin B. Jacob

Edwin Binyon Jacob (hereinafter Grandpa) was born in 1868 in Cork. His parents were Charles Henry Jacob and Sarah Elizabeth Jacob. I think at that time they lived at No. 4 Hawthorne Place, College Road, Cork. The family business was a traditional grocery shop at No. 41 Princes Street in Cork. I can remember visiting the shop in the mid-1930's and the typical fragrances of a grocer's shop, in particular the smell of raisins. I would then have been 4, 5, maybe 6 years old. Edwin was the eldest of five children. Then came Thomas Bewley Jacob, Joseph Binyon Jacob, Louisa Pearman Jacob and a twin sister of Louisa called Lucy who died aged about three. In due course "Uncle Tom" and "Uncle Joe" managed the shop in Princes Street, until the 1940s, when Joe died and Tom retired to Dublin. Tom had three sons, Jack, Henry (Hal) that died very young, and Basil. Joe had one daughter, Doreen. "Auntie Lulu" married Henry R (Harry) Gorsuch, and they had four sons, Henry, Edwin, R ("Bobs") and Maurice. By the 1930s the Gorsuch family had settled in Inniscarra, Co Cork, at a beautiful spot beside the river Lee.

I don't know much about Grandpa's schooling though I think that he finished it at Wigton School in the Lake District of England, and then became a student teacher at Wigton. In 1891, when he was 23, he was invited to join the staff of Newtown School in Waterford and accepted. I have the original letter of appointment signed by Edward Garnett. I am sure he made a very good teacher. He was kind, patient and had a wide breadth of knowledge on all sorts of subjects. He was particularly interested in botany and, on occasion when he had the boys out for a walk and one of him asked him what such and such a flower was beside the road, he would say "well, that is roademsidem communis". In other words, he didn't know what it was but it was a fairly common roadside plant! Photographs of him at that time show he was starting to go bald and had a moustache (which he wore for the rest of his life).

He clearly became an integral part of the Quaker community in Waterford which, in those years, was numerous and strong. He would have become known to Thomas Newenham Harvey, the proprietor of two businesses, one of which was a printer called N. Harvey & Co.

The other was a services business called Harvey & Son. At that stage this was mainly a house agency that specialised in looking after the estates of Waterford families owning a number of houses that were rented out - rents were collected and repairs were organised by the firm, as well as Insurance, an Emigration Agency, and Stockbroking. Harvey & Son also included the Waterford Working Men's Penny Bank. This had been started by a Harvey forebear in the mid-1800's so that people in Waterford could save their small surplus and earn some interest on it, and could withdraw it for Christmas, or whatever else they might need it for. The "Penny Bank" (which had a full Banker's Licence) continued until 1974 when it was acquired by the City of Dublin Bank Limited. T. N. Harvey had no-one in his own family to succeed him. Clearly he thought highly of Grandpa and left him a half share (with Louis Jacob) in Harvey & Son, and thus began half a century working at 12 Gladstone Street.

The Whites were one of the strong Quaker families in Waterford at that time. Ernest Albert White and Sarah Holmes White his wife (who came from England) lived at 1 St. Andrew's Terrace near Newtown School.

An attractive young Quaker from Halstead in Essex called Jessie Elizabeth Baker came to help look after their eight children (including Lucie Dorice, the fifth, and Kenneth Coleby, the eighth, who is mentioned in Chapter Nine in connection with my father, Charles). Edwin and Jessie would have seen each other quite frequently at Meeting for Worship and other times, and they fell in love and married in 1902. They set up house at No. 15 Percy Terrace, a modest redbrick house just off John's Hill and quite near to Newtown School. On 5th April, 1903 their first-born Charles Shuttleworth Jacob (my father) arrived and during the next few years the family expanded with the birth of Bernard Binyon Jacob, Dorothy Elizabeth Jacob and, in 1910, Marguerite Moss Jacob, their fourth and last child, by which time, for health reasons, they had moved to Tramore.

Jessie E. Jacob

"Grandad" Baker, Jessie's father of Halstead, Essex.

Jessie (Baker) Jacob's parents, "Grandad" and "Little Granny" Baker, with her brother Geo and sister Win.

A Jacob Family
Tramore in the 1900s

Uncle Geo Baker and his wife Aunt Eunice, 1930.

Elizabeth (Little Granny), Jno (Grandad Baker), and driver Uncle Geo Baker.

At first they temporarily rented a house on Tivoli Terrace near the railway station and then moved to "Midvale", a relatively new four bedroomed house at the other end of Tramore which they rented from the Walsh family for the ensuing 50 years or so. The Walsh's lived in the other half of the semi-detached house. Florrie and Ena Walsh were still there when Weston and I were growing up, and we knew them well, but the two households were quite content not to impose themselves on each other.

MIDVALE

Jessie (hereinafter called "Granny") entered into the life of the community in Waterford but kept up a lively correspondence with her sister and brothers in Halstead. Our generation always referred to them, as Auntie Win (short for Winifred), Uncle Lance, Uncle Ted (short for Edward) and Uncle Geo (pronounced Jo, short for George).

Grandpa had a very considerable influence on his growing children, and in his late seventies my father Charles Jacob wrote the following about him. It gives a good pen-picture of his father.

(In the following section in italics, where the words "father" and "mother" are used it is of course Charles speaking of Edwin or Jessie)

"I think that the first seven years of my life were largely moulded by the fact that my brother Bernard was very seriously ill as a baby and required a good deal of my mother's attention for several years – my early impressions of our family life mainly centred on my father. Of course my mother was always part of the family scene – I see her in my mind's eye clearly, making brown yeast bread in the kitchen at 15 Percy Terrace and can still get the rich smell of the loaves as they were turned out of the tin. The kitchen was at the end of the hall and the big coal range seemed to fill the end wall, shining with black lead, the copper water pipes polished and looking very satisfying somehow in the soft light of the oil lamps.

"My earliest picture of father (I can only have been about 6 years of age) is again in the warm light of an oil lamp this time in the Percy Terrace sitting room, and the lamp with its white glass shade over a cut glass bowl for the oil, supported on a polished brass pillar rising from a strong and heavy metal base.

A Jacob Family
Tramore in the 1900s

Father and I were sitting at a table, and he was making a clock face for me to learn to tell the time. He had a nice piece of three-ply wood (about 8 inches square), which he had sand papered smooth, and covered by a piece of azure paper which he had pasted on. He drew a circle in Indian ink using a rather elaborate compass which I think came from a very old set of drawing instruments, each in a special slot in a shagreen covered case, which was old and treated with the care which its age and usefulness deserved. He divided the circle into twelfths, and the figures were put in. Then father took two clock hands which he had made from corset whalebone and had filed a point on each, which we then bolted to the centre of the clock face with a tiny nut and bolt, and so I learned how to tell the time.

"In recalling these impressions I realise how very fortunate I am to have had such a home. My mother, making nutty flavoured brown bread which looked nice, and smelled nice, her kitchen with the soft light of the oil lamp, the big warm range with bright polished edges and copper pipes, and my father and I working on the table in the circle of light. And while it was being made I was told all about whales and whalebone. All so simple, but lasting, and cared for, and orderly – and I felt privileged to be part of it.

"On Sunday mornings father and I would walk down via John's Hill, Michael Street and George's Street to the old Quaker Meeting House, a few yards from the quayside and the River Suir. Our Sunday morning meeting for worship was an important part of the week.

"Some time previously father had told me about the "Father Matthew", a steam tug which J. Ernest Grubb of Carrick-On-Suir had bought for towing barges from Waterford to Carrick with all sorts of merchandise (except alcoholic drink) for his shop and warehouse in Carrick. It was the first (and only) steam tug on the Suir above Waterford and was a low lying shallow-draft craft with a powerful engine. On this occasion father had made sure that the "Father Matthew" would be in Waterford, so we walked round by the river on the way home and down onto a pontoon where he showed me the tug and explained her excellent features. I can remember well the look of the boat but I was rather disappointed because she had no Captain's Bridge and no distinctive funnel. I must have been told a good deal about the boat because I was well aware of Ernest Grubb's courageous venture in buying her, and the increased traffic she could handle, being able to pull the barges whatever the state of the tide or current (the Suir is tidal up as far as Carrick). Maybe she did away with the need for horses for towing – I don't remember.

"Another "after Meeting" adventure I recall equally clearly. Mother had put up a sandwich lunch for us and father and I walked down along the river quays again and this time to the ferry hulk which was just beyond Reginald's Tower. From here a regular ferry service brought passengers across the river to a slip near the Abbey Church. The ferry boat was a heavy beamy craft with two oarsmen rowing with a large and clumsy sweep to each man. I was interested in the diagonal course the boat had to take rowing across the current. Our object on the Kilkenny side of the river was to visit a railway carriage shed which later became the Tyresoles factory building. Here father sought out the caretaker of the shed and gave him, I think, a half a crown (two shillings and sixpence) and in return we were let in to the shed where we saw two rows of carriages all polished and clean and we were allowed to climb into a first-class compartment to eat our sandwiches there. The caretaker man and father had a good old chat about railways generally and carriages and engines. The Rosslare line had been opened not long before and some of the carriages specially built for that express service were in the shed as far as I can remember. At any rate, the man was very pleased that somebody had been sufficiently interested to visit him and his carriages and I remember him as a nice, polite and interesting man!

"We then walked a half a mile along the Rosslare railway line to Cromwell's Rock and inspected the big boilers and pipes and pressure chambers where the railway sleepers for this new line, had been treated with creosote under steam pressure, to protect them from rotting. Then we walked back to the ferry and so home again - it was a nice sunny day and we saw a great many interesting things concerning the river and the railway line, which father pointed out to me and explained.

"From the back windows of No. 15 Percy Terrace we could see down over South Parade to the gasworks. Every now and again a cloud of steam and smoke arose, whenever the retorts were being emptied of their coke. Father took me down one afternoon to see this operation but I don't remember much about it except the heat, the steam and the smell. He showed me the big gasometers, and explained how they rose and fell with the quantity of gas in them, and the chains and pulleys and counterweights that offset the weight of the big cylindrical upper half of the gasometer, as it rose and fell with a water seal that prevented the gas from escaping. All this was interesting, but what really caught my imagination and what I can still remember clearly, was his experiment to show me how the gas was driven off when the retorts, full of coal, were heated, leaving coke behind.

"First of all we went to the shop of a tobacconist on Waterford Quay who was a client of my father's. Here we bought a long stemmed "Churchwarden" white clay pipe. This had to be brought home with great care so as not to break it. Then father produced a small lump of pipe clay which he had got from the clay pipe factory in John's Lane. The next step was to choose some small lumps of clean shiny coal and hammer them into small pieces. These were loaded into the bowl of the pipe and sealed in by a good capping of pipe clay. This gave us a retort and father made a nice red fire in the sitting room and into this placed the loaded pipe bowl with the long stem of the Churchwarden sticking out to the front through the bars of the grate. The red hot coal was carefully raked around the little retort and we watched the end of the pipe stem very intently. Nothing happened for quite a while, and we began to wonder whether all was going as it should, when a little wisp of smoke appeared. Great excitement!

A Jacob Family
Tramore in the 1900s

Father lit a match and applied it and the coal gas burned with a whistling flame shooting out from the pipe stem. It was all very exciting and completely successful and was a dramatic demonstration of an interesting manufacturing process. You can imagine how the brightly burning flame shooting out of our simple apparatus in our darkened sitting room provided a memorable picture for a young lad. Incidentally, the manager of the gasworks was also a friend of father's, through his work at the office.

"Looking back I think this was a wonderful exercise in the development of awareness in a young boy of 8 or 9 years and confirms my feeling that father must have been a very good teacher when he was at Newtown.

"Another Waterford business that opened up an aspect of life that was of great interest to me was a small iron foundry owned by Ben Graham and his brother situated through an archway beside the Clyde Shipping Company office on Waterford Quay near the Post Office. I think I must have asked him what was "pig iron" because one day I was taken to the foundry on the occasion of the tapping of the furnace when the red hot molten iron was drawn off and ran into a series of moulds in the sand of the floor of the foundry which ran in parallel lines and right angles so that when it cooled it was in the pattern of a litter of piglets. We had to keep well away from this operation because any dampness in the sand would have caused a small explosion that would have spattered molten metal around and might have damaged things including us! The possibility of this was fully explained to us by Ben Graham and so we realised how the red hot liquid iron could be lethal. After that I took a special interest in the manhole covers all round Waterford to see which were produced at Grahams Foundry.

"Father was always interested in ships, especially big ships such as the Atlantic liners that called regularly at Queenstown (now Cobh). Because of this he applied for appointment as Waterford Agent for several of the larger shipping companies. He had a fairly steady business with them and became known as an Emigration Agent – so much so that in about 1918 he received a stern warning from the local IRA (Irish Republican Army) telling him to do no more booking of Irish young people to America or else he would attract Republican attention!

"Of course, as a shipping agent, he received invitations from time to time to visit the big ships at the company's expense. One such invitation came from the Orient Line to visit one of their newest vessels, the Orsova, in Tilbury Docks London. Anyhow, father decided to accept and he greatly desired to have me with him although I can only have been about 8 years old. The company were very sympathetic provided that I would be fully insured against every possible eventuality. This was got over and we set out by the "Great Western" steamer direct from Waterford to Fishguard and on to London. When we got to Tilbury Docks there was a good deal of shunting backwards and forwards with trains on the other lines, and we finally drew up alongside the big ship. She seemed immense to me. Up the gangway with us and then we were soon led into the dining saloon and given a sumptuous meal, but the only aspect of this that I can remember is that, for the first time in my life, I had soup with little bits of what seemed to be to be baked custard floating in it. After the meal father (and I) with all the other agents were taken on a tour of the accommodation. The whole adventure made a great impression on me and I can remember various details very clearly though it was over 70 years ago.

"In our Sunday walks along the quayside, father pointed out to me a number of very fine logs of mahogany which were moored to the floating pontoons down by the old Adelphi Quay [note by PRJ - now, in 2008, these pontoons have been replaced by a yacht marina, having been in the meantime used for many years in connection with lairage for the cattle, which were then exported on the Great Western to Fishguard]. He explained to me that these logs were left in the water for a year or more, so that all the sap would be washed out of them, and they would then be slowly dried out by Graves & Co. Limited (timber merchants). Father knew the proprietors of Graves and he got permission for us to see over the big shed with all the saws and planing machines in it. Graves had only recently installed an engine which drove the fans in a system of ducts from all the machines so that the sawdust was sucked away and piped to the "gas" engine where it burned and drove a big flywheel providing the power for all the machinery. I had never seen a planing machine and the circular saws that cut up the big logs - they were rather frightening, making a shrill noise as they worked. The timber (mostly deal) was cut into planks, and all the other sizes that the building trade required. For flooring the planks had then to be planed with tongues and grooves.

"Graves were the largest builders' providers in Waterford. At one stage they had an inviting notice outside their gate which said "Graves Are Open"! Much of the timber they processed and sold, came by sea from Scandinavia and elsewhere, so they built a jetty of their own to accommodate the ships, on which they had a small electric crane. Waterford was one of the first cities in Ireland to have its own electricity station (before the ESB) which was situated by the river, beyond Waterpark College, not far from Newtown. This station had a short but useful life, for a few years, and then it was acquired by the ESB. In due course Graves graduated to a much larger crane for unloading the timber. Harry Elmes (whose father was one of the proprietors of Graves) told me that strong objection was made to the company installing this crane by the Labour element on the Corporation, who maintained that it would mean that fewer men would be employed unloading the timber from the ships. The Labour element in Waterford campaigned vigorously but ineffectually against the crane, and there was some unfortunate high feeling on the matter." (This is the end of Charles's reminiscences of his father, Edwin).

A Jacob Family
Tramore in the 1900s

It is natural for my father, Charles, in his latter years to have written down his memories of my grandfather (Edwin) and not of my grandmother (Jessie) because even after he "left home" Charles remained closely involved with Grandpa. They worked together in Harvey & Son from the early 1920's to the early 1960's. Nevertheless Granny was an important part of his life before he left home, and I will say more about her later.

Grandpa was the quintessential solid Victorian middle class man, quiet, utterly reliable, of complete integrity and a man of habit. He was deliberate in all that he did, never fussed, just got on with things, kind, considerate and with never a hard word to, or about, anyone. Money making was not a priority for him. Married in his mid-thirties, by the time I first knew him (in the mid 1930's), I was 3 or 4 and he was about 67. By that time the top of his head was bald, but he was still very active! He liked gardening, vegetables being his main concern. He had a friendly rivalry with his distant cousin Willie who lived at the other end of Tramore over the progress of their tomatoes. Grandpa had a small greenhouse. He was a devotee of the compost heap which he called "the pile" – it was long, rectangular, and not enclosed. He would cut off and use the compost at one end and put fresh vegetable material on the other end and when the cut face reached about half-way he started piling fresh material back at the beginning again. Every autumn he collected leaves from the footpath outside the gate, picking them up and putting them in the wheelbarrow with two ply-wood "hands". Weston and I used to help him with this when quite small. He always carried pocket scissors with him and used these to snip off any trailing brambles that were growing out of the hedge, so that pedestrians would not get scratched.

Between the vegetable garden, and the front garden and gravel, there was a long, straight lawn edged with roses and herbaceous plants called the "grassy walk". At the foot of the vegetable garden there was the "hut", which was his workshop, his storage place for garden tools and everything to do with his bees. The garden included some not very productive apple trees and a small forest of raspberry canes. The top of the grassy walk opened on to the "back grass" which was surrounded by a clipped macrocarpa hedge. When Weston and I were small boys we made a "den" under one end of this hedge and spent a lot of time there in the summer – our secret place.

For many years Grandpa kept bees – at one stage up to 12 hives. His calm temperament was ideal for a beekeeper. I will never forget the smell of beeswax, the acrid smoke from the smoker in which he used rolled up corrugated cardboard, and the cloth impregnated with carbolic. We would put on veils and, if the bees weren't too angry at the time, EBJ would show us how the frames worked, how to spot the queen bee and the queen cell, how to deal with surplus queens, the building up of the cells by the workers, the brood cells and the honey cells, the separator and the "super", the sections for "section honey", etc. I don't remember ever wearing gloves, so I think he must have been very careful that we didn't come too near at the wrong time.

Jessie (Baker) Jacob, Charles S. Jacob, James S. Baker. c. 1904.

Geo, Lance, and Ted Baker (Jessie's Brothers).

A Jacob Family
Tramore in the 1900s

Lance and Becky with Kathleen (KB).

There was great excitement in the autumn when the frames containing honey were brought into a warmed-up kitchen, the caps sliced off with a special knife, the frames inserted in the rotary extractor and the handle at the top of the extractor turned round and round so that the honey ran out of the cells by centrifugal force and, lo and behold, came out of a tap at the bottom of the extractor cylinder as golden liquid flowing into the ready waiting jars. It was exciting, hot, everything got sticky, and the odd few bees that had come in with the frames were all too inclined to sting.

Many years before a well had been drilled behind the house, and there was a hand pump standing about five feet high with a long curly-ended handle. The water was mainly used for the garden, and a long pipe delivered the water to "the pond" which was simply an old cast iron potato boiler, possibly from the time of the famine, sunk near the top of the grassy walk, from which buckets of water could be taken. It always had a wire netting cover to stop small children from falling in.

Also, at the back of the house, there were usually some logs for chopping. Henry Ford is reputed to have had a motto "He who cuts his own firewood warms himself twice".

Midvale had a small enclosed back yard with a coal shed, and an outside flush toilet which was never used. As a small boy I couldn't understand why anybody would want to go outside to use the WC.

Among my earliest memories of Grandpa are of him sitting beside the fire in the sitting room after his evening meal with a drawing board on his knees and the canvas for a woollen hearth rug clipped to it, knotting the wool carefully and patiently according to the pattern. He had a natty little gadget that you held in one hand and turned a handle with the other hand and fed the ball of wool in at one side and exactly the correct cut lengths of wool came out the other side. Perfect occupational therapy for a very small boy.

As I am sure was the case in many families, the monthly arrival at Midvale of the National Geographic Magazine was eagerly awaited by us boys.

At meal times I often found myself sitting beside him. We would all say a silent grace before the meal with our hands resting on the table and he would put his hand over my wee paw thus enveloping it in a most comforting manner. We were always intrigued by his oval shaped silver serviette ring which, when rolled across the table cloth, went up and down like a yo-yo. He always wore a waistcoat and, at meal times, would tuck the corners of his white linen serviette (they were never called table napkins in our family) into the armpits of his waistcoat, keeping the serviette from slipping down, and thus protecting his clothes from any spillages.

He was very patient, forgiving and non-judgmental when, aged about six, I purloined one of his razor blades from the bathroom to do a bit of wood carving – I sliced a hunk of skin off the knuckle of my forefinger in the process, and I imagine he thought that was sufficient rough justice!

A Jacob Family
Tramore in the 1900s

Waterford Friends outside the Meeting House, about 1925.
Top row from left: Bernard 3rd, Charles 9th.
Front row from left: Dorothy 2nd, Kathleen, 3rd, Jessie 4th, Marguerite 9th.

The Jacob Family 1934.
Back: Bernard, Jessie, Edwin, Dorothy, Charles, Doreen,
Front: Philip, Weston.

He normally rode his bicycle to the Tramore Railway Station, put it in the bicycle van (which had in a previous existence been a van for carrying coffins) and then cycled from the Waterford Railway Station to the office. In his latter years when he got a bit arthritic, he had a special step fitted to the rear hub so that he could mount the bike more comfortably.

During the troubles in 1921/2 Grandpa was respected by both sides – once one side tried to extract money from him at the office but he managed to persuade them against it.

In 1939 when it became urgent for anyone with any Jewish connections to leave Middle Europe, Quakers in England facilitated many refugees to enter their country and some were then sent on to Ireland. Grandpa undertook to meet refugees arriving at Rosslare and accompany them to Ardmore where a house owned by Sir John Keane of Cappoquin was made available as a temporary stopping place – this reception centre was looked after by Mary and Ruth Odell that I have mentioned elsewhere. Two of the refugees, Fritz and Mirza Marckwald, stayed at Midvale with my grandparents for quite a while to improve their English, and our family maintained a close friendship with them until they died in Waterford many years later. Also, on the outbreak of World War II, Bernard (Bun) and Sally Jacob (who by then lived in Saffron Walden, Essex) asked EBJ and JEJ could they look after Bun and Sally's adored baby Ann until things in England looked safer. So, for a year or two "Baby Ann", a most attractive little girl with curly blond hair and a ready smile, was a great addition to the Midvale and Summerville households, until it was deemed safe for her to re-join her parents in England. Anne is the Author of Chapter 13.

In the late 1940's the two Misses Robinson, (aunts of Florence Bell) who lived near to Midvale, (and who both worked in Waterford) bought a new car and offered to bring Grandpa to the office in Waterford every day, which was gratefully accepted. Sometimes I got a lift too!

One of my father's regular reminiscences when he was nearing the end of his life was a remark made by Maxie Halley, a well know Waterford solicitor, "if there is one man I'd trust completely to look after my affairs it would be Edwin Jacob".

During the period after our mother died Weston (aged 5), and I (aged 3), were often looked after at Midvale for part of the day. On one occasion we arrived at Summerville on our own, having walked, and crossed the road, by ourselves (all of 200 yards), and Weston explained how we had managed by saying "I minded Philip and Philip minded me".

I find it harder to recall memories of our grandmother, Jessie Jacob (or "granny" as we invariably called her). This is strange because we were in her care for much of the two years between my mother's death and my father's marriage to Stella, but of course I was only 3 or 4. Midvale was near our home, Summerville, although it was necessary to cross the road on the way. It was not a very busy road, albeit the main coast road, but there was a crossroads on the way with vehicles coming downhill to it from three directions at speed.

A Jacob Family
Tramore in the 1900s

Granny knew her Bible well, had a strong faith, and put it into practice in her own life, but did not press it on others. I still treasure the Bible she gave me on my 21st birthday. She was a real beauty when young. She was very good at befriending friends, neighbours and acquaintances if she felt they could do with a helping hand or were lonely. One fortuitous result of this was our friendship with Mrs. Lily Finnegan, a widow who lived on Love Lane a few hundred yards from Midvale. She was from Ireland, had got married and then emigrated to Canada but sadly her young husband was killed by a burglar shortly after, and she then came back home. "Mrs Lily" was a natural teacher, and Weston and I went to school in her little bungalow until we were 8 or 9 years old. This gave us a first rate grounding in reading, writing, sums, handwork, geography, good manners and everything else that it is useful for a youngster to know (except outdoor sports!). I particularly remember making little models of steam engines, carriages and other things out of matchboxes, matchsticks, pieces of cardboard, cotton reels, elastic bands, gum, etc. In her tiny garden she had what she called the "look-out" which was a wooden platform about three feet square and three feet high with a railing round it and a ladder up. This was the Captain's Bridge, or the Nobleman's Castle, or anything else we pretended it to be.

Among the people that Granny befriended I remember Annie Rodgers, Katherine Walpole, Ruth and Mary Odell, Cherry Robson, Maggie Byron, and also of course Fritz and Mirza Marckwald – about whom I will say more later on.

Granny was a wonderful letter writer – almost every day she sent off at least one letter in the post – her handwriting, which she tossed off at great speed, was little more than a succession of circles so it took quite a bit of interpreting! Granny never lost her sense of wonder at the world around us – she loved looking at the stars at night, and on the few occasions when the Northern Lights, or aurora borealis, appeared, she was enraptured. Highlights of the many times that Weston and I stayed at Midvale for shorter or longer periods were Granny's rock buns with raisins and sultanas which she tossed off in a twink and we thought were delicious. We also loved "dip" which was simply fried bread dipped into fried tomatoes. As part of her "healthy eating" regime, Granny used to get special health foods from Heath and Heather, some of which we thought delicious, especially their fruit and nut cake. If ever she had an upset tummy she would simply fast for a couple of days and was then right as rain (though I wondered at that tender age why something should be right as rain – I preferred the days that were not raining). In common with many of her generation Granny wore her hair in a bun. Not surprisingly Granny was a great admirer of Gandhi and she also thought highly of Smuts in South Africa – she used to talk to Weston and me about world affairs quite a lot. She was a supporter of the Friends' Service Council, the organisation through which British and Irish Quakers channelled their (mainly overseas) aid programmes. Grandpa was also a life-long and committed Quaker.
He served as Yearly Meeting Clerk for a period, and was chosen as a participant in a significant visit by Irish Quakers to Meetings in the USA.

For some years Mrs. Crowley who lived three or four miles away near Garrarus Strand helped to do the housework at Midvale. She was an elderly countrywoman of the best type – salt of the earth, and one of the last remaining shawlies, using a black shawl over her head and wrapped around her as standard outdoor garb. Mr. Crowley was a very competent handyman, in spite of the fact that his left hand had not grown properly and was the shape of a potato with five small sprouts out of it. He amazed me by being able, with this left hand, to push a nail into timber so that it would stand up ready to be hammered home. Another member of the Crowley family worked all day every day drawing sand and gravel by horse and cart from Garrarus Strand to the public road, where it was transferred into lorries.

Ellie Cahill

Then there was Ellie (Cahill). Ellie lived on Poleberry in Waterford near the train station, and was left a widow when her children were quite young. She came to Midvale every week to help Granny in the house. Her youngest, David, sometimes came with Ellie and spent the day at Midvale too. He was in the garden one day when EBJ was digging, and the fork turned up some worms. Young David pointed at them and said "Wurrums, wurrums, loog-er-um". This has become a favourite saying in the Jacob household. Ellie had a daughter called Frances who had an artistic bent and later became a designer for Waterford Glass.

The milk was delivered to Midvale by Katie on behalf of her brother Peery in his cart, being drawn by a donkey called Julia, which was exhorted to greater effort by saying "G'won Jooolya" – this was one of Marguerite's favourite memories in her later years. One day Peery, when asked did he think the day's weather was going to improve, looked up at the sky and then after a pause said with great gravity "She's strugglin' ma'am".

Katie on the milk cart drawn by Julia the donkey, 1930.

A Jacob Family
Tramore in the 1900s

Granny sometimes brought us to visit Mrs. Elmes at her attractive house in Ballycarnane (but pronounced Ballycarney), a few hundred yards up a lane behind Midvale. We were regaled there with delicious scones buttered and jammed.

Every Sunday morning when leaving the house Granny would pick a sprig of sweet briar and pin it to her lapel, and thus was able to enjoy the fragrance all through Meeting! Midvale was a very welcoming place, with the open smiling faces of Clematis Jackmanii around the porch, and the hallway with an old-fashioned wind-up phone and a cuckoo clock standing on the hall cupboard. The cuckoo clock is now in my possession and is still in good working order. In the sitting room small boys were allowed to drape a rug over the back of the sofa to make a "den". Small boys were also encouraged to keep the gravel raked. Upstairs the beds had eiderdowns and soft pillows and on special occasions a fire was lit in one of the bedrooms too (which gives me the horrors to think about now). It was luxury personified. Apparently once when I, as a very small boy, was given a birthday present of nice new shiny Wellington boots I was found later, fast asleep, lying on one of the beds wearing nothing but the Wellington boots. A family of swifts nested under the eaves and the screeching sound of their calls as they flew around the end of the house is now as clear in my memory as if it was yesterday.

Arum lilies and red hot pokers are two flowers that always make me think of Midvale. There was a substantial latticed wooden summer house in the garden which could be opened up to let in the fresh air. I believe this was used for my father's convalescence as a boy after a serious illness. When Granny and Grandpa's four children were grown up but had not yet left home I am told they had great fun, when doing the washing up, lustily and tunefully singing a whole variety of songs together. Charles was usually called "Chas", Bernard "Bun", Dorothy "Pol" and Marguerite "Mossy"

In 1939 a first cousin of Grandpa, Annie Jacob, of Colwyn Bay in North Wales, died and, to his surprise and grateful pleasure, left some good furniture to Grandpa and also some money which enabled him to buy a house in Dublin for Marguerite and Jack Skelton who had just been married.

"Fast forward" to the mid-1950s. Granny and Grandpa moved into Summerville when my father and Stella moved to Waterford. Before long however Grandpa became too much for Granny to look after and he had to move to a nursing home, in Dublin. He died in 1958, but not before his first great-grandchild Owen was born. Owen is the eldest of Brigid's and my family (and by pure coincidence his fiftieth birthday is at the end of the week in which I am typing these words). Granny lived on for a while with Mrs O'Byrne, in Dublin, on Upper Leeson Street, and Marguerite visited regularly, but then moved to Waterford and was looked after by Charles and Stella at their newly built house, Ard Mor, until she died in 1963. Sadly, her declining years were not a happy period for her, first moving from Midvale, which had been her home for 50 years, to Summerville, then Grandpa having to go into a nursing home, then his death, and the various other moves and changes that became necessary.

Halstead, Essex, Jessie Jacob's home town.

*Edwin and Jessie Jacob.
in front of the Garden Room, Summerville, 1955.*

A Jacob Family
Tramore in the 1900s

Dickie Beale on his 499 cc Ariel Motorbike, about 1930.

Bull Nosed Morris Car 1930.
Back row: Marguerite, Edward Baker of Halstead, Walter Gough (car's owner).
In car: Dorothy Jacob, Weston Roberts (Kathleen's father) Lily Finnegan, Jessie Jacob.
Front row: Bernard and Edwin Jacob.

Young Friends Camp.

A Jacob Family
Tramore in the 1900s

*Marriage of Charles Jacob and Kathleen Roberts (centre front),
at Enniscorthy Meeting House, 14th September 1927.
Bernard, Dorothy, Lizzie, Tom, Lulu,
Edwin, Jessie, Marguerite.*

*Back: Marguerite, Bernard, Kathleen, Charles, Dorothy.
Front: Jessie and Edwin.*

Chapter 2

Charles, Kathleen, and Stella Jacob
Weston and Philip's Early Years

Edwin and Jessie Jacob's first child, Charles Shuttleworth Jacob (my father), was born in 1903. His middle name, Shuttleworth, which has caused amusement down through the years, will be explained at some later date in my notes on the family tree. Because his brother Bernard had poor health when living in Waterford, the family moved to Tramore before 1910, and "Midvale" became their home. My father had a serious dose of Scarlet Fever at "Midvale" but was successfully nursed back to health, though I believe his eyesight was affected and was the reason he had to wear spectacles.

It was a lively and happy household. Father, Bernard, Dorothy and Marguerite got on well together, and Bernard in particular was a live wire. They enjoyed walking, swimming, camping and cycling. Father particularly remembered one summer when they camped near the "Metal Man", two or three miles from Tramore along the coast. There were also close connections with Newtown School, and with the headmaster James Clark and his family - one of whose daughters, Susette, later married Hubert Poole – the Pooles remain good friends of our family after many years.

In due course he went as a boarder to the Quaker school, Bootham, in York, which he enjoyed and benefited from. He was given the nickname of "Azcoom" when he arrived. The previous term the school play had been on a biblical theme and one boy with a broad Yorkshire accent had to speak the line "and Jacob has come" so when Jacob arrived next term the nickname was almost automatic.

After leaving school he started work in Harvey & Son, primarily looking after the stockbroking business while his father, Edwin B, looked after the expanding travel agency, Thomas Frederick Harvey Jacob (cousin Frederick) looked after the house agency, and all three had a care over the Waterford Working Men's Penny Bank and the insurance agency. During the 1920's father was active among young Friends, both on a local basis and among Quakers all over Ireland. He was obviously a good organiser and I still have his camping notebooks and lots of photographs of the different campsites, mostly in Co. Waterford, with bell tents, bicycles, primus stoves, the lot. His particular friends in Waterford were Norman Baker, Dickie Beale and Eric and Malcom Grubb. There was an active walking club in Tramore called the "Crimson Ramblers". One local wag said "Yes indeed, they start off as Scarlet Runners and by the time they return home they are Virginia Creepers".

One of the firms with whom Harvey & Son did stockbroking business was Hillman & Catford in Bristol. They "made a market" in many of the more frequently traded shares. It emerged that Hillman & Catford were not very good at keeping their books.

Some concern was felt, so Father went to Bristol and spent many months there helping to sort things out. He felt at home with the Quaker Community in Bristol and he began to take notice of an attractive young Friend, Kathleen Emma Roberts, who was the daughter of a pharmaceutical chemist Weston Roberts and his wife Agnes. Weston Roberts had spent the first decades of his life in Enniscorthy Co Wexford, and "his" chemist's shop beside the river at the old bridge still had the word "Chemist" painted on its wall until about the year 2002, though he had moved to England more than a century before. Charles and Kathleen's relationship blossomed, and after he returned to Waterford they were married in 1927 in Enniscorthy Meeting House.

Kathleen, who as well as being a qualified pharmacist, was talented artistically, played the cello, was good at calligraphy, and was also an illustrator. They set up house in "The Limes" on Johns Hill, Waterford, occupying a flat that was made available to them by one of cousin Frederick's family. After that they acquired a cottage in Tramore, "Summerville". It had no "mod-cons" so a modest flat-roofed extension was built which included a hallway, bathroom, toilet and coal house. This cottage was conveniently near Midvale, about 200 yards down the road, handy for babysitting and other family support from my grandparents.

Kathleen and Weston

By this time Weston had arrived (on 7th September 1929) and on 8th July 1931 I myself was born. When I was about six I was fascinated to learn that I had actually been born at Midvale in my grandparents' double bed, a lovely old iron Victorian bedstead with traditional brass bed knobs. I was given the name Philip Roberts Jacob, after Kathleen's brother who had recently died, while prospecting for oil in Venezuela.

In 1934 my mother went into the County & City Infirmary, on Johns Hill in Waterford, for what should have been a simple operation for gallstones. Unfortunately complications developed and, very sadly, she died, leaving my father with two little boys aged 5 and 3. My grandparents were wonderfully supportive and Weston and I spent short or longer periods at Midvale for the next two years.

I don't remember much about my mother, except three episodes which are crystal-clear in my mind. One is of her using the green painted iron-framed mangle, on the front lawn, squeezing water out of the washing before pegging it onto the clothes' line.

Postcard of an oil "gusher" sent from Venezuela, by Philip Barritt Roberts to Kathleen Jacob (nee Roberts) 1929.

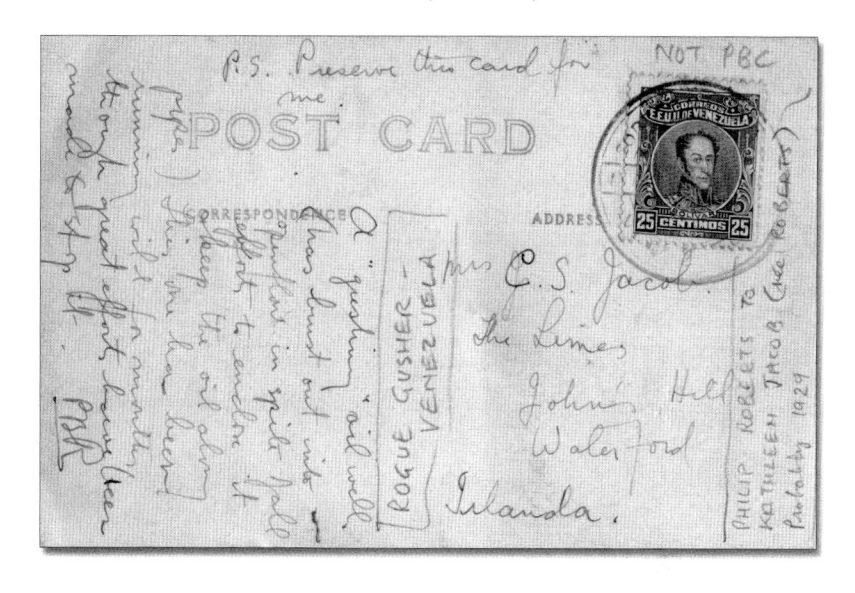

*Philip, Kathleen, and Weston in Summerville garden 1933.
Note Flanagans (Waterford fishmongers) carrying bag on bike.*

Charles Jacob on a country walk with Philip and Weston 1933.

The second is of her on her knees on the bathroom floor, using the pastry board on which to mix up some coal tar ointment for sore skin behind my knees and on my elbows – I have always had very dry skin. She had trained as a pharmacist when working in her father's shop in Bristol. The third was mother gently extricating a blackbird from some netting which had been put over the strawberries in the vegetable garden. This act of rescue was done with great gentleness and the bird flew away happily. It is a memory that I cherish.

One of Granny's nieces, Kathleen Baker, known to all as KB, came over from England to Tramore to look after the house and its two small occupants for a while. Then Miss Williams (her Christian name Mildred was never used) came to look after us. She was a wonderful person, kind, competent, intelligent and meticulous in all things, especially in making sure that the two little boys in her charge had impeccable manners!

It was a very sad time for Father, although as a three year old I did not really understand what had happened and it had little adverse effect on me. I think Weston, nearly two years older than me, was much more affected and developed a sense of insecurity. However, life went on and after a year or so Father started noticing a teacher at Newtown School who was approximately his own age called Stella Maloney. Stella was music mistress, games mistress and senior mistress, one of an excellent team of teachers assembled by Arnold Marsh to work with him in resuscitating the fortunes of Newtown. She was also very attractive, lively, good-natured, generous and with a great sense of fun. She came from the small town of Radstock in Somerset.

Stella Maloney c.1936

It must have been in the first half of 1936 that Father proposed marriage to Stella and, although they were deeply in love by that time, Stella was not at all sure that she would be able to manage two small boys and a household, having had so little experience of such things in her life up to that time.

It was arranged that our Auntie Pol would act as chaperone for a fortnight's holiday with Charles and Stella and us two boys in a camp coach in Dorset that summer, during which the engaged couple would see how they got on together and whether Stella could cope with Weston and me.

Portisham Bottom Camp Coach, 1936.

The train station at Radstock, Somerset, Stella Maloney's hometown.

The camp coach was one of a number of railway coaches which had been converted into holiday homes and parked on unused sidings at various locations throughout Britain. Ours was at the station in a tiny hamlet in Dorset called Portisham Bottom. In the West Country dialect it sounded like "Poshum Bohum". It was an idyllic spot and we had a great holiday, with various members of the family and friends including Dorrie White coming to stay for shorter or longer periods. I particularly remember Father buying a small elastic band powered "Frog" model aeroplane and flying it, without a great deal of success, in a nearby field. I was fascinated by the railway linesmen that passed through every few days on the rail tracks, on a crude platform on four wheels, powered by two men pushing two horizontal handles back and forth, connected to cranks on the axle, thus propelling the "vehicle" while they inspected the track.

One day we visited Weymouth and had a trip in a sleek varnished mahogany speedboat out into the bay to see the German liner "Bremen" that had previously held the Blue Riband for the crossing of the Atlantic. That day we spent some time on the strand and for no particular reason I buried my sandals but forgot where, and they were never found. Later on that day I had to be carried (I was only 5) because the pavements of Weymouth were too hot with the sun beating down on them for my little bare feet. Another day we went to Chesil Bank, that extraordinary long beach that stretches for miles towards Portland Bill, with uniformly rounded pebbles, big at one end of the beach and small at the other. There are two villages not far from Weymouth, one called Abbotsbury and the other called Swanage. I enjoyed seeing the swans at Abbotsbury, but was puzzled and disappointed to learn that there were no swans at Swanage.

Another day we went to meet some friends in Dorchester and had afternoon tea in the hotel grounds there. There was a very annoying girl of about my own age there, and I pushed her into the stream that ran through the hotel garden, much to everyone's consternation. Back at the camp coach I was furious because in dishing out the tinned fruit salad there weren't enough cherries to go round, and I didn't get one. One mealtime we were given junket for pudding, and I didn't like junket so I refused to eat it. I was told that I would sit there until I did. I sat all afternoon. In the end I won because the grown-ups' patience ran out before mine did and I was "let off with a caution".

In spite of everything the experience of the camp coach was deemed a success and that October Stella and father were married in the Methodist Church in Radstock, the small coal mining town between the Mendip hills and Bath, where Stella had been born and brought up. Stella's father, Bertram Crewe Maloney, was a grain merchant and flour miller with mills in Radstock, Frome and Shepton Mallet. He was a perfect example of a sound and solid citizen, with a friendly and generous nature and an impish sense of humour – on one occasion he apparently asked one of the children at tea-time what was written on the underneath of the mug the child was holding, whereupon the child of course turned the mug upside down and the milk spilled all over the table.

A Jacob Family

Tramore in the 1900s

*Charles Jacob
with Philip and Weston 1934.*

The Marriage of Charles Jacob and Stella Maloney 1936.

L to R
Back Row: Bernard Jacob, Jessie Jacob, Bertram Maloney, Edwin Jacob.
Middle Row: Mrs. Maloney, Dick Beale.
Front Row: Trena Maloney, Charles Jacob, Stella Jacob (née Maloney), Dorothy Jacob.

Just Married!, Charles Jacob and Stella Maloney 1936.

Philip, Charles, Stella, Weston, Jacob, October 1937.

Bert was amused but his wife wasn't! Stella's mother was also a real example of what a mother should be. We called them Grandpa and Granny Loney. Grandpa Loney delighted Weston and me by arranging a trip around the town on the fire engine (he was captain of the Fire Brigade) and we felt very important on this enormous red vehicle with polished brass radiator and fireman's ladder on top. Stella had two brothers and three sisters, Conrad and John, Freda, Mollie and Trena.

When the newly-weds disembarked from the Great Western steamer onto the Waterford quayside they were met by a contingent of Newtown pupils, each with a hockey stick held aloft to form a "tunnel of honour" under which Charles and Stella had to pass. Being a Waterford business-man he was mildly embarrassed, but Stella was tickled pink.

(I don't know that it matters, but it is intriguing that the men from four generations of our family in Ireland, have married English people, or at least people born in England. Charles Henry Jacob to Elizabeth Binyon from England; Edwin Jacob to Jessie (Baker) from Halstead; Charles Jacob first to Kathleen (Roberts) from Bristol, and then to Stella (Maloney) from Radstock; Phillip Scanlan to Kathleen (Sedgwick) from Derby; Weston Jacob to Hilda (Shaw) from Manchester; Philip Jacob to Brigid (Scanlan) born in Nottingham (but became an Irish citizen as an infant). In addition Cousin Willie Jacob married Edith from England.)

SUMMERVILLE

After Charles and Stella were married life at Summerville reverted to normal and very quickly Stella mastered the art of running a household and looking after Weston and me. Being a music teacher Stella tried to teach me the piano but I was a hopeless pupil and gave up about eight years later!

Stella had with her a hilarious book by W Marchant Jones about "Jarge Balsh". She read to us from this with a broad Somerset accent, with which of course she was thoroughly familiar. "Jarge" (which is West Country for "George") was an imaginary countryman living a few miles from Stella's home in Somerset. We enjoyed this hugely, especially when she got to the bit where the local milkman woke them up every morning whistling "I'm for ever blowing bubbles…" and she sang and whistled it for us. She instinctively knew what a youngster would enjoy.

A Jacob Family
Tramore in the 1900s

*Charles and Stella Jacob at Summerville,
October 1937.*

*Weston and Philip Jacob
in 1937.*

*Bertram Crewe Maloney,
Captain of Radstock Fire Brigade.*

*Radstock Fire Engine 1937,
with from left, Weston, Philip, and Stella Jacob.*

Father had a series of motorbikes - two Rudges, one of them a Rudge "Multi", and a Sunbeam. The "Multi" had infinitely variable gears, being belt driven, with adjustable V-shaped pulleys at each end. As one contracted the other widened, thus altering the ratio by forcing the belt up or down the pulley wheels. Grand in theory, but in practice it chewed up the belt in no time flat. He bought the Sunbeam from Horace E. Sexton, who lived in a house called Brockenhurst in Tramore. Horace was the proprietor of a grocery shop called "The Central Stores" in Waterford. Jim Sexton was Horace's son and Michael and Jonathan are his grandsons. Horace kept the motorbike immaculately, and handed it over with its original owner's handbook. On one occasion when Father was on holiday in West Cork and Kerry the motorbike developed gearbox trouble at Derreen between Bantry and Killarney. Father stopped at a one-man garage where the garage-man dismantled the gearbox, discovered which spare parts were necessary, looked up their identification details in the handbook, wired the manufacturers in Britain, and received the necessary parts the following day by post. The man then proceeded to reassemble the gearbox. By that time he had imbibed a little too much alcohol, but he succeeded in reassembling it, all the while muttering to himself "little to big, big to little, little to big, big to little ...."

THE SILVER BULLET

Sunbeam was an interesting marque – the company had started as a lacquering service, and was bought over by the Sunbeam car company who wanted to acquire the lacquering expertise. Father had a series of sidecars, one of which was made of aluminium, in a streamlined shape, and was known in the family as the "silver bullet". On the occasion of my birth he was hurrying along the road between Waterford and Tramore to see his newborn and went round one bend so fast that the sidecar lifted off the road and gave him a real fright. Whenever the sidecar was detached he kept the motorbike in the wooden shed (which we called the workshop) in the garden at Summerville but this meant pushing it up a plank over the big step from the roadside pavement and then pushing it up another plank at the top of the garden path into the workshop – all a bit of a palaver. Strange what apparently small and insignificant things stick in one's memory from an early age!

Some time in the mid-1930's he decided that he should have a motorcar so he bought an ancient Jowett, with a horizontally opposed two-cylinder engine, from the Penrose family for the large sum of twelve pounds ten shillings. It was old, but on the whole it did the job all right. It had a folding canvas hood which had to be treated with special liquid every so often. This liquid was made up by a Mr. Walsh in a laneway behind the old Meeting House in Waterford and CSJ christened the liquid "Walsh's Patent Concoction". The car itself was christened "Daisy", and had both the gear lever and the handbrake mounted outside, on the running board, so one had to put one's hand out through the cellophane flap, which formed the right hand window, to change gear. The handbrake acted by tightening a collar round the propeller shaft. When Daisy was ultimately scrapped the bench-type front seats were kept and for many years were used as a bed in the cottage in the Comeraghs.

"DAISY"

Stella was driving Daisy once, with me as a passenger, from Tramore to Waterford. As we were passing Kilbarry Bogs there was a sudden loud bang. We thought we saw something flying through the air, to the left of the car. We stopped, walked round the car, but didn't notice anything wrong. We couldn't see anything on the road either, and were about to get back into the car when one of us said "Look!" and pointed to the left hand front wheel. The mudguard had disappeared - its bracket had broken, it dropped onto the revolving wheel, and was thrown into the air, over the wall, landing yards away, and was hidden in the rushes like Moses. So we resumed our journey, none the worse, but short of one mudguard.

Daisy's successor was a Vauxhall 10, pale grey with red upholstery, registration number Z8470, bought with money left by Cousin Annie of Colwyn Bay. CSJ and Stella then borrowed a caravan from Tommy Gallwey and drove to West Cork and Kerry, where they parked beside the strand at Castlegregory and had an idyllic holiday – the first they had had, away from home, since they were married. The Vauxhall was then laid up during World War II in Paddy Scanlon's garage. After the war it was sold, but almost immediately it gave the new owner trouble. As Paddy Scanlon said "She ground to a halt and the gear-box broke and ended up in giblets on the road".

Vauxhall Ten car and Caravan on holiday in Dingle before W.W.2

Kelly's Hotel Rosslare.

In the mid thirties it was decided to re-roof Summerville – the slates were slipping – so we all moved into "Slievebloom", a very fine new bungalow on the sea road. This had been built as a summer holiday house by Sam and Winifred Pim and they very generously lent it to us. We set up our model railway on the parquet hall floor. Robert Jacob came to visit with his working model steam engine, fuelled by methylated spirit. His engine got up such a head of steam and speed going down the straight that when it got to the curve at the end it tilted over and fell off the tracks, and the methylated spirits spilled out onto the floor, but somehow disaster was averted.

Back at Summerville, where space was at a premium, there were two storage cupboards in the roof spaces, one christened "the hen run" and the other "stalky bird". The reason for the first name was obvious but I never fathomed the reason for calling the other "stalky bird".

That brings back memories of when I was much smaller – enticing the next door cat into the meat safe outside the back door of Summerville (do you remember the outside meat-safes covered with perforated zinc? No refrigerators in those days!) with a saucer of milk and then shutting the poor cat in so that it could drink all the milk – it was not amused. Another time a workman asked me could he borrow a "cold chisel". I was the only one around at the time and I had no idea what he meant (I thought he was saying "coal chisel") so as we had a hammer with a pointed end for breaking up the lumps of coal I handed this to him, but he didn't think it funny.

For my fourth birthday Granny took us for a couple of days to Kelly's hotel in Rosslare. I was given a golf tee and it became a treasured possession, probably also because it made me feel like a grown-up. To make it a special occasion a birthday cake had been brought from Tramore in a tin. It was probably for my fifth birthday that I was given a present of a small plasterer's trowel. It was my favourite possession for years, I think this was also because it made me feel grown-up to have a real workman's tool.

Granny did her best to give respite to whoever was looking after us at Summerville, one time taking us to Ardmore where we stayed in a hotel and visited Ruth and Mary Odell. Weston and I discovered a little shop at the sea front that sold particularly good ice-creams. One morning, bright and early, we made our way down to this shop and knocked on the door loud and clear looking for our ice-creams. The proprietor, who lived on the premises, was not a bit amused when she finally was woken from her sleep and came to the door to find two small boys clamouring for ice-cream at that hour of the morning.

On another occasion Granny took us for a few days to Helen Jacob in Lismore. Helen owned a farm and had a lovely old thatched farmhouse which she ran as a B&B. Granny was horrified when Helen's farm steward took Weston and me out on a rabbit-shooting expedition with his 0.22 rifle. I think Weston was about 7 and I was about 5. The thing that particularly remains in my mind however was the stomach-turning sight of squirming maggots infesting sores on a sheep's skin. Horrible.

We spent some hours on another day in the barn rigging up a Heath Robinson mousetrap which, we hoped, would lead mice to fall into a biscuit tin and be unable to escape. Predictably we never caught any. Also at Helen Jacob's I was hoisted onto a Shetland pony at the top of the sloping lawn. The pony then bolted down to the bottom of the lawn, turned sharp left and of course I fell off. The result was a large triangular rip in my nice new grey flannel trousers – shorts (as boys didn't graduate to long trousers until their teens in those days). It put me off riding for life.

Another few days away with Granny were spent at a little village outside Wexford called Killinick to stay with Maggie Byron. It was the one and only time that I have slept on a feather mattress. I thought it was luxurious - it hugged my little body and was ever so cosy. There were peahens in the garden, they made an awful row, and laid eggs but hatched no chicks. It was explained that that was because there was no peacock around, but I was too young to understand the full implications of that. Nearly 70 years later Brigid and I were passing through Killinick and stopped. I went into the pub, asked did anybody know which was Maggie Byron's house, and a kind man was able to direct me to it, though it had been sold, presumably after Maggie Byron or her family died, and was now in different hands. Apparently in the meantime it had passed through the hands of a Captain Poole who was related to the Enniscorthy Pooles, and was senior captain of Irish Shipping for many years, including the Second World War. Most of these childhood memories would have been when I was between four and nine years old.

Father had a habit of building a new shed whenever we ran out of space in the house. First there was a coal and wood shed in the back yard. Then there was another to keep the turf dry. There was already a corrugated-iron-clad workshop. Then, when the Maguires came the Garden Room (much more than a shed!) was built, and shortly afterwards another corrugated iron one for our eight bicycles, with room for more turf. A few years later another shed was erected to keep Dreoilín dry over the winter. Quite a conglomeration!

Weston

Philip

Father was not a natural gardener (though Stella was) but he knew the name of our lantern tree "Tricuspidaria lanceolata". The name appealed to him, and he lost no opportunity to tell people that was its name.

Weston and I on the whole were very healthy, but I do remember getting a bad dose of jaundice, losing a lot of weight, and being a bit sorry for myself. When small, we amused ourselves with wooden bricks, rubber minibrix, meccano, making wee models from scratch, and reading "Two little Savages" and books on Woodcraft Chivalry (which father preferred to Scouts). We loved Stella reading to us, including from a book on knitting, with pictures of dropped stitches that took on a life of their own and disappeared through cracks in the floorboards.

Weston developed a passion for listening to the wireless (a good HMV one) and he spent hours sitting on a "dumpy" with his ear to it absorbing the latest music. Then, and later, the programmes included Sandy McPherson on the theatre organ, Monday Night at 8 is on the Air, In Town Tonight, Henry Hall, Tommy Handley in ITMA (It's That Man Again) and many others.

In Summerville my bedroom was up the steep narrow stairs, on the left hand side, and our parents were in a slightly larger room to the right at the top of the stairs. On birthdays and at Christmas Father, the night before, tied all the presents at intervals on a very long piece of string, and piled them at the bottom of the stairs. Next morning we all sat up in our parents bed, and the string was hauled up bit by bit, with great excitement guessing whose present would be next.

There was only standing room in the centre part of the upstairs rooms, with the area under the eaves being curtained off and used for storage, etc. One of the treasures was a wooden box containing things sent home by my Uncle Philip Roberts from overseas. There was an ostrich egg, an emu's egg, the rattles from rattle-snake's tails and things like that.

I was always making things with my hands, and I particularly remember illustrating and colouring home-made Christmas cards. I had a book produced by the Van Houten Cocoa Company with blank spaces in which one inserted tokens that came with packets of cocoa until one had a full book. My book never got filled up, perhaps because "we grew up on Fry's" as the advertisement said. The particular theme was heraldry and I remember learning all the heraldic terms, some of which I remember to this day.

On the lathe that came to us from Uncle Fred Jacob of Bray I made a variety of things. Harry Giles, one of the handy-men employed by Harvey & Son, paid me the compliment of asking me to make him a couple of boxwood, spinning-top shaped, "tools" for opening up the ends of a lead water pipe to receive another pipe-end before they were soldered together. I also had a commission from Tommy Maguire to make a set of oak side plates for his house in Woking (they used wooden utensils whenever they could). For these I used timber from a furniture factory, offcuts from some church pews they were making. He paid me very well for them, much to my delight.

I made a wee round wooden box, and gave it to Granny, who graciously accepted it, thinking it was a present, and wasn't best pleased when I said "That will be sixpence". The best wood we had for turning was lime, kindly given to us by Bob Alesbury of Edenderry, a gentle giant of a man who had been at school with Father and who had a delightful wife, Doris, who was tiny. I made wooden balls the size of a hockey ball which Weston and I "dribbled" round the Newtown Cove Road with our hurley sticks for exercise, but the balls were not elastic enough and broke the hurley sticks!

The bed in which I slept when I was small was a "bed settee" which, in theory, was wide enough for two people. Aunt Dorothy came to stay with us for a few days for a family wedding, and she and I slept side-by-side on the bed-settee. She was quite a sizeable lady, and she weighed down one side of the bed so much that many times during the night I found that I had rolled down on top of her, and had to kick myself back up to my side of the bed. I think neither of us got much sleep. My room was immediately above the kitchen, and on occasion when visitors came for an evening meal the coffee beans were ground in a coffee grinder which made a loud noise, and woke me up. We had a good box of marbles, and it was fun to start these bouncing down the stairs and onto the tiled hall floor below – it is remarkable how high a good glass marble will bounce on a hard tiled floor.

Arnold Marsh quite often came to visit and one lunchtime he was winding up pieces of string in a particular way. As a small boy I said to him "Do you think that is the best way to do it?" and his amused reply was "I don't think it is, I know it is!" When Father and Stella got married both the staff and the Old Scholars were very generous. An excellent built-in wardrobe was given for our hallway, and a well made "climbing frame" for the lawn and for two small boys to climb all over. Weston and I used it a lot and pretended it was all sorts of things like ships and castles and forts, etc. A tradition had grown up that the Newtown and Mountmellick Old Scholars' Association Reunion Weekend was at Whitsuntide, and on Whit Sunday all Old Scholars were invited to Summerville for afternoon tea. Scores of Old Scholars would turn up and swarm over the house and garden. It was always a great occasion.

About this time Weston was given a pet tortoise. It only moved very slowly, like all tortoises. Weston had just become a fan of the game of cricket. That season Wally Hammond was the outstanding batsman, but scored runs very slowly indeed. Weston christened the tortoise "Wally".

Turning my mind back to my bedroom, I remember going to sleep night after night with the sound of corncrakes' calling coming through the open skylight, which was the only window. I had many nightmares which featured either tigers or lions coming in through that skylight, probably because on one occasion a prowling cat looked in at me through it. When alterations were done to Summerville, before moving in, the upstairs window of my parents' bedroom was enlarged. This meant the chimney in the wall was unusable, and a new chimney was installed on the outside of the wall, made of asbestos piping. In due course soot built up on the inside of this pipe and on at least one occasion when the soot caught fire the asbestos burst off in patches, sounding just like a shotgun, and scaring the living daylights out of Stella.

Both my parents enjoyed music. My uncle Philip Roberts (after whom I am named) had left us a good EMG wind-up gramophone which used special triangular cane needles (trimmed with a special snipper) on 78 RPM records, and which had an enormous (in my eyes) horn protruding from the top of the cabinet. There were also box after black box of classical 78 rpm records of a high standard and listening to these this gave me a good grounding in classical music. Father was in a choir called The Glee Hive and Sir William Beresford was in the bass line. I thought this very posh! Father once took the part of the Mikado in a production of Gilbert & Sullivan's eponymous light opera and for months he went around the house singing snippets from that tuneful work. Stella won first prize at a fancy dress party for her appearance as "Carmen" – she really did look smashing in red and black, with a mantilla and a flowing black lace veil.

Wilfred Lamb in those days was on the committee of Newtown School and frequently stayed with us overnight. As a small boy I enjoyed making mud pies in the garden. I once invited – nay ordered - Wilfred to stand on the hardened mud pie telling him it was quite safe and was strong enough to take his weight. He was a sport and did as requested!

Father's first cousin Doreen (his Uncle Joe's daughter) was quite a formidable, but very kindly, person and was an army nurse. We were not allowed to call her Cousin, or Aunt – just plain Doreen. I am told we boys always pronounced it "Dreen". She was very good to us, and when she came home on holiday from Sierra Leone or India or wherever she had been posted, she brought generous presents – a tricycle, a big box of Meccano or suchlike. On one occasion she took Weston and me to Waterford (all of eight miles on the bus) and to a watchmakers where she bought each of us a wrist-watch. I had just learned how to tell the time. Coming back to Tramore again on the bus I apparently walked up and down between the seats and asked each person would they like to know what time it was. When they (of course) said "yes please", I stretched out my arm, looked at my wrist-watch and proudly told them the time, much to their amusement.

When in Waterford we occasionally saw the "Stanley Steamer", a coal delivery lorry, chuff, chuff, chuffing along the street with smoke and steam coming out of its funnel and the red hot coals clearly visible under the boiler. It had solid rubber tyres and gave many many years of reliable service.

The triumvirate of Norman Baker, Dickie Beale and Father wanted to do a bit of touring on the Continent, and bought a green open Peugeot "tourer" car. It was long, and as it had to be housed in the garage at Midvale, the garage had to be lengthened. It also tended to get stranded at the top of hump-backed bridges if the hump was too high. It was christened the "Green Dragon".

Doreen Jacob
1920's

Philip Barritt Roberts
1920's

Uncle Joe, with Doreen (far right) and her Austin 7 car, late 1930's.

Richard Nichols, a Quaker from Dublin, came to stay with us, and became acquainted with it. Intrigued with its name, when he got home he wrote a wonderful letter to Weston and me about the adventures of the Green Dragon, with splendid illustrations of a green dragon on the highways, breathing fire, all in green and red ink. We were absolutely thrilled, and kept the letter as a most prized and precious possession for years. Father never went on any touring expedition in it, and I seem to remember the others didn't either. Maybe it was a White Elephant, not a Green Dragon.

At one stage he became keen on beagling, and sometimes took us boys along too, though of course we were only able to follow the hounds for a relatively short period. When we were old enough to cycle a few miles we used to go to Pembrokestown, outside Tramore, to a lovely clear swift-flowing stream with masses of watercress. As well as being very tasty watercress is supposed to have lots of vitamins and this was approved of in a family that believed in healthy eating. During the War years we had a series of picture charts showing the level of vitamins in most fruits and vegetables. The winners were blackcurrants and wild rose hips, and purple sprouting broccoli respectively. To help with our intake of fruit (and our "regularity") a large box of dried nectarines was acquired – I liked them a lot.

The venue for the annual Tramore Point-to-Point horse race was not far from Pembrokestown – it was exciting to watch. The Waterford Hunt traditionally met on St. Stephen's Day in the car park beside The Grand Hotel and as a great friend of my father's, Tommy Gallwey, regularly hunted, we used to watch the hunt setting off. Also great excitement!

Father developed a particular interest in the remarkable Malcomson family that had built a large cotton mill in Portlaw in the early to mid 1800s, and who then also developed a major shipbuilding business in Waterford, but all of which collapsed later that century. Clogs to clogs in three generations. By the time his researches ended he could have claimed to be the world expert on the Malcomsons. He was inordinately proud of Waterford Port, too, and knew the harbour engineer William Friel well.

Tommy and Nona Gallwey's son, Dayrell, was almost exactly the same age as I was. They lived in an attractive house called "Fairlinch" near Midvale, and even nearer to Sunnycroft where Mrs. Lily Finnegan lived. Dayrell and I became good friends and spent a lot of time together. Then the Gallweys moved a couple of hundred yards down Church Road to a rather larger house called "Rocklands" and I continued to spend a lot of my time with Dayrell there. Tommy Gallwey had been in the British army and had medals which Dayrell showed me with great pride. He told me one of them was the VC, but that was wishful thinking on his part! With a military background, it was not surprising that Dayrell, though normally a most friendly and mild-mannered boy, at one stage persuaded me that it was a brave thing to do to kneel in a patch of nettles, and it would be cowardly not to, so I did. I have never forgotten the pain that it caused, but I never held it against him.

Marguerite Skelton and Richard Nichols, at Powerscourt Gate Lodge, 1936.

Old Waterford Port.

Their garden ran down to the wall beside the Doneraile Walk, with seats looking out over Tramore Bay which we pretended were the bridge of a ship. Rocklands had a kind of orangerie which they termed the "Winter Garden". At one stage it housed a monkey in a cage, at another a parrot (but it didn't talk much!). Beside the Winter Garden was another large room in which Tommy had a model railway erected on shelves around the perimeter, but I think it was a bit too complicated, and I don't remember having much fun with it. Tommy's wife Nona produced delicious afternoon teas for us, but first prize for freshly baked scones with raspberry jam and cream must go to Dayrell's Granny Kenny, in her spacious Victorian house "Bellair". It was always a treat visiting her – we had fun playing in the garden, where I particularly remember huge clumps of pampas grass.

In the mid-1930's Sir Alan Cobham had become famous with his "Flying Circus" and on one memorable occasion this came to a large field somewhere between Waterford and Tramore. His small planes gave a marvellous display of simple aerobatics, the star attraction being an autogiro, the predecessor of the helicopter but with the added advantage that if the engine stopped the autogiro would simply glide back down to the ground under perfect control.

Around that time the distinguished archaeologist Jacquetta Hawkes (wife of J.B. Priestley) excavated a double ring fort, or maybe giant's grave, on a hilltop at Harristown near Belle Lake between Waterford and Dunmore. I think it was established that it was in use in two different periods about a thousand years apart. Father had an abiding interest in antiquities, and we were often taken to see ogham stones, cromlechs, giant's graves, raths etc, and the "sugar loaf" which intrigued us – a large rock standing upright in a field which is believed to be the core of a mini volcano (but I have my doubts). On one occasion we accepted an invitation to stay in a wooden hut sited near Woodstown Strand owned by Arthur Graham (whose sister Sally married my Uncle Bernard). I seem to remember it was rather crude, without many creature comforts but with lots of midges and we didn't go back! While there I was intrigued by the series of wooden poles which formed a traditional salmon fishery far out in the shallows beyond Woodstown Strand. I couldn't quite understand how it worked – one of life's mysteries. About then Arnold Marsh, who was Headmaster of Newtown School, acquired a small cottage as a "getaway", tucked into a valley near the sea, just north of Creaden Head near Dunmore, beside the little strand of Fornaught.

Any chapter about our parents would be incomplete without mention of Jenny, though her arrival in 1945 was a bit later than most of the reminiscences recounted here. Jenny (now O'Sullivan) contributed chapter 12. She was a delightful, pretty little girl, with lovely curly hair, and was a wonderful addition to the family. I was still a boarder at Newtown School then, and took great pride in showing off my sister to everyone!

Sir Alan Cobham's Flying Circus 1933.

Jenny with the van "Joey".

For no particular reason a memory from years before comes into my mind. Father had always been keen on hill and mountain walking and had a cherished pair of leather mountain boots with hobnails. One Christmas instead of a turkey we had a goose, and this produced a good jarful of goose grease, which he used successfully to keep his boot leather nice and supple. Surplus grease was foolishly poured down the kitchen sink, and congealed in the wastepipe, the clearing of which was incredibly messy and smelly, and I still feel queasy even thinking about it.

A minor feature of life in Ireland that was then common deserves mention. When there was a bereavement in the family most people sewed a black diamond-shaped patch onto their upper sleeve for a period, and used special black-edged notepaper and envelopes for correspondence.

The time came when Weston and I had to have our tonsils out. This was done by T. O. Graham (nick-named "the butcher") in the Royal Victoria Eye and Ear hospital in Dublin. We were together in a semi-private ward. Weston spotted that the nurses had their names on name-tapes inside the cuffs of their blouses, and pulled their legs by calling them by their Christian names from that time on. They loved it – Weston always had a way with the girls.

Later on I had an operation for a hernia from which I had been suffering, in the Meath Hospital in Dublin – it was done by a superb surgeon, Victor Lane. The Meath was near the centre of Dublin, and the sound of ringing bells from numerous churches on a Sunday morning was marvellous. My hernia prevented me from playing games at school, or swimming, for two or three years, which meant that I never really learned how to swim well, much to my regret.

TRAMORE PIER

Tramore was a great place to grow up, especially with parents that had such a wide diversity of interests. One place that we never grew tired of was the "Rabbit Burrows", the local name for the extensive sand dunes at the end of Tramore Strand. We used to adore climbing up and then running down the long sandy slopes, lying in the sun out of the wind, watching the burnet moths with their red and black wings and bodies; the blue, yellow and white wee butterflies; getting prickled by the sea holly; enjoying the wild pansies, etc. Just beyond the Rabbit Burrows is a narrow channel called the Rhineshark where the sea rushes into a lagoon (the "Back Strand") when the tide is coming in, and rushes out again when the tide is falling. It is a genuinely dangerous place, and a great fear of approaching it too closely was instilled in us. This was effective in keeping us away from it. We were also interested in the long lines with baited hooks which were laid on the dried out strand by locals at low tide, to catch bass when the tide came in. I don't know how many they caught – probably not many. Just the other side of this channel was a big house owned by another branch of the Gallwey family called "Corbally Mór" but we never visited it. For many years, until 1911 when the natural defences of the sandy spit that backed the strand were breached, what is now the "Back Strand" was quite dry. It was the site of the Tramore racecourse and of an army shooting range - but that was long before my time. Nowadays apparently quite a few sailing boats come up the Rhineshark on a flooding tide and anchor in the lagoon behind the Rabbit Burrows, where there is enough water for them even at low tide. It is a perfectly sheltered anchorage.

LAUNCHING THE CANOE

Mention of the Rabbit Burrows reminds me of the fun we had with a folding two-man kayak-type canoe which was given to us by Basil Jacob in the late 1930's. Early one Sunday morning father, Weston and I carried it down to the pier in Tramore, got on board, and paddled across the bay, landing through the small waves (it was a very calm morning) on the strand at the Rabbit Burrows. We pulled the canoe up to the high tide mark, and had our picnic breakfast in the sunshine. We then turned round and paddled back to the pier again full of fresh air and the excitement of adventure. There were gannets circling round above the bay, and we joked that they might mistake a silver mark on the canoe for a fish, and would dive on us. They didn't.

On another occasion the canoe was packed up and transported to Lismore where father reassembled it, and paddled down the Blackwater to Cappoquin, Weston and I got on board, and all three paddled on down the river, but not as far as Youghal. At one stage Weston and I were lying down inside the canoe, out of sight, for a while. We then re-emerged just as the canoe was passing a farmer in his field, who was mightily surprised to see two young chiselers suddenly appearing, and a hilarious conversation took place between him and Father.

Another adventure was when the canoe was packed up and taken to Blackstoops, a house owned by the hospitable Ivan Yates and his wife Millicent (who was a Quaker from Waterford). We pitched our tent there, just upstream from Enniscorthy, and next morning set off down the river Slaney with the tent (Father's treasured "Palomine" made by Black's of Greenock) and provisions on board so that we would not starve. When passing under the old bridge in Enniscorthy the water was slightly too shallow for our heavily laden canoe, and it got stuck. Father had to step out into the water and push it off. Fortunately he was able to get back into the canoe again without losing his balance and falling in. We paddled gently down the Slaney, with the current, until it was time to find a camping place for the night.

Our progress was assisted by the falling tide, but this resulted in yards of deep mud banks between us and the nearest field by the time we stopped, which we hadn't anticipated. I can't remember exactly how we got ashore, but we did, and slept soundly. We woke early the following morning to find a large congregation of swans on the river. They were magically pink in the early morning light, a sight I will never forget. We managed to get back into the canoe again and paddled on down to Wexford town where, once again, we found the tide was out and there was a lot of mud, but it didn't stop us from reaching the slipway.

For a period the canoe was kept at the Boat Club in Waterford, just across the river Suir from Adelphi Quay where the Great Western had its regular berth. One particular day Father, Weston and I pushed off in the canoe from the slipway and paddled upstream with the rising tide, under the bridge. Before getting to Granagh Castle we entered a small tidal tributary, known as the Kilmacow Pill. (The word "pill" is a West of England term for a tidal tributary flowing into a river – the King John's River in Waterford is just such a waterway and it is always known to Waterford people as "the Pill". There is also a village called "Piltown" a bit further up the river Suir). We got a mile or two up the Kilmacow Pill, turned round, and returned on what was then the falling tide to the boathouse, where we lifted the canoe out. Father, in his enthusiastic way, told the boatman how we had got on and that we had got right up to Kilmacow. When at last he paused the boatman looked at him quizzically and said "And tell me, Mr. Jacob, did you have trouble with the Customs?" Father was silent for a moment and then threw his head back and burst out laughing – he always enjoyed a harmless leg-pull, even if he was the butt of the joke.

While on the subject of water, I should mention how important "the pier" was in our lives as children – it was only a couple of hundred yards from Summerville down Cove Road. From late spring to early autumn there were always a number of boats moored there, fore and aft. If a major storm was in the offing it was necessary to haul the less robust boats up onto the pier because it was a tidal pier with hard sand and if the swell became big enough it would come round the end of the pier and bash the boats up and down at mid-tide. The "Equinoctial Gales" in September seemed to be the worst storms each year. The grand old man of the pier was Mike Brien, who in his heyday used the Puffin, a good seaworthy motorboat, but one which I only ever saw in its shed. The Murray family regularly fished; Jack Whalley (a painting contractor from Waterford with a hare lip) had a seaworthy motor-sailer called the "Sea Hound"; the Church of Ireland Canon Staunton's white painted sailing dinghy "Minx" (normally sailed by George Chapman, as the Canon had become too old) always looked smart. In due course we had our own 10 foot dinghy, a small butty varnished sailing dinghy with a broad stern which we called "Dreóilín" (which is Irish for "wren"). To his glee my father discovered that the Latin for the common wren was "Troglodytes Troglodytes Troglodytes". Thereafter the boat was often simply called "TTT". When Weston and I were small there was a little shop at the pier. One winter it was damaged in a gale and never re-opened. We managed to squirm into it through a crack, and found the remains of a box of peppermints which had become liquid and made the place smell of mint.

Mike Brien once received a telegram from a Scottish laird, who was keen on shark fishing, with the message "To Mike Brien, Tramore – Are there any basking sharks in Tramore Bay at the moment? Please reply by return" to which Mike sent the reply "There is only one basking shark in Tramore Bay and that is yours truly Mike Brien". Mike Brien used to roar with laughter when he told this story.

The road to the pier went down a narrowish cleft, but wide enough at one point to have a couple of houses on each side, the roofs of which were about level with a road that ran along the top of one side of the little valley. When my Uncle Bernard was a boy he managed to lob a stone down the chimney of the Kielys' house and unfortunately it landed on a china teapot over the fire, breaking it into smithereens. The irate owner came out and shouted up at Bernard, who confessed. The upshot was that Bernard's father (our grandpa) bought a nice new teapot for the Kiely family and all was forgiven.

For a short while Stella had help in the house from a woman called Eily who lived at one end of the Doneraile Walk, nearest to the pier. Eily is only memorable for one thing – when telling about her mother being startled by a mouse and almost losing her balance, Eily said "Me mother nearly lost her stand-up"!

A Jacob Family
Tramore in the 1900s

Red Cross Group 1945.
(Including 4th and 5th from left, Stella and Charles Jacob).

First Tramore Town Commissioners 1948.
Charles Jacob, far left front row.

Father, in true Quaker fashion, was happy to do his bit for the citizens of Waterford and Tramore.

- He was one of the first elected Tramore Town Commissioners, and was immediately made Vice-Chairman. He had had no intention of standing for election, but was persuaded to do so.
- He was at various times Secretary and President of Waterford Chamber of Commerce – Weston and I were goggle eyed at his substantial gold Chain of Office.
- He was a great fan of Canon Hayes who started "Muintir na Tíre", a national voluntary organisation dedicated to promoting the process of community development, particularly in rural areas, based in Bansha, Co Tipperary. He liked to tell the story that he felt encapsulated Father Hayes' philosophy whenever there was dissention in the community, as follows. 'A man had fallen into the river. A passer by managed to grab his hand, but he had a false arm, and it came off. So his would-be rescuer tried again, and caught the man's leg, but it too was false, and came off. Exasperated, the good Samaritan said "If you won't stick together I can't help you" '.
- And of course at various times he had a wide variety of responsibilities among Quakers, including being Clerk of Yearly Meeting, and Secretary and Chairman of the Newtown School Committee.

Muintir na Tíre Rural Week, Waterford, August 1945.
Charles Jacob, Father Hayes, Martin Breen, Prince Ferdinando Caracciolo.

A Jacob Family
Tramore in the 1900s

THE COTTAGE

Chapter 3

The Cottage in the Comeraghs

    I don't know whether Norman Baker, Dickie Beale or my father had the idea of renting "the cottage" but it was a very happy thought and it gave immense enjoyment for years – probably the happiest of all my memories from the mid-30's to the mid-40's. It was one half of a semi-detached farm labourer's cottage dating from some time in the 1800's. It was owned by a local small farmer called Peter O'Connor from whom it was rented at 12 shillings and six pence per quarter. He was elderly and became bed-ridden, and when receiving his quarterly payment he sat up in bed with his bowler hat on. The cottage had a porch in which logs for the fire were kept, and a living room the full height of the cottage but with only a very small window. The fireplace was large and open and had a fan (made by Pierce of Wexford) situated four or five feet from the hearth. A wheel about 18 inches in diameter with a handle for turning it was connected with the fan itself by a belt. The fan was half buried in the floor and the current of air from it went along a pipe and came up under the middle of the grate so it was possible to start a fire quite rapidly, and whenever it died down a few turns of the handle would produce the necessary draught to get the flames going again. On the other side of the fire-place a doorway led to two small bedrooms, above which, and behind the chimney, was "the loft" on the floor of which three or four mattresses, and later on the bench seats from Daisy, (the old Jowett car), meant that it was possible for six or eight people to stay. The item of crockery that I thought most interesting was a "moustache mug", probably brought home from Germany, with a china "moustache guard" across part of the open top, to stop a droopy moustache having a bath in an overfull mugfull of coffee. There was of course no running water, no electricity and no toilet facilities. The well was down the hillside through a few small fields half filled with bracken. Washing water was obtained in buckets from a stream which ran beside the road a hundred yards away. The road ran along beside the cottage following the contour of a small foothill of the Comeragh Mountains (spelled Damh Beg but pronounced Dov Beg). Between the road and the small wood that skirted the hill was a necklace of small fields. For some years the toilet arrangements were simply to cross the road and the small field, and over the wall into the wood. Later on, when we children got a little older, an outside "bothy" was constructed beside the Cottage which held an Elsan chemical closet. Lighting at the cottage was mainly by candle – I don't remember oil lamps being used much.

    The first thing to do when we arrived at the cottage for our holidays was to light a good fire and air the mattresses and the bedclothes, which included wonderful brown sheepskin rugs which were ex-army surplus from the First World War. The cottage stood in a small field, with outcrops of rock, one of which was the shape and size of a small whale, and was known as the submarine.

A Jacob Family
Tramore in the 1900s

At the Cottage in the Comeraghs 1940.
Stella Jacob, Susan Maguire, Dorothy Jacob, Elizabeth Maguire,
Tim Maguire, Philip Jacob, Anne Maguire, Weston Jacob.

Charles and Robert Jacob,
Camping atop the Comeragh Mountains 1938.

Surplus visitors would sleep in tents on the one or two level patches of the field. At the beginning of every season, at Easter time, Dickie, Norman, and father, plus anyone else such as Robert Jacob and Jim Sexton that wanted a bit of a diversion, would arrange to buy a tree from the owner of the little wood. Cross-cut saws were then put into action and enough logs sawn and split to last through the summer. The tree trunk was sawn into rounds which could then be split with an axe, or with a sledge and wedges. On one occasion someone had the bright idea of rolling one of these rounds down the field but of course it went out of control and gathered speed, and when it jumped over the wall near the cottage it narrowly missed one of the motorcars – first of all consternation, and then great hilarity. As an amalgamation of the names Beale, Jacob and Baker, the cottage was given the name "Bejakers".

A hundred yards away was a small hill-farm owned by the Drohan family. Mr. Drohan was by then fairly elderly but Mrs. Drohan was very active. She was a wonderful, friendly, motherly person, always wore black with a shawl, and had a broad smile and an equally broad Waterford accent. Her apple cake was absolutely delicious. Her daughter had left home to become a nun, and two or three of her sons (Willie and Joseph are the ones I remember) looked after the farm, which had a few cows that we were taught to milk. Sometimes we were lucky enough to get a lift on the pony and cart, about a mile down the steep rocky road which ran beside the Mahon Stream, with the churn of milk being taken to the creamery at Mahon Bridge. We were fascinated by the working of the creamery and were sometimes regaled with a mug full of pure cream – how we weren't sick I can't imagine! On our way back up the hill we sat beside the churn which by then was full of hot buttermilk and sometimes we brought our freshly washed handkerchiefs and spread them out on the churn to dry and to be "ironed".

At Mahon Bridge there was a rather run-down shop owned by a Mr. Power where we would buy bread, butter, matches and other necessities of life. The shop was neither hygienic nor well stocked! Behind the shop were the remains of a mill with quite a large iron mill-wheel. I think it was originally owned by the Penroses – but it had not been working for many many years. The Mahon Stream was not big enough, and was only a spate stream, so the mill cannot have been economic.

At the Drohans' farm we had great fun in the hayloft but what I remember best was chasing the hens to make them lay their eggs on the run – when first laid a hen's egg has a rubbery coating and it bounces along the ground, taking a few minutes before the shell hardens and becomes brittle. The hens were fed a meal made mainly of ground-up yellow maize and this became "yalla male" when spoken in the local Waterford accent.

We spent our days exploring the foothills, inspecting the turf cuttings, picking blackberries and, in particular, fraochans (otherwise known as bilberries or whorts) which we then cooked up as part of our daily diet. Sometimes, when we were old enough, we went cycling to Kilmacthomas or Kilrossanty for foodstuffs, medicines, etc.

A Jacob Family
Tramore in the 1900s

*Drohan's Farm in the Comeraghs,
with two Jacob and two Drohan boys at the entrance.*

*At the Comeraghs 1941.
Back: Jim Sexton, Robert Jacob, Charles Jacob.
Front: Weston Jacob, Anne Maguire, Elizabeth Maguire, Philip Jacob.*

I was particularly intrigued by a hydraulic ram installed by Miss Heather who built a cottage just along the road – I thought it wonderful that the energy of water coming down the hillside in a small stream was able to force a small proportion of the water back up again and into the water tank in the roof of her cottage – perpetual motion of the simplest kind.

But best of all was spending time by, or in, the Mahon Stream which tumbled down the hillside through a small wood beside the road to Mahon Bridge. There were some quite good bathing pools, and we always tried to increase their size by shifting rocks and building dams, not with any great or permanent success, but we felt like real engineers. The favourite bathing place was christened the "pools of Moab".

Very occasionally there would be a major expedition to Coumshingaun Lake or, when we were a bit older, up to Crotty's Lake and Crotty's Rock. Crotty was apparently a local highwayman who robbed the rich to give to the poor, like Robin Hood, and when he was chased by the authorities he would retreat up the mountain to Crotty's Rock from where he was able to observe his pursuers. Once or twice we got to the top of the Comeragh Mountains. On one occasion father and Robert Jacob mounted an expedition to spend a night on the highest point of the Comeraghs, Knockaunapeebra. They planned it meticulously, and as they had to take all their food with them to the top of the mountain they took what they believed provided the most nourishment with the least weight – RyVita, raisins, etc. They had great fun, behaving like professional mountaineers and excited schoolboys all at the same time.

The cottage in the Comeraghs came into its own from 1940 on, by which time I was nine and Weston was eleven, and the Maguire children then joined us – but more of that anon.

Over the back of the Comeragh Mountains is the Nier Valley where every second family has the surname Wall and all the others have the surname Brick, so a person is always known by his own name and that of the dominant close relative. For instance a man would be called "Thomas Wall Michael Brick".

Father was great for getting into conversation with local people, and on one occasion, when he asked a local farmer "Have you ever been up to the top?" was met with the rejoinder "And why wouldn't I when I own the whole bloody mountain?".

On another occasion a Comeragh mountain farmer was describing how some energetic woman hillwalker walked up the mountain "She went over the mountain like a bloody lion". (It may have been Dr. Mary Strangman who was our family doctor up to the early 1930's – there weren't many women doctors in those days. She was quite tough.)

Years afterwards Father was reminiscing about a mountainy family in the district, possibly one of the O'Neills who I understand were the last remaining native speakers. When the hen laid an egg the mother said to the son "Well, you can have it for breakfast tomorrow. How would you like it?" And the son said "With a comrade".

Apparently the O'Neill clan had a war cry "lamh laidir abú" (pronounced "lawv loijer aboo") which being translated means "(the) strong hand uppermost". We children (including the Maguires) thought this was a perfect motto, and for years we used it as our own private war cry among ourselves.

The Maguires and Jacobs play at the "Pools of Moab", Mahon River, Comeragh Mountains, 1940/41.

Chapter 4

Tramore in the Thirties and Forties

We'll start from Summerville. Turn left outside the gate and downhill, on Cove Road, the first cottage immediately beside ours was Mr. O'Connor's, a retired farmer, of slender means and a quiet nature though he did get a bit cross when some of the stones fired by Weston and me with our catapults either hit him or went very near. His garden extended up beside ours but was considerably wider. When he died, father acquired the property, christened its back garden "the Haggard" and grew vegetables, kept beehives in the garden, and later on built a very simple shed in which our little sailing boat Dreoilín wintered. After Mr. O'Connor died we discovered the remains of an early Rover motorcar in his tumble-down garage, but it was too far gone to refurbish or rebuild. Later on Doreen acquired the cottage from father, but he kept the Haggard. Doreen then left the cottage to Ann Jacob. Ann now calls it simply "Mansfield" and uses it for short holiday stays and for lending to her friends. It was let out for many years to Ray & Catherine Finnegan, but they moved out some time ago.

Next down on the left was Mike Brien and then the house where Kathleen and Bridie lived, respectively the daily house-helps in Summerville and Midvale for a number of years. Then "Juverna", the O'Sullivan's house – they had a flourishing bottling plant in Waterford. Later on one of the daughters was a renowned "eco warrier". Then the steps up to the Doneraile Walk, created in Tramore's hey-day many years before as a very civilised seaside walk above the cliffs. It even had a café, but that was long ago. Across the road from Kathleen and Bridie's house were the Kielys – they were part-time fishermen from the pier.

Back up to Summerville gate, opposite which lived the Murrays who had one of the larger fishing boats at the pier and a very attractive thatched house – rather more than a cottage. They too were the unwilling recipients of catapulted stones. Almost next to the Murrays lived Miss Haskins, a retired nurse who came into her own when the Maguires came to stay with us – she often asked us children over for tea and showed us mementos from her years abroad, including a very nice set of Mah Jong pieces made of real bamboo (and she taught us how to play Mah Jong too).

Turning right, up Cove road, from Summerville gate, first on the right was "Cobh Lodge". The elderly occupant died in the late 1930's and my father bought the house. It, too, was originally a modest single storey cottage, but a two-storey extension had been added to the rear. I remember a young couple called Hyde with two small children living there for a couple of years first of all, and then Jim and Veronica Sexton. They were wonderful neighbours and their parties were renowned for delicious sustenance and innovative and enjoyable party games.

A Jacob Family
Tramore in the 1900s

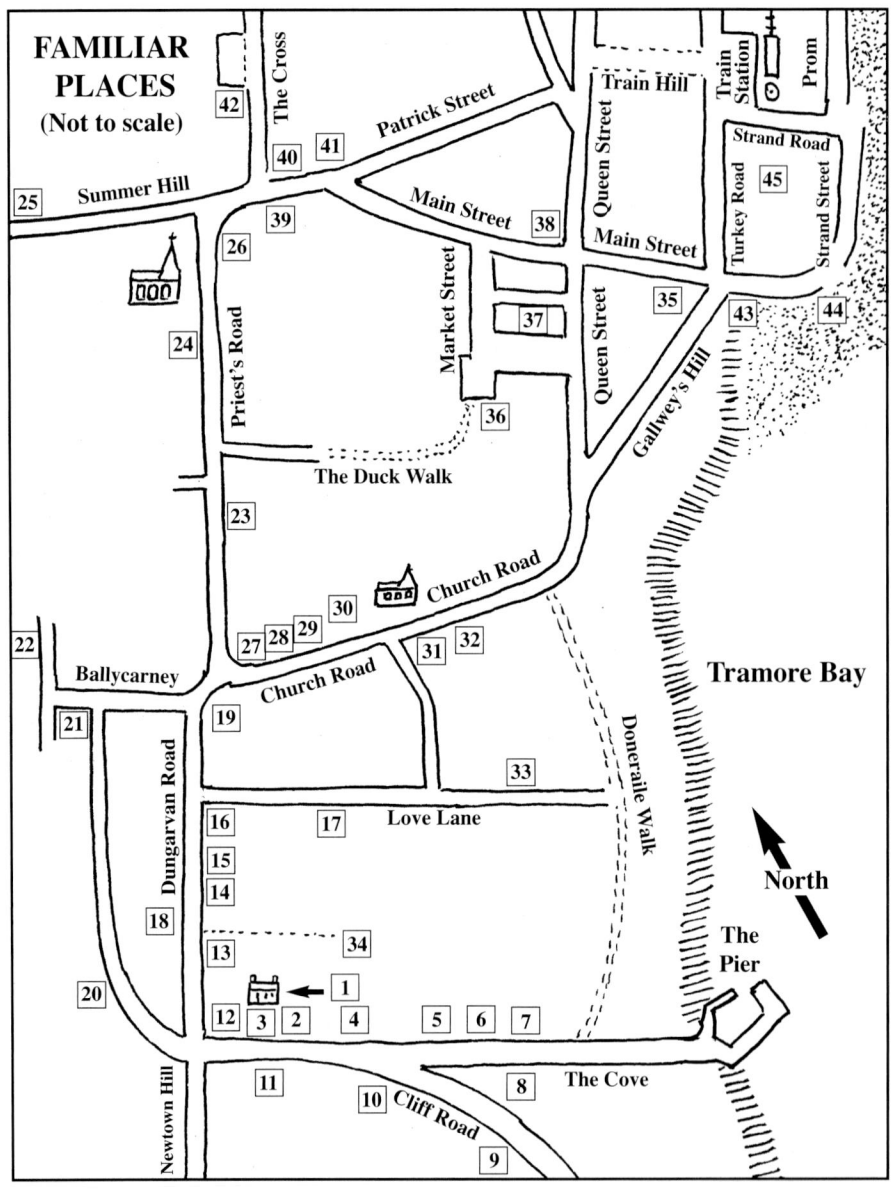

FAMILIAR PLACES
(Not to scale)

Map locations (as labelled):
- 42 — The Cross
- 40, 41 — Patrick Street
- 25 — Summer Hill
- 39, 26 —
- 24 — Priest's Road
- 38 — Main Street
- Queen Street
- Train Hill
- Train Station, Prom
- Strand Road, Turkey Road, 45, Strand Street
- 37 — Market Street
- 35, 43, 44
- 36 — The Duck Walk
- 23
- Gallwey's Hill
- 30 — Church Road
- 27, 28, 29, 31, 32
- 22 — Ballycarney
- 21, 19 — Church Road
- Doneraile Walk
- Tramore Bay
- 16, 17, 15, 14 — Love Lane
- 18, 33
- Dungarvan Road
- 13, 34, 1
- 20, 12, 3, 2, 4, 5, 6, 7
- The Pier
- North
- 11, 10 — Cliff Road, 8 — The Cove
- 9
- Newtown Hill

(1) Summerville.
(2) Cove Lodge.
(3) Cottage.
(4) Mansfield.
(5) Mike Brien.
(6) Kathleen and Bridie.
(7) Juverna.
(8) Kiely's.
(9) Slieve Bloom.
(10) Miss Haskins.
(11) Murray's.
(12) Paddy Kiely's Shop.
(13) Ritz Pub.
(14) Maggie Beyont.
(15) Miss Jones.
(16) Fernville.
(17) Mrs. Finnegan.
(18) Midvale.
(19) Gallwey's (Fairlinch)
(20) Misses Robinson.
(21) Carroll Grubb.
(22) Mrs Elmes.
(23) Jim Cusack.
(24) Fergusons.
(25) Pumping Station.
(26) Nell Paxton.
(27) Mostyns.
(28) Kennedys.
(29) Dickinson's.
(30) The Matchbox.
(31) Fred and Betty Chapman.
(32) Gallwey's (Rocklands).
(33) Garda Barracks.
(34) Villette.
(35) Storrars.
(36) The Forge.
(37) Grand Hotel.
(38) Post Office.
(39) Lodge's Grocery.
(40) Lodge's Hardware.
(41) Reddy's Garage.
(42) Phyllis A. Baker.
(43) Shalloe's.
(44) Bathing Boxes.
(45) Atlantic Ballroom.

Beside that was another small cottage which father bought when the occupant died, and where for a year or two I had a lathe that had come from "Uncle Fred" Jacob in Bray, and where I did quite a lot of wood-turning. "Uncle Fred" had used it among other things for making bandage-winding machines in the first World War (or was it the Boer war?). That brings us to the crossroads.

Turning left onto what is now called Dungarvan Road, and going up Newtown Hill, the first house was rented by the Goodfellow family (a name which, as a small boy, I found very amusing). There was a son called George Goodfellow a bit older than Weston and me, who later became a clergyman. Later on Billy and Maria Glass and their three children Hjordis, Brian and Olaf rented the house while Billy was steward of Major Carew's estate at Ballinamona, half way to Waterford. Maria, like Veronica Sexton, was a past master at organising children's parties. A bit further up the hill was Seaville House occupied then by Robin Cooper-Chadwick (of the Penrose family), and at another time by a Mrs. Malcolmson and more recently by Terry Crosbie and his wife (née Malcolmson). Then came a narrow laneway which led to Joe Brown, his wife Mollie and sister Dorrie. Joe and Dorrie were distinguished golfers and hockey players respectively. Later, Joe developed a shop, the "Cove Stores", at the cross roads. Next to the lane was an attractive house called Beechmount, where from 1942 Fred and Betty Chapman (parents of Joy and William) lived. That was about the extremity of the village of Tramore. Coming back down the hill again the first opening led to the golfcourse which was created in the early 1930's – Weston and I used to roam around picking up lost golfballs, but I am afraid we didn't return them. Any of them that were damaged we removed the covers and unwound what seemed like miles and miles of thin elastic rubber which surrounded a little bag of some unidentified liquid. I wonder do they make golfballs like that nowadays? Next downhill was Sam Morris's house. He and my father were contemporaries and got on extremely well together, though from utterly different backgrounds. Sam owned a coal merchants business in Waterford under his own name, which was confusing as there was a totally different and much larger coal and timber business owned by another Morris family in the city. One of Sam's exploits earlier in his life had been trying to get a free seat at the circus, climbing under the edge of the circus tent only to be roared at by a clown who had a face painted on the back of his head, and hair covering his actual face through which he was looking straight at Sam.

At the bottom of the hill, on one corner of the crossroads, lived the local Garda, O'Sullivan by name. On rainy days he played Pooh Sticks with Weston and me down the stream at the side of the road. He also played Pitch and Toss with his friends and defended his action by saying that was the best way to hear about everything that was going on in the village. The corner shop at the crossroads, on the right, was then owned by Paddy Kiely, a retired post master. He was a very short man, but he made up for that by having a quite remarkable girth!

A Jacob Family
Tramore in the 1900s

Tramore Pier.

Cove Road Tramore. c. 1930.

When I was a small boy it was still the era of sugar being weighed out into blue paper bags, butter being carved, with butter "hands", off the large lump (which had been tipped out of the butter box), then being patted into shape, and weighed carefully on the scales. Biscuits were of course loose in glass-topped Jacob's biscuit tins. Bread was mainly turnover loaves wrapped in newspaper. Small quantities of tea, salt, bullseyes, etc. were packaged in cones of newspaper twisted on the spot. Ice-cream was always between two wafers and tuppence bought a fine fat one. The corner shop was never the same again after Paddy Kiely sold it! Then came the Ritz Pub. It was a small tumble-down thatched premises, with a garden out the back which ran along behind Summerville and on summer evenings the loud talk and laughter often kept us awake. After that a longish drive between two houses led to Villette where another branch of the Chapman family lived – Fan who was by then a widow, her daughter Betty who was mildly mentally handicapped, and her son George, who had a gammy leg. Fan and Granny were great friends and often visited each other. Villette had a large pond, or small lake, surrounded by trees and a very large free-standing garage in which Canon Staunton's sailing dinghy, "The Minx", spent each winter – George Chapman used to sail it for (and with) Canon Staunton during the summer. Next up the road was another little shop kept by "Maggie". This was just across the road from Midvale (Granny and Grandpa's house). The Jacob family always referred to her as "Maggie Beyont". Unfortunately her shop was the reverse of spick and span and we were enjoined not to buy anything there, which was a bit hard on poor Maggie.

Then there was "Suntrap" where an elderly Miss Jones and her dog lived. She had the thinnest legs I have ever seen in my whole life, accentuated by her shoes being a size too big. She was a good-natured soul. My pet memory of her is when she was at a musical evening at Summerville and my father played a record of Ravel's Bolero with its hauntingly repetitive theme that gets gradually faster and faster – Miss Jones got a fit of the giggles which turned into uncontrollable laughter but fortunately she calmed down before it was necessary to throw a bucket of cold water over her. Further along the road was "Fernville" where Ernest and Hester Pitt and their family (Elizabeth, Philip and Gavin) were for a few years. Ernest's business was Bell's, the chemists in Waterford (a huge gold painted bell hung outside their shop front) of which Maud Bell's husband had been part-proprietor until his death. Arthur Westcott Pitt then became the driving force. Arthur was a very strong swimmer, lived in Dunmore, and was renowned and admired for having his own private plane and landing strip. He had a strangely flat nose and the story was that he had dived into the swimming pool at Bootham School in York when there was no water in it, but I think that was just a leg-pull.

Between Fernville and the next house "Fairlinch" was Love Lane where Mrs. Lily Finnegan taught Weston and me and Dayrell Gallwey, and later on Fritz and Mirza Marckwald, the three R's and great deal more besides, in her little cottage, "Sunnycroft". Further on down Love Lane was the old coastguard station which, by this time, was the headquarters of the local Gardaí Siochana, and incorporated a storage shed for the breeches buoy rocket apparatus for getting a line onto ships wrecked on the coast. Once or twice we were privileged to see the local lifesaving crew practising at the Metal Man. To mimic a ship's mast there was a tall pole with steps bolted on to each side which we had great fun climbing – we called it the "Monkey Pole". At one stage Leslie Crumpton lived on Love Lane - he built an IDRA 14 foot dinghy in his garage. Love Lane ultimately opened out onto the Doneraile Walk, along the top of the cliffs, where there was an old gun emplacement and the ruins of a tea-house.

Back now to the crossroads near Summerville and up the new road (then the "Yellow Road") through the field behind Midvale where the Misses Robinson had built an attractive bungalow. One worked in Graves' timber business in Waterford and the other in the Bank of Ireland branch on the Quay. About 1947 they bought a smart new green Austin A40, and as Grandpa was really too old to travel to the office by train, but wanted to remain involved in the business, they gave him a lift in every day for a few years. I was lucky enough to be given a seat most days, as well. Further on up that road, in what amounted to a small village, called Ballycarney (or Ballycarnane) lived old Mrs. Elmes, and also old Mrs. Grubb (known in our family as Mrs. Leepy Grubb because her husband was called Leopold) and her daughters Kathleen and Carroll. Sixty years later, at the time of writing this, Carroll has just died, aged 99.

Back down from Ballycarney, past Veale's and the high wall of Morrissey's Manor House and farm. At the top of Church Road is Fairlinch where Dayrell Gallwey lived. Going on down Church Road three adjoining houses were home to the Mostyns, the Kennedys and the Dickinsons. Mr. Kennedy was an Irish teacher in Waterford, and always known as Professor Kennedy. His son Paddy was a friend of Weston's, memorable for thinking that Hippocrates was what you call the big boxes in which hippopotamuses are transported. Kenny Dickinson, when quite a young man, decided he was going to emulate Smiths Crisps and started manufacturing potato crisps under the name "Ken's Crisps" which he packed and sold in second-hand Jacob's biscuit tins. Some local wag used to say Ken was ripping people off with "a ha'p'orth of crisps in a thruppenny packet". Inexperience and lack of scale led the business to fold up after a few months.

Then there was a tiny little square house built by Marion Poole (called "The Matchbox"), later occupied by Emily Bennis (a Friend) when she moved to Tramore from Limerick. Then the Church of Ireland National School which was occasionally used as a court-house. Once a year CSJ was called before the Court and fined five shillings for not having Weston and me vaccinated – our mother had a conscientious objection to vaccination. I can't ever remember being inside the Church of Ireland, beside the schoolhouse, but it sticks in my memory because it was considerably older than the Catholic Church at the top of the town. The story goes that the Parish Priest at the time invited the then most renowned church architect to visit him in Tramore, took the man on a long walk around Tramore, ultimately stopping in front of the Church of Ireland, and said to the architect "now I want you to bate that". The architect duly obliged, and some short time afterwards, in about 1860, a fine Gothic Revival Catholic Church rose in a commanding position at the top of the town, appropriately at the end of Priest's Road, from where it is a landmark for scores of miles around. The Church of Ireland was certainly beaten in the size stakes!

Fred and Betty Chapman lived opposite the Church of Ireland before they moved to Beechmount. I have a clear recollection, when I was about six, of passing by their house on the way to Meeting on the Sunday after Christmas and being told by my father that there had been a happy event in that household on Christmas Day, a little girl was born, and was called Joy after the day that was in it. Joy is now Joy Simpson, and we see her every Sunday at Monkstown Meeting.

The other side of a laneway beside Chapman's was an imposing terrace of Edwardian houses called "Atlantic Terrace". The laneway led to the Tramore Tennis Club, then past bungalows where among others Annie Rodgers, Katherine Walpole, and Charles Bacik lived, (he re-started Waterford Glass in the 1950s, more than a century after the original glass works closed). The laneway met up with Love Lane at the old coastguard station.

On down Church Road from Chapman's was "Rocklands", to where the Gallweys moved from Fairlinch – I have written more about them elsewhere. Then a large house occupied by the two Misses Elwyn, aunts of Bob Doupe. When they died, Bob and Hope Doupe inherited the house and lived there for a while. Opposite was a neat little cottage where Miss Coulter lived – the retired teacher from the Church of Ireland National School. Then, on the sea side of the road was the gate to the Doneraile Walk, and beside that Smoky Joe Walsh's house – he was the proprietor of the Munster Express. He had a delightfully unorthodox (perhaps even eccentric) daughter Miriam. He was chief reporter for his paper, copy writer, editor and production manager. This enabled him to ensure that in virtually every edition of his weekly paper, there appeared a fine photograph of Smoky Joe himself. Then two lovely houses below the level of the road, at the top of the cliff, with wonderful views over the bay, one of which was run as a guest house by the YWCA. On the other side of the road the Spencers built a house and in the spacious garden they set up large greenhouses and grew tomatoes, though whether it was a commercial success or not I don't know.

On down the steep Gallwey's hill one could, if one's brakes didn't fail, stop and go into Shalloe's shop. It was a quintessential seaside resort shop with all the cheapest toys one could imagine, which in those days included Japanese-made tin cars of no quality at all. Little did we think that within a few years Japan would be making far better toys, cameras, motorbikes, cars, etc. than those being made in Europe. Just before Shalloe's there was a small enclave of houses nestling under a bit of inland cliff. Douglas and Ruth Storrar and their two boys David and Martin lived here for a few years – he was the Financial Controller of Allied Ironfounders, one of the few heavy industries in Waterford. Douglas was a small man, with a domed bald head. They were the kind of people that our family enjoyed being with, and on my marathon cycle tour in 1950, after a half-year in London, I visited them in their house in Wellington, near Malvern and the Wrekin.

BATHING BOX

Past Shalloe's shop, towards the sea, on Strand Street, on a slipway, stood the bathing boxes (on their cast-iron wheels), though I never remember one being used for bathing, even by a gentlewoman with an old-fashioned sense of modesty! In their heyday the bathing boxes had been drawn by horses over the hard sand and into the sea to where the water was two or three feet deep. Here, too, behind the sea wall was the Atlantic Ballroom and, in the summer season the roundabouts and bumping cars and three-card tricksters - and occasionally Duffy's circus. Duffy's only had a tiny circus tent, but I enjoyed the performances mightily, especially the clowns. I am still a sucker for a performance by a good clown!

Past the bathing boxes and the Atlantic Ballroom, and beyond the broad slipway was "The Prom". This promenade backed the beautiful broad strand, with its superb fine sand, which stretched on for what seemed to small children like miles, to the sand dunes, usually called "The Rabbit Burrows".

The strand is of course the reason for the name Tramore – in Irish "Big Strand" is "Tráigh Mór" pronounced "Traw More".

At the end of the Prom stood "Ocean View", a large house owned by the Moores. Mr Moore was the Bank Manager. A branch of The Provincial Bank of Ireland was the only bank in Tramore, and so Mr Moore was an "important person". He was also a character. He cycled to work every day, but sometimes the wind blowing along the Prom was rather strong, so he devised and made a windshield for his bike, its two sides meeting in the front at a sharp angle. It was not long before all Tramore gave Mr Moore the name "Split-the-Wind". Ocean View was also a Guest House, popular with visitors to the seaside resort.

A few yards further on there was a stone building which had originally been the lifeboat house, where the voluntary lifeboat was kept. This service largely owed its existence to Edward Jacob who had been appalled at the loss of life from sailing ships foundering and breaking up in Tramore Bay if they had unfortunately mistaken it for the safe haven of Waterford Harbour a few miles to the east. Edward (1843-1924) was "Cousin Willie's" father, and Robert and Anna Jacob's grandfather. The worst recorded wreck was the "Sea Horse" in 1816 when 363 persons were drowned. There was for many years a stock of warm blankets in this shed, ready to wrap round the lucky survivors of shipwrecks. By the time we were children this shed was closed, and in the doorway an elderly lady sat with her Primus stove, offering a different kind of service. She provided a constant supply of boiling water for picnickers to use for making their tea, for a modest charge. She was known to everyone as "Gertie Boiling Water".

Energetic souls would walk on from this point, either on the strand or on the sand and shingle spit between that and the Back Strand, (or Cúl Trá, pronounced 'cool traw') to reach the "Rabbit Burrows". We had many happy days there running up and down the sand hills, looking at the tiny blue and yellow butterflies, and the yellow and blue miniature pansies, and trying to find the kitchen middens we were told had been discovered there, but had obviously been covered up by blown sand.

Return now to the bathing boxes and the Atlantic Ballroom, up Strand Road, a hundred yards back from the strand lies the Station Square, and what was the terminus of the Waterford to Tramore Railway. Opposite the station was a shop called Manahan's that sold good ice-creams, and behind that a terrace where Willie Watt's mother lived. Willie was proprietor of the Waterford Sack & Bag Co, but was more famous for his superb tenor voice. He broadcast and recorded on many occasions. Before joining the Sack & Bag Co he had spent some time in Harvey & Son with EBJ learning about office work, a fact of which I was inordinately proud. Beside Manahan's was Train Hill – very steep, and not suitable for cars. One of the two "carriers" in Tramore, Willie Brown, was based on the square, with a brown horse, and a cart, though I cannot remember us using his services.

The little seven mile long Waterford & Tramore railway dating from 1863, which was never connected to the mainline system of Ireland, was a real feature of Tramore life. It was used every day by commuters, and in summer crowds would come at weekends from Waterford, particularly to enjoy the wonderful long sandy beach and have their picnics, with the inevitable sand in the sandwiches. Because the train simply went backwards and forwards between the two terminuses on a single track there was a turntable for the engine at each terminus.

THE DAY THE ENGINE FORGOT TO STOP

On one famous occasion the engine driver, probably because he had enjoyed someone's hospitality not wisely but too well, forgot to stop when he got to Tramore Station, the engine overshot the turntable, and landed on its six wheels on the roadway three or four feet below the level of the railway line. All Tramore turned out to see the result and the episode was the subject of jokes for years afterwards.

DERAILED AT "PERRY'S HILL"

On another occasion a more serious accident occurred near Perry's Hill, about two miles from Tramore, when a different engine toppled off the rails and landed on its side at the bottom of the embankment. I was quite small, but remember clambering around it.

Waterford and Tramore Railway Train, July 1934.

The Motorcycle Ice Cream Man, Tramore.

A Jacob Family
Tramore in the 1900s

The two "guards" were characters – Christy Falconer and Paddy Madigan. Five minutes before the train was due to leave the guard on duty would ring the "five-minute-bell". The "one-minute-bell" was rung on a smaller handbell and the guard would then walk across Railway Square to where he could see up Turkey Road towards Gallwey's Hill. If anyone was running to catch the train departure would be delayed until the passenger was safely on board.

When I was nine or ten I caused amusement on the train by knitting socks, scarves and gloves for UK Merchant Seamen to help the "War Effort" (SKJ had organised knitting parties at Summerville for this purpose, and I had joined in). 50 years later Heather Swailes (from England) asked me was I from Tramore, and when I said "Yes" she said "Are you the person who as a boy knitted socks on the Waterford-Tramore train", and when I said "Yes" again she said "My mother was a Jackson from Tramore and used to talk about you". There's fame! We boys smoked on the train (but I didn't like it, and was put off for life). One day some jokers lifted Tim Maguire up onto the old style netting luggage rack for the duration of the journey. The last train ran on 31st December 1960.

Years before, the two daughters of Aubrey Harding (an Ulster Quaker), Sylvia and Muriel – later married to two Jess brothers - were on holiday at Willie & Edith Jacob's house, overlooking the railway just outside the station. They knew what train Grandpa would be on, and every morning looked out the window to see him waving his handkerchief at them from his carriage. He later gave them a present of a box of handkerchiefs embroidered with the days of the week.

Tramore was the seaside holiday resort for countless families from the hinterland, Kilkenny and Tipperary in particular, so there were a number of small hotels. However, it is not the hotels that I remember from my boyhood days as much as the dentist. He saw patients once a week in the front room of a house opposite the railway station. He had very little equipment – the drill was treadle-operated, and it was quite a feat to use the drill for delicately enlarging cavities while manipulating the treadle. When it was necessary to administer an anaesthetic, he would fill a syringe with some liquid (Procaine I think), would stand back from the unfortunate patient, and would squirt the liquid onto the gum where the anaesthetic was needed, thus freezing it. Every filling he put in was amalgam, which he would squeeze between his fingers and thumb to mix until it squeaked before stuffing it in the cavity . His name was Mr. Jennings, and was christened "Jellybags" by my father and his siblings many years before. He was a precise old-fashioned grey-haired little man in a tweed suit, with a small moustache, who was certainly not at the cutting edge of dental technology.

Next along Lower Branch Road was the Majestic Hotel, painted white, and the subject of a magnificent reproduction in icing sugar for some special occasion - but I can't remember what. After that, the back of the Meeting House and then a terrace which included Mabel Jacob's residence – she was cousin Willie's sister and lived to a ripe old age.

Then there was "Easton" where cousins Willie and Edith Jacob lived and Robert and Anna grew up. Edith was an intelligent, attractive, able person, born and brought up in England. She was then ever so slightly intimidating, perhaps a wee bit grand, but in her latter years softened and was beloved by all. When I was ten or twelve I was invited one day to dinner with them and we had soup to start with. It was served with bread on the side plate, and I knew it was not good manners to break up the bread and put it in my soup but I said as much to Willie and Edith and, bless them, they said it was perfectly all right!

Next was "Powerscourt" where the Bells lived. Fred Bell, who was a Quaker, died in 1941, leaving his wife Maud and children Robina (later Chapman), Henry and William. Maud was very hospitable. I remember the wonderful Christmas parties there, the blazing and welcoming fire in the hallway, the big dog, and all the wonderful goodies at tea time. Now, in 2008, Ross and Robina (Bell) Chapman live in Newry, Co. Down and William and Florence live in Sandyford, Co. Dublin, all four being very active in Quaker affairs. Henry's family live in Australia – he himself died a few years ago.

At this point Upper Branch Road (which comes down the hill from the centre of Tramore) merges from the left with Lower Branch Road (which is really the main road to Waterford). On the right hand side is Tivoli Terrace, to where Granny & Grandpa and their family moved initially from Percy Terrace, Waterford. Further on along the Waterford Road, lived two stalwarts of the Tramore Singers when Stella was conductor, Captain Doyle in the bass rank (who suffered a heart attack and died when lifting up one side of a car while somebody else changed a wheel), and Jim Tobin, an anchor-man among the tenors.

Then there is a right turn at a crossroads (now a roundabout) that takes one back down Old Riverstown Road to the sea, past Zoe Brabazon's house, yet another member of the Tramore Singers. From here one was able to see the remains of the small grandstand of the old Tramore Racecourse that had been flooded in 1911 when the sea broke through the sand and gravel spit which ran from Tramore to the "Rabbit Burrows" and Brownstown Head.

Now, back to where Upper and Lower Branch Road meet, we head towards the centre of Tramore. First the front door of Powerscourt, then the back entrance of Easton, then the Quaker Meeting House which was built in 1869, where we went to Meeting for Worship every Sunday. It consisted of one quite large room divided by folding doors and simple "facilities" and is now leased to the Tramore Development Agency. We went to Meeting regularly, and were perfectly happy even though there was Sunday School only very infrequently. Grandpa would come in with his hat on, sit down on the elders bench, and place his hat on the seat beside him. Cousin Willie (Jacob) would sit beside him and regularly read a passage from the bible. Cousin Edith (Jacob) would usually either sing or recite a hymn. Cousin Mabel (Jacob) would usually speak, with an evangelical message. Others sometimes contributed. Occasionally I got fidgety, and once when I was about six I dropped a marble by mistake – it rolled right across the wooden floor. Auntie Pol was sitting beside me - her disapproving "vibes" were powerful and gave me a real guilty conscience. On Sunday afternoons Cousin Mabel had a gospel meeting in her house, but it wasn't my "thing" – I only attended once or twice.

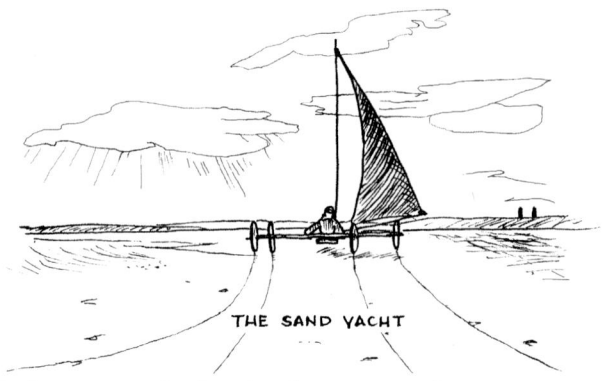

THE SAND YACHT

Being built on a very sloping site, there was rough storage space under the back of the Meeting House. There Father, Robert Jacob and Jim Sexton stored their sand yacht, which they had themselves made in 1940 out of timber and old bicycle wheels. The first time out on the strand they took a corner too fast and the wheels buckled right over which was disappointing but did not put them off. They got stronger motorcycle wheels instead – these were better but made it a bit heavy. Neither father nor Robert knew the principles of sailing, but they had a few laughs, and then before long abandoned the project. The steep sloping Meeting House "garden" was used to grow potatoes during the Second World War.

Another few yards along the road lived Ernest Chapman, at 1 Rosebank Terrace. His children Belle, June and Colin were more or less the same age as Weston and me. His wife had died some years earlier when they were still living in Annestown but by this time they had a wonderful Quaker relative from England called Dorothy Darton looking after them. She was in the same mould as Veronica Sexton and Maria Glass – kind, totally competent, excellent cook, excellent seamstress, great at organising children's parties – she was a real addition to the community. She ran a small primary school in the house and her pupils included Joy Chapman, William Bell, Tim Maguire, Colin Chapman and Pete Langley. I think prior to living here Ernest and his family had been for a short time in one of the two houses beside Smoky Joe's, called Cliff View, though presumably not the one that was a guest house run by the YWCA!

A few yards further on, on a hairpin bend, where Pond road meets Upper Branch Road, just past the top of Train Hill, was a small hall or assembly rooms - I seem to remember this is where election counts took place. Horace E. Sexton's house was at the far end of Pond Road. (Horace was Jim Sexton's father). He was proprietor of The Central Stores, a high-class grocery on the Quay in Waterford. My father bought Horace's immaculately kept Sunbeam motorcycle about 1930.

Moving along Queen Street towards the centre of Tramore was Torpey's the butchers, and then Jim Halligan's electrical goods and repair shop (yet another of the bass members of the Tramore Singers). Jim had a gammy leg. Then came Greer's cake shop, and the crossroads with the main street. Down to the left was Fox's Pharmacy and the Provincial Bank.

Straight ahead was Molloy's the butchers, Jim Stubbs (cobbler) and the Grand Hotel which was in a dominating position. Some decades previously it must have been where the cream of Tramore's summer visitors stayed, but by this time the place was already showing signs of being the relics of old decency. My chief memory is of the head waitress Mary who was a diminutive woman with her hair piled high on her head, but with an undoubted air of authority. As children we always wondered whether birds actually nested in her hair. I have been reminded that across the road from the hotel was Patsy Power, Tramore's best taxi-man, who lived in an unbelievably small dwelling, but I don't think we as a family ever availed of his services. Beside the hotel was Market Square, used as a car park (and for the Waterford Hunt meet on St. Stephen's Day every year). From the other side of this car park ran an alleyway and another small square, one side of which consisted of the Assembly Rooms, where the Scouts met. The forge was in the opposite corner. As boys, Weston and I were fascinated by the operation of the forge - the fire, the bellows, the anvil on which the blacksmith hammered the red hot horseshoes into shape, the tongs with which he picked up the horseshoes, the way he held the upturned horse's hoof between his thighs and the sizzle and smell when the horseshoe was burning onto the hoof. And we couldn't understand why the nails being driven into the hoof weren't causing the horse great pain. All very fascinating for a small boy. From the fourth corner of the wee square ran the "Duck Walk" (often used by us as a pedestrian short cut).

The Misses Flaherty had a drapery on the little street behind the Grand Hotel, Market Street, and here also was Mr. Flanagan, shoe mender. He was a kindly soul and when Stefan Feric was showing Weston and me how to make catapults in 1939 very kindly supplied us with bits of upper leather for making pouches, and wax-end for tying the pouch onto the elastic. Some time later, on the same little street, the Rex Cinema was built – nothing more than a great big barn!

Starting from the crossroads again and going up Main Street (which is quite steep) we often went into the Post Office (which doubled as a telephone exchange and a haberdashery and wool shop). The telephone operator/postmistress/shopkeeper had a switchboard that was operated by plugging two cables, one for the caller and one for the recipient, into holes in the switchboard. On one occasion she received a call for Granny (who lived at Midvale at the top of the town), but there was no reply from Midvale, so she asked the caller should she try Mrs. Jacob Easton because she saw Mrs. Jacob Midvale passing by about twenty minutes before and perhaps Mrs Jacob Midvale was on her way to visit Mrs Jacob Easton. That is the kind of service one doesn't get nowadays!

Further up was a garage with a petrol pump, on the footpath, operated by hand that had two glass containers each holding a gallon which filled up alternately and when emptied into your petrol tank you knew how much you had bought. In those days also there were excellent metal two gallon petrol cans with brass caps which some cars carried as a spare strapped onto the running board. I had one, but years later someone took a fancy to it, and it disappeared. The street also had a chemist (Hogan's), a haberdashery (Martin's), and when we were boys the Torrie family opened the L&N grocery (short for London & Newcastle Tea Stores) – this was a forerunner of the supermarket. The manager was Charlie Matthews, but he left, I never knew quite why, and set up a grocery later on under his own name.

Plunkett's (butchers) were opposite and then Goodwin's (greengrocers) with a really pitifully small selection of vegetables. The small dark brother looked after the shop, and the tall thin one had a milk round in the village from whom we in Summerville bought our milk. He had a bicycle and a small milk churn on the front of the bike with half-pint and one-pint dipping ladles. He was a good-natured bloke and always gave a little bit of extra milk which he called "a tilly for the cat". In those days most people bought potatoes from some local smallholder who grew more than they needed themselves, and it was the same with cabbage and carrots, though in Tramore there was also a slightly simple soul called 'Stasia who sold vegetables from a string bag, trudging from house to house on foot. She wore a grubby old mackintosh raincoat, down to the ground, and an old out of shape trilby felt hat pulled on like a cloche.

The rest of Main Street was mostly small dwelling houses. Near the top was Reddy's Garage, and one of the rather larger enterprises in Tramore, Lodge's. On the right-hand side of the street was Lodge's hardware shop and on the left their bakery and grocery. The baker's van called round to houses in Tramore every day. I remember a cafuffle once, though it wasn't fully explained to me - I think one of the van-men had been taking money from householders for bread he had delivered, and putting it in his own pocket.

Take a right turn after Lodge's and you are on The Cross Road that passes the racetrack on its way to Waterford. A hundred yards along this brings you to Sweet Briar Park. Here lived a Quaker called Phyllis Ada Baker, Norman Baker's sister, the name always in full to distinguish her from her sister-in-law Phyllis M Baker. She had a wonderful "museum" of interesting things, which she was very good about showing to two small boys. At the very top of Main Street there was a small Methodist Church, beyond which towered the fine edifice of the Catholic Church.

Straight on beyond the Catholic Church Summer Hill passed by the pumping station in which a "gas oil" (or diesel) engine thumped away, bringing Tramore's water from Carrigavantry Reservoir. Carrigavantry is one of three lakes, not very far apart (Carrigavantry, Ballyscanlon, and Knockaderry which is the reservoir for Waterford).

Turn left between the Methodist and Roman Catholic Churches and one is on Priest's Road. Nell Paxton lived in about the fifth house. Her husband had died leaving three small children, Peter, Timmy and Millie, about the same sort of age as Weston and me. Nell, a very attractive lady, had a good and well trained soprano voice (and was in the Tramore Singers). Strangely, years later, Mrs. Massey, one of my landladies in Dublin came across Peter Paxton – he was musical and was then an organist there. Up a small cul-de-sac nearby lived Mrs. Phillips, Nell Paxton's sister. Then there was a group of handsome houses with a common front gravel in one of which lived the Ferguson family. Mr. Ferguson was an auditor and accountant in Waterford and his children, Donald, Daphne, June and Keith were about our age. Daphne was a couple of years older than I, attractive, vivacious, an excellent hockey player and was then at Bishop Foy School in Waterford. I worshipped her from afar. Later on Donald inherited the business but I believe it folded up – I can't remember why. (Forty years later I was at a horticultural lecture in Dublin and, lo and behold, the speaker was Keith Ferguson!)

Then, on the left-hand side, started the "short cut" (the Duck Walk), by which we nearly always walked on shopping errands to the middle of "town". It conjures up in my mind a picture of me, aged about seven, wearing short trousers, and one of the khaki coloured rubberised cotton fabric raincoats typical of that period, on a cold rainy winter day, with a string bag containing the family groceries from the L & N.

Further on the right-hand side of Priest's Road, "Endsleigh" where Jim and Veronica Sexton settled when they left Cobh Lodge. And across the road from them Pat (short for Patricia) O'Sullivan, a champion Irish golfer for many years.

Up a cul-de-sac Dr. O'Donnell who was Stella's GP, – by that time I think Dr. Mary Strangman was no longer around. Then Jim Cusack's little shop (another member of the Tramore Singers, and a very good tenor).

And that completes my mental tour of the little town where I grew up so happily.

From time to time Father's play with words and local phrases pops into my mind.

- He was fond of saying that apprentices in the old days were given "lodging and the run of their gums", i.e. they were given a bed to sleep in and food to eat.
- He was very proud of the Waterford "blaa", a special kind of soft round flat bread bap made only in Waterford.
- Whenever he got a letter written in Irish he would try and read it out but he was not an Irish speaker and instead of "A duine uasail" he would say "A dwiney weasel", and at the end of the letter where it said "Mise le meas" he would say "Meazy leh Meaz".
- A snail was always a "shellacky bookie". Fifty years later I was browsing in Dineen and discovered that a slug in Irish is "seilide" and if it has its house on its back, it is a "seilide buaice".

- And telling about a man who arrived in a donkey cart, got out of it at the front door of the establishment where he was staying for the night, and said to the porter "Boy, extricate the quadruped from beneath this vehicle and stabulate him. Donate him an adequate supply of nutritious aliment, satiate his thirst with the usual element, and when the aurora of morn shall illuminate the Oriental horizon I shall award thee a pecuniary compensation for thy most amiable hospitality".
- Oralia is a little town in Canada that is said to be pretty, and he would relate how one man passing through it for the first time read its name as "you really are", but by the time he came back he had changed his mind and read it as "you're a liar".
- There apparently was a firm of solicitors in Sligo called Argue and Phibbs, later joined by a new partner called Rooke, so it became Argue, Phibbs and Rooke.
- And the well known case of the Skibbereen Eagle, a small local newspaper in West Cork, which in 1897, when Russia was pursuing policies disapproved of by the western nations, solemnly declared to a British statesman, in an editorial, that it had "got its eye both upon him and the Czar of Russia". So the Western World stopped worrying.

Fritz and Mirza Markckwald 1940.

Chapter 5

1939 – A Watershed Year

In 1939 refugees started to arrive from Nazi Germany, the war broke out in Europe, and I started at Newtown School. Hitler's determination to rid the countries under his control of Jews, and anyone that had any connection with Jews, prompted the formation of networks to enable threatened people to seek asylum elsewhere. In the United Kingdom Quakers received many refugees from Germany, and from Austria too as there was a Quaker Relief Centre up and running in Vienna. A committee that included Quakers was also formed in Ireland and offered to take a small proportion of the refugees that arrived in Britain. One of the routes by which they came was from Fishguard to Rosslare. My grandfather, Edwin B. Jacob, became responsible for meeting them at Rosslare and then accompanying them to Ardmore where there was a Reception Centre, which I have mentioned in the Edwin B & Jessie E Jacob chapter.

The first two refugees I remember were Fritz and Mirza Marckwald. After a period in Tramore staying at "Midvale" with Edwin and Jessie Jacob, during which they learned some English with Mrs. Lily Finnegan at her tiny primary school that Weston and I attended, Fritz and Mirza moved to Galway where Mirza got a job with a small hat-making company, " Les Modes Modernes". As Mirza was a skilled seamstress she made good use of her time there.

The story of "Les Modes Modernes" is interesting. Serge Phillipson was born in Warsaw in 1902. His family moved to Berlin in 1904/5. Serge married Sophie Orbach. To escape the hostility towards Jews in Germany they moved to Paris in 1929/30. Sophie's brother had moved to Paris earlier and had formed a small hat factory "Les Modes Modernes". Serge joined the firm in 1933. In 1935 an Irish Government Minister and an Irish businessman arrived in Paris seeking companies that might set up subsidiaries in the west of Ireland, and create jobs. They visited "Les Modes Modernes" and in 1935 Serge moved to Ireland and formed "Les Modes Modernes" in Galway.

Some years later, after the war, Fritz and Mirza benefited from another instance of continental expertise developing a business and creating jobs in Ireland. Charles Bacik and Miroslav Havel arrived in Waterford from Czechoslovakia, with the commercial objective of setting up a glass-making, blowing and cutting operation. This expanded greatly over the ensuing decades as "Waterford Glass". Charles was the technician and "Mickey" the designer. They started in a simple box-like concrete block building near the Kilcohan soccer ground in Waterford, and employed Fritz as financial controller and salesman. He continued in this position for a number of years.

Also in 1939 a young man called Stefan Feric arrived from Austria and stayed with our family in Summerville. He was a student who had not finished his medical degree. We were told that he swam across the Danube to get away.

Although it seemed to us boys like forever, he probably only stayed with us for six or nine months. Father took Weston and me to Dublin to collect Stefan from Philip Somerville-Large's house, Vallombrosa in Bray, and we came home via a visit to the Kings River (where the Poulaphuca Dam was under construction, and behind which Blessington Lake was created), and that night we camped on the slopes of Keadeen Mountain. Stefan was a bright, active individual and enjoyed this introduction to the countryside of Ireland. He was very good with Weston and me. We were enthralled at how he could carve, with his penknife, a chain with interlocking links from a rod of seaweed. He taught us how to make catapults. His mother, who remained in Austria, knitted a very good navy blue polo-necked pullover and sent it over for me – I wore it for years. Stefan ultimately managed to finish his degree here in Ireland, and ended up with a responsible job in a major food company in Dublin, got married, and lived happily for years in his adopted land. I owe my life to him because one day when he had accompanied us to Tramore Strand for a swim I got into difficulties in an unexpectedly deep channel, but was not yet able to swim. Stefan spotted what was happening, hauled me out, and saved me from drowning. Fortunately he was a strong swimmer. (The reason I had not yet learned to swim was that I was still not allowed to play games or swim following my hernia operation).

*Stefan Feric with Philip and Weston,
camping on the slopes of Keadeen Mountain Wicklow, 1939.*

At first, the outbreak of war in September 1939 on the Continent of Europe, had a minimal effect on Ireland (which remained neutral throughout the war, thus infuriating Winston Churchill). Gradually, however, even in Ireland white bread became a thing of the past, rationing came in, no bananas, no oranges, very little butter (except when one could get "country butter" which was bright yellow and very tasty), coal and petrol were virtually unobtainable, cars were laid up, and a good many people cut and harvested turf for themselves – it became the universal fuel. Some people for whom cars were a necessity used big square bags of gas tied to the roof of their car, and others a "gas converter" (like a mini gas-works!) bolted to the front or back of their car. Hayboxes were used to assist in cooking, and make-shift "cookers" were made out of metal drums packed with sawdust with a hole down the middle that acted as both fireplace and chimney when the sawdust was lit. Everyone was trained in air-raid precautions, we learned how to use gas masks, there was a black-out so that no lights were shining at night that would act as beacons for enemy aircraft. Some businesses ground to a halt, but on the whole people managed surprisingly well.

In September, 1939, I started at Newtown School aged eight, as a day scholar, in the class then known as "Transition". By this time Weston and I both had bicycles. Weston's had previously been our mother's, a BSA man's bike with a cross-bar so that she could have a child seat on the cross-bar - my father had one on his too. (The letters "BSA" were the initials of the cycle's manufacturers Birmingham Small Arms). My own bicycle was a brand new blue "Elswick", and was my pride and joy. We would cycle to Tramore Station, put the bikes on the train, and then cycle from Waterford Station to Newtown School. There is more about the school in another chapter.

Either before the outbreak of war, or shortly afterwards, Tommy Maguire, who was Senior Partner of the firm S.C. Maguire & Co., Stockbrokers, in London (through whom our family business of Harvey & Son transacted its stockbroking in London) made a request to Father and Stella. They asked if things got nasty and bombing started could Tommy and Norah's four children move from their home in Woking to Ireland, and stay with us in the peace and safety of Tramore - until hostilities ceased if necessary. Bless them, my parents said "Yes, of course", and when things hotted up in 1940 four weary children arrived at crack of dawn one June morning at Summerville's front door. They were obviously somewhat apprehensive and bewildered, but it wasn't long before Stella, in the wonderful way that she had, made them feel completely at home. Thus began an unforgettable period for the Jacob family.

The youngest was Timothy (six), then Susan, the same age as me (eight), Elizabeth, always known as "Buff" (twelve) and Anne, (about fourteen) who was very conscientious and felt a responsibility for her siblings.

Summerville was a small house, so arrangements were made for some of the Maguires, and sometimes Weston and me, to sleep elsewhere, mostly at Midvale, but also sometimes billeted with a kind elderly bachelor called Mr. McCarthy who lived on his own in a bungalow next door to Midvale.

A Jacob Family
Tramore in the 1900s

The Maguire Family at Summerville, 1940/41.
Susan, Nora, Anne, Tommy, Elizabeth, Tim in front.

"The Garden Room" Summerville.
Susan Maguire, Weston Jacob, Tim Maguire, Philip Jacob,
Stella Jacob (in shadow) on right, 1940.

It was decided to build an extra room in the garden at Summerville, so Hamiltons the builders were called in at short notice and created what became known as the "Garden Room". It had a flat roof so that the view from the upstairs window of Summerville would not be obscured. The Garden Room helped to relieve the pressure on space, but even so, fitting in eight people (and feeding them) was quite a feat – for instance there was only one bathroom and one (fortunately separate) WC in Summerville! In order to make room for the Garden Room the corrugated-iron roofed wooden shed which we called "the workshop" had to be moved. Mr. Crowley, the handyman from near Garrarus, was called in to give help and advice. He looked at the construction of the workshop and said "Well, we'll take off the ridge piece, we'll saw the shed right down the middle, we'll carry it in two halves and then nail it together in its new position". CSJ was tickled pink by this simple solution and the job was duly done with little or no hassle.

Buff, in particular, was energetic and a live wire. She had been in the Girl Guides in Woking, had begun to learn the piano there (and played "Marche Militaire" confidently and very loudly), and had an aptitude for mathematics and numbers (at dinner one day she asked "Does anyone know what four consecutive numbers add up to 10?" and then told us the answer, namely 1, 2, 3 and 4. I was only a beginner at maths, and was duly impressed).

We made a small tree-house in a small tree in the front garden at Summerville. One or two of us that had a commercial streak would go to Paddy Kiely's corner shop, buy a packet of Smarties, open it up, count how many there were, and then sell them in small lots to the others, making a small profit each time.

Under the eaves in my bedroom upstairs there was a curtained-off storage space where we made sufficient room for a "den" for Elizabeth, Weston and me – it was called "Estibuff" – "Est" from Weston's name, "i" from my name and "buff" from Elizabeth's. This was rather hard on the others, but I don't think it caused too much resentment.

Bicycles were procured for the Maguires and this enabled Elizabeth, Weston and me (and sometimes Anne) to cycle the twenty-five miles to the cottage in the Comeragh Mountains where we happily spent, without adults, what seemed like months but was probably only a couple of weeks, in the summer. I was nine or ten, but managed to play my part. We agreed on a rule, when cycling, that none of us was to forge ahead, especially riding up hills, when the younger members of the party couldn't manage it – any perpetrator would be barracked with shouts of "show-off". We all lived an active, largely outdoor, life, tending for ourselves, and many years later the Maguires said how much they appreciated having been exposed to all this, as they had previously led a largely sheltered suburban life in Woking. For my part I regard this period, when our family became three girls and three boys, as one of the most enjoyable and formative periods of my life. I don't apologise for repeating my admiration for the way our parents (and particularly Stella) coped so well and made sure that everyone had a full and satisfying time.

Although it seemed like a much longer period, a year and a half after they had arrived, Anne, Susan and Timothy returned home to England. Elizabeth was in the middle of an exam cycle, and stayed another year or so in Ireland. A friendship that she formed with Desmond Hall at school remained alive and some years later when they were both in Africa they decided to get married and settle in Ireland. We still keep in touch in Des who lives in County Waterford, and also of course with Susan and her husband Kit, and Tim and his wife Eva, living in England. Susan in particular appreciated what she saw of the Society of Friends, and she and members of her family have been active among Quakers. Kit has been in the forefront of very advanced research into a particular aspect of cancer, and in addition has been Secretary of the Pugwash Group, of which you have probably heard. Tim's career included sea-faring, business, and ordination in the Church of England. He has done, and still does, much excellent parish work.

The friendships forged then have lasted ever since. Sadly the passage of time has taken its toll, and Anne and Elizabeth have both gone from among us.

Tramore Strand at dusk.

Chapter 6

Along the Coast

Out Summerville Gate if one turned left, and then right at the V-junction, one found oneself on the coast road looking across Tramore Bay to Brownstown Head and looking down a hundred feet at the sea below. The first house on the right was the Pims' house "Slievebloom" that I have mentioned in Chapter 2. During the war we sowed potatoes in their back garden but they were "Golden Wonders" which the little black slugs adore and it wasn't a success. There was a tall swing which I once fell off and twisted my back rather badly, but never told anybody. A flock of lapwings – a very attractive bird – frequented the field beside the house. A special design feature of the house was small sized roofing slates. Unfortunately this was inclined to let the rain creep in when winter storms were raging. Architects sometimes get things wrong! At Easter one year John Brigham, Headmaster of Newtown who also taught French, arranged a residential "French weekend" for our class in preparation for the Intermediate Certificate exam. He had put together an innovative and intensive tuition weekend, but in the short time available it didn't do much for our ability to speak French!

We often bought potatoes from a cottage next door to Slievebloom. As a small boy sent to collect a stone of spuds I realised how heavy it could get, trudging home! The "Giants' Scratch" was a bit further on – here, on the low cliffs beside the road, were bare rocks with some distinctive long straight cracks across them. This, we were told, was where giants had filed their fingernails, thus making the scratches.

Next was "The Guillamene", the men's bathing place, and then Newtown Cove. This cove had a disappointingly stony little beach but fortunately the locals had created a concrete apron along one side, and high and low diving boards at the sea end of the apron. These diving boards had to be dismantled before winter arrived, otherwise they would be destroyed in winter storms. In my late teens I often cycled out here before breakfast to have a swim, though I was never a particularly strong swimmer. Behind Newtown Cove was a wooded glen. Just inland from this was a large old house where Nellie Hynes lived. She was a very able and intelligent woman and was elected to the Tramore Town Commissioners on the first count, when they were originally set up. (So was father). Half a mile nearer to Garrarus was Kate Rockett's pub, not a place that we frequented!

A cliff path led from Newtown Cove to the "Metal Man" less than a mile away. Below this path the coast was very rocky, and on one occasion Robert Jacob showed me a place where he sometimes swam from the rocks. I did likewise, on my own, a number of times thereafter. I certainly didn't appreciate what a risk I was taking and I would not dream of doing it now. Just before the "Metal Man" was the Monkey Pole, mentioned in another chapter.

The "Metal Man" is Tramore's icon, standing atop one of the three whitewashed pillars that had been built on Newtown Head in 1823, as a reaction to the wreck in 1816 of the Seahorse and the drowning of hundreds of men and women in Tramore Bay. Across the bay, on Brownstown Head, there are two black pillars, and further east again stands the historic Hook Lighthouse, a single pillar, painted with bands of black and white, at the entrance to Waterford Harbour. These landmarks were there long before the Metal Man was put in place. Viewed from the sea the three white pillars showed up well against the land behind, the black pillars showed up against the sky, and the Hook with its bands of black and white was distinctive in its own right. These made it easier to determine which was Tramore Bay and which the entrance to Waterford Harbour. Of course that was not much good on a black dark night, or when there was fog, and over the years a number of sailing ships foundered in Tramore Bay. Robert Jacob's great-grandfather, Edward, was very much involved in forming a lifeboat service with volunteer oarsmen which saved many lives in the 1800's.

The "Metal Man" itself had been made in England for an Exhibition, and was then acquired for Tramore. A Jacob forebear liked to tell people that he had once stood on the "Metal Man"s head. When asked to explain how, he would say, "Well, you see, it was on the quayside in Waterford waiting to be transported to Tramore, lying on its back, and I climbed up onto it and stood on its head there". To hop three times around the Metal Man pillar without stopping guaranteed that you would get married within a year. This didn't work for me until I was 25.

THE METAL MAN

Then, a bit further on, was the "Puffing Hole" where, if the tide and the wave conditions were right, a great vertical spout of water like a geyser would be propelled from a hole at the landward end of a particular cave. We were always warned not to go too close to it because in 1861 Robert Jacob (the "R" of W & R Jacob Biscuit Manufacturers) and his friend James Walpole were swept out to sea and drowned at that spot, presumably by a freak wave. Further on again, Garrarus Strand was hopeless for bathing – very stony and exposed. Mr. & Mrs. Crowley lived nearby.

Along the Coast

Dunabrattin Harbour, with old coastal schooner, in background.

Dunabrattin Head.

The next strand, Kilfarassy, was a bit better for bathing, but no great shakes. Another half mile on, a walk across two or three fields and down a grassy cliff, there was a delightful secluded cove that we as a family called "Veale Strand". There is no truth in the contention that this was because a dead calf had been found on the strand – it was called after a family by the name of Veale that farmed nearby. This place was a real favourite of ours, father loved swimming and picnicking there and so did we all, including the Maguires. Next along the coast came Annestown with its lime kiln, its strand, its tidal islands, and its very steep village street. The Galloways lived on the left-hand going up. A few years ago they turned their house into a most delightful small "Country House" hotel where Brigid and I have stayed once or twice. At the foot of the steep street a side road leads to Dunhill and a castle that always intrigued us – built on a steep bluff above the road, it must have been quite impregnable, though now in ruins. The story is told of one time when under siege, with the enemy trying to batter down the door, the lady of the house poured boiling porridge down on top of the attackers, which successfully drove them away.

Next point of interest on the coast is Dunabrattin Head and Boat Strand, and to the delight of father, a promontory fort (he had a "thing" about promontory forts!). The cliffs are quite high here, but there is a narrow twisty road down to a small quayside where for many years a coastal sailing schooner landed cargoes of coal from south Wales. The crew unloaded the coal onto the quayside using the boat's spars as derricks – altogether a hard way to earn a living. Nearby the McCoy sisters had a farm, and I think in addition ran the Munster Dining Rooms in Waterford on behalf of Friends – cheap meals for the poor and destitute. The Torrie family from Waterford built a superb holiday bungalow at Dunabrattin which we envied greatly!

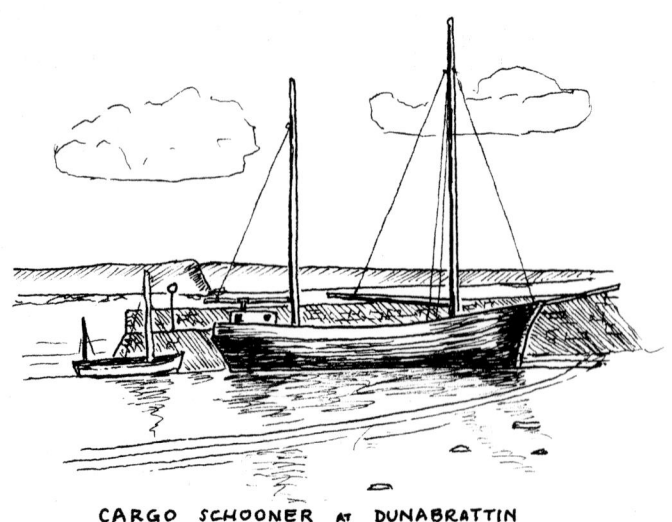

CARGO SCHOONER AT DUNABRATTIN

At the right time of year, from here to Bonmahon there were carpets of sea pink and white sea campion along the cliff tops beside the road – a spectacular sight. The remains of copper mines that were worked many years previously were a feature of this part of the road, too. In ruins by the 1930s, they have now been turned into a tourist attraction. At the village of Bonmahon the Mahon river flows into the sea. It comes all the way down from the Mahon Falls in the Comeragh Mountains and Mahon Bridge (near where "the cottage" was), via Kilmacthomas (always called by locals simply "Kilmac"). Cousin Frederick had a holiday cottage in Bonmahon – the first cottage in the terrace. Next along the coast is the inlet, the sandy cove and attractive village of Stradbally. The river Tay, whose source is in the Comeraghs in the coum to the west of the Mahon Falls, flows into the sea here. It used to be said that Stradbally was for the "gentry" and Bonmahon for "ordinary people" like us.

Further on this remarkable coastline produces another long strand, at Clonea, and then comes the big inlet of Dungarvan Bay. Dungarvan was a rather run-down small town in those days. It had the celebrated Ring Irish-speaking college nearby, the charismatic head of which, the "Fear Mór" by the name of Ó'hEocha (Irish for Haughey), was well known to Grandpa. I think they had various business dealings together. The Irish College is now flourishing again. Beyond Dungarvan, near the end of Helvick Head, and beside the little fisherman's harbour, Hubert and Suzette Poole had built a wooden hut. Weston and I once spent a holiday with them there. Their daughter Beryl was about Weston's age, David was about my age and then came Donald and Christopher. Christopher was very small and had just learned to talk – when asked his name he would rattle out "Tritter Mahdin Pool" (his middle name was Martin). That was about as far along the coast as we ventured in those days.

Waterford Friends pinic near old copper mine workings at Bonmahon.

A Jacob Family
Tramore in the 1900s

Newtown School Main Building, 1937.

Chapter 7

Newtown School

Not surprisingly Newtown looms large in my memories up to when I left at the age of 15. Indeed, since that time too. My grandfather became a teacher in 1891. My father and his brother and sisters went to school there, and he was on the School Committee and Secretary and Chairman at various times. My brother and sister and I went to school at Newtown, and so did our own four children, and now three of our grandchildren are there. I was on the School Committee and so was Brigid. Stella, who married my father when I was five, after my own mother died, taught music and games, and was senior mistress. For a period, her brother John was at the school as a pupil, and had the distinction of building himself a tree-house in one of the trees at the end of the rugby pitch. Arnold Marsh, the Headmaster, showed how much he encouraged enterprise and originality by allowing John to sleep in it provided he was up in time for breakfast!

Arnold Marsh 1890-1972

Newtown School was founded in 1798 for Munster Quaker children. The fine Georgian house bought from Sir Thomas Wyse that year and now standing on 17 acres of grounds is still called the "Main Building", though it is now joined by many and various school buildings. Arnold Marsh arrived in 1926, rescued the school from closing, and through the force of his personality and the help of some of his own resources gradually built up numbers and by the time I arrived there were 90 pupils. This made for a "family" atmosphere and small classes. Numbers are now well over 300.

Arnold retired as Headmaster, and left, in 1939, the year I first went (not cause and effect!). By then he had married my mother's first cousin, Hilda Roberts. Arnold had a big voice. The story goes that one day, in the garden, he wanted to see Mr. Burke so he let out a bellow "Burke!". Five minutes later Mr. Burke appeared. "Where have you been?" says Arnold. "In the gate lodge having my lunch" says Mr. Burke. That was all of four hundred yards, with substantial buildings in between. Some shout! Arnold was very proud of the school herd of Kerry cows, reckoning their light weight would prevent their hooves from cutting up the playing fields. Stella always maintained that she had taught him how to drive a car - she had one herself that she called Blue Peter. The first lesson he went like the wind, never slowing down. He said Stella never told him he could take his foot off the accelerator!

John Brigham became Headmaster in 1939, the year I started at Newtown. He was English, and exceptionally young to be the Head of a school. It was still the era of school caps, and royal blue blazers with green braid around the edges and the school logo on the breast pocket.

A Jacob Family
Tramore in the 1900s

Whitsunday 1937, "Old Scholars Tea" at Summerville, with Weston and Philip on top of the climbing frame.

Newtown School Prefects 1947.
Back: Elizabeth Gray, Philip Jacob, Sheila Tyrrell, Edmund Lamb,
Front: Patricia Maclachlan, Michael Illing, John Brigham, Cilla Telford, Malcolm Maclachlan.

I was in "Lower Transition" for my first year. The next year was "Upper Transition" which was housed in what had been a greenhouse beside the laboratory – as cold as charity in winter and rather hot in summer.

I was studious and enjoyed learning, and in those days had a good memory and could absorb facts and figures. I think I must have been rather a prig, which is probably confirmed by the reaction of fellow pupils, in my first or second year at Newtown, when I displayed in the annual exhibition of handwork a number of things I had made, and produced my own labels for them on special paper with calligraphy (crude I suspect) which I had done with a genuine quill pen created from a goose quill. I was gently teased for being a "show-off".

For the first year or two I was a day scholar, travelling on the train from Tramore to Waterford and back every day. In due course I became a boarder, which suited me very well and saved a lot of wasted time travelling. When the Maguires arrived of course they also went to Newtown. We all had bicycles, and for rainwear some ex-War Department oilskin jackets and trousers were obtained to keep us dry. When the Second World War really became serious, Newtown made arrangements with Lismore Castle that, if the need arose, the school could be evacuated to the Castle where it would be relatively safe from bombing, but that never became necessary, although it would have been rather fun and modestly exciting. Father was deeply involved in discussing potential arrangements with the Cavendishes.

When fuel started to get short Newtown laid in a stock of turf, and a huge stack of it was installed on the "terrace". This was a reserve and in the end not much was used - it ended up as an enormous mound of peat mould, as the turf weathered rather badly over a period of years. Heating the school at that stage was a real problem, and all sorts of timber, turf and other things were burned in the school's boilers, while we pupils were sent out for a run between classes to get our circulation going. What with the cold, and of necessity a poor diet, chilblains were the order of the day and very itchy and sore they were too.

During some of the war years Newtown was without a caretaker for part of the summer, so we as a family moved in. It was great to have all the facilities available just for us!

The staff that I remember best include:-

- Billy Boggs (Maths) a stickler for discipline, a good rugby coach, inclined to have favourites among the pupils, particularly those who were good at maths, and inclined to be less supportive of girls and their efforts than of boys.
- Lester Smith (Science & Geography) was one of the team of enthusiastic teachers that Arnold Marsh had built up that were all forward thinking and prepared to be unconventional. Mr. Smith (for some reason nicknamed Smegs) was a good teacher and an excellent role model. He once said to me, after a pupil had made a superb glass model of the human circulatory system, that a teacher's proudest moment was when a pupil could do something better than he could himself.

Another of his pearls of wisdom - one has to be specially nice to people that one doesn't really like. Prior to coming to Newtown Smegs had worked in a factory in Lancashire and then became a geography teacher. He was prone to digressions in class, such as relating how a local dignitary visiting his school in Lancashire had asked a pupil in geography class to tell him about "Egg-wiped". Flummoxed, the child had to be told that the man meant "Egypt". Many of his stories began "Now when I was at the chemical works …." He was the prime mover in the annual school plays and put a great deal of thought and effort into them and got many pupils involved. He was keen on handball. He complained that he couldn't afford to run a car because it would cost nearly £1 a week (which was quite a large proportion of his salary). And he avowed that too much washing was bad for one – it washed away the skin oils (the girls wrinkled their noses at this statement).

- Mr. Fraser, ex-Royal Navy, the gymn teacher, when we made a mess of something, would say "the idea was good but the execution was crude", and exhorted us constantly with the encouragement "it's that little bit extra that counts".

- Rex Webster (English, Latin and games), his wonderful bass voice, his multitude of talents, his sarcastic comment to a pupil that made a mess of answering a simple question "saw-dust is too good for your brains, they must be made of cold porridge".

- Eileen Webster (née Halliday) (History and English) who was respected by everyone – a friendly and supportive person and an excellent teacher.

- "Mocky" Malone, the Irish teacher when I arrived, who had an unorthodox approach to exams. His son Ailbe was a pupil, short of stature, with even shorter legs, but able to win "the mile" with his legs going so fast they were simply a blur.

- Mr Foster (FEF) who arrived after a series of other Irish teachers, and became a tower of strength to the school for many years. A good teacher, a limitless supply of energy and common sense, and an ability to maintain discipline without excessive sanctions. I had difficulty remaining quiet in class, and I'm afraid often said things *sotto voce* that I thought were clever or funny. FEF once responded "Oh, Jacob, will you stop being so facetious". FEF was brought up on a small farm, where everyone helped with the chores, and there was no "slacking", so he always put his heart and soul into what he was doing. CSJ praised this type of person by saying he "had mud on his boots".

- Mrs. King, the kindly soul who had a care over all our clothes and was monarch of the "Sewing Room", where she comforted countless small homesick children and kept them warm.

Stella Maloney's car "Blue Peter" at the beach 1935.

*"All aboard"! The same car "Blue Peter" at Newtown School 1936.
Stella Maloney (later Jacob) a teacher there at that time is at the wheel.*

A Jacob Family
Tramore in the 1900s

Philip Jacob woodworking at Newtown School, aged about twelve.

Stella Maloney (later Jacob) 1923, before her Newtown School appointment.

Newtown School pupils and staff, 1997.

Other memories:-

- A number of good horse chestnut trees in the grounds, and the game of "conkers" being played enthusiastically.
- The swimming bath, which was simply made of concrete, and given a good coat of lime wash before being filled at the beginning of the summer - it looked like pea soup and smelled of chlorine.
- School walks every term, and school excursions every year, maybe up the River Barrow by barge as far as one could go, or to Cahir by train, or some other interesting place.
- Making two or three inch long models of ships at my desk in class and selling them to fellow pupils for sixpence a piece. Philippa Murphy sat at the desk in front of me, and was known to turn round and sweep all my model making stuff onto the floor. Served me jolly well right.
- The Forestry Club hut at the end of the playing fields where club members had many an evening relaxing beside a good hot open log fire.

Although I played rugby and hockey, tennis and cricket, and enjoyed them I was only mediocre. In athletics, there was not much rivalry between individuals, but great rivalry between the clans - in those days green, red and blue. Both Weston and I were blue. He was captain of the clan one year.

I liked working with my hands and it was a boon having the carpentry workshop available. Once a week prefects were invited to "Prefects' Tea", alternating weeks with Mr. Brigham (Headmaster) and his wife Pat, and Lester Smith (Senior Master) and his wife Annie. These were excellent occasions for stretching the mind, and we had poetry readings, play readings, discussions, and a jolly good tea as well.

John Brigham lived in an attractive old house overlooking the River Suir previously owned by Lady Lushington. The next gateway led to another gracious house, "Holmacre", where Helen White lived. She was an elderly Quaker related to the White family with whom Granny had started her life in Ireland, and it so happened that the family of Gordon Brickenden, one of my school-friends, also had a connection with her. She was very kind, and often invited Gordon and me to afternoon tea on a Sunday. Gordon had a very good imagination, and persuaded me that he was in process of building an aeroplane at his home near Dublin. When I spent part of the Summer holidays with him there he was strangely evasive about the existence of the plane, and was unable to show it to me!

In my second last year a classmate from a farming and sporting background smuggled a shotgun into school, and he and I made some gun-powder in the laboratory. I think we only managed to fire the gun once. Mr. Burke, the head groundsman, heard it and said to my friend afterwards "That was the hell of a fine report!". Although I suspect staff were aware of what had happened, not a word was said on either side.

A Jacob Family
Tramore in the 1900s

I had started on the school ladder quite early, and managed to keep pace, so when I did my Leaving Cert. and left I was still only 15 years old. A boy called Michael Illing and I were the first "form" to do the Leaving Cert. at Newtown.

It was a very happy period of my life, with plenty to do, plenty to stretch the mind, good companions, staff that were good teachers and good people, the reverse of authoritarian, and who encouraged enterprise among the pupils.

A few more disjointed memories.

- The sun recorder on the top of the roof of the Charles E. Jacob block - a spherical glass ball that concentrated the rays of the sun onto a cardboard strip and, when shining, burned a track on the cardboard.
- A unique forty foot ladder used for fixing gutters and things on the main building.
- Timothy Maguire, when 7 or 8 years old, waiting for the rest of us to get out of class and riding around chatting with Johnny Burke on the horse and cart which served the small farm on the school grounds.
- Blowing myself up in the lab one evening when trying to mix some gun-powder, burning off much of my hair, and burning my face and hands quite badly. Fortunately the school nurse, Nurse Elder by name, was ex-Army and knew exactly what to do – she lathered my burns with bright yellow Acriflavine, and took me into the school infirmary (the Nest). After a few days I had recovered enough to go back into class. Lester Smith, the Science Master, dealt with my indiscretion with exactly the right mixture of reprimand and sympathy. I could have been expelled, but instead I learned a lesson which I have never forgotten.

Punishment was by conduct marks and order marks, and led to detention on a Saturday afternoon, writing lines. Talking in the dormitories after "lights out" had for years been dealt with by some fairly hard belts of a slipper on one's bottom, but that died out before I left. Sometimes running a certain number of times round the playing fields was substituted for detention and lines.

Ivan Allen is one of the best known past pupils, and became a farmer and then a hotelier at Ballymaloe. A few years ago when Valarie (Weston's younger daughter) and her family and I were staying at Ballymaloe Ivan came over to our table, welcomed us, and told Valarie that Weston was the first baby he had ever given a bath to. He then explained that when he was at Newtown, many years before, the "domestic science" class included boy and girl pupils and when the day came to give them a lesson in how to bath a baby, Weston was borrowed for the purpose.

"Exeats" were a system of allowing and controlling boarders who wished to to leave the premises on half days (Thursdays and Saturdays) and on Sundays for particular reasons. I made good use of these, going "down town" every Thursday to see my father at 12 Gladstone St., and from time to time going aboard the old Waterford Port dredger, the "Portlairge" (which is the Irish name for Waterford).

The chief engineer was Jim Moir. He was always happy to show me how the boilers, the steam engine, the controls from the bridge, the crane and grab that lifted the mud, and everything worked. The smell of grease, coal smoke, sea water, and mud, and the sound of the grab's chain rattling out and then being winched in again will stay with me for ever. On a number of occasions I wangled my way aboard the "Fastnet", the "Skerries" and the "Rockabill", the three black-funnelled coastal steamers of The Clyde Shipping Company that had a regular freight service up and down the Irish Sea. No roll-on roll-off in those days, nor containers.

I was not so lucky with the "Great Western", the ship that plied back and forth between Waterford and Fishguard, taking mostly passengers and cattle. She was built specially for the Waterford route, and as the River Suir is a bit shallow, she had to have a rather flat bottom. This led to her rolling a lot if there was any appreciable swell. Father used to tell of Bernard, travelling years before on the old Great Western, when asked what the small hinged watch net beside the bunk was for, replied "Oh that's to put your eyeballs in".

A favourite place to visit was the control tower of the Waterford Bridge when a ship was about to go through and a lift was imminent – I was fascinated by the lifting mechanism and the whole procedure.

With all these memories I imagine you will realise that I view Newtown through rose tinted spectacles, and why.

The Great Western, Waterford to Fishguard Ferry.

A Jacob Family
Tramore in the 1900s

Weston and Philip sailing at Caragh Lake 1944.

Chapter 8

Caragh Lake

One of the long-term benafactors of Newtown School, a Cork Friend called Wilson Strangman, had established a "Camp" beside an old stone cottage at a seldom-frequented spot at the far end of Caragh Lake in Kerry, supplemented in summer with some ex-army bell-tents. Each year he would invite a group of boys to spend a week or a fortnight at "Camp" and this was the highlight of the year for many of us. There were a couple of rowing boats, toilet facilities were simply a deep hole excavated among some rhododendron bushes, and as it was a private part of the lake clothes were not obligatory. We swam, fished, sailed, rowed around and made excursions up the river to visit Mrs. Quirke's shop where we bought dozens and dozens of eggs, bread and butter (sometimes tasty bright yellow "country" butter, which was not rationed) etc. When frying eggs for twelve people over the open fire back at "Camp" we would break 24 eggs into an enormous frying pan, and then cut them apart when cooked. About then Ivan Allen had started growing tomatoes commercially at Imokilly Orchards, near Shanagarry where Wilson Strangman lived, and baskets of tomatoes would be sent down by train. These had to be collected from Caragh Lake railway station which meant some of us rowing to the inhabited end of the lake, perhaps two miles, and going ashore to collect this welcome addition to our food supply.

My times at "Camp" were during the war years when cars were laid up, so we all arrived on the railway which ran from Farranfore Junction to Cahirciveen. (This branch line was closed a few years later, and an airport has replaced the Farranfore railway station). We then transferred into one of the "Camp" boats and rowed back to "Camp". The local family, the McGillycuddys, had a care over "Camp" in off-season. Dick Fletcher had built a sailing boat shortly before, when in his last term at Newtown, and it was transported to "Camp". Unfortunately it was built of elm, and elm twists up in fresh water like a fried rasher of bacon, so voyages in it consisted mainly of frantic bailing to keep the boat from sinking. There was one attractive island we often visited, just a large hump covered with pine trees, and this was christened "Pudding Island". Up the river that feeds into the lake there was a small hotel, the Glencar Hotel - sometimes used by visitors to "Camp", but never by us "Campers". Wilson Strangman himself adored that part of the world and often spent holidays tramping over the mountains, staying in hay sheds when night overtook him, and enjoying the simple warm hospitality of Kerry folk. It was regarded as a great privilege to be invited to "Camp", and we all enjoyed it immensely.

A Jacob Family
Tramore in the 1900s

King Edward VII visit to Waterford, on the 2nd May 1904.
Some onlookers were bitterly disappointed because the King was not wearing a crown.

Chapter 9

Harvey & Son, 12 Gladstone Street, Waterford

From the year 1900s when Grandpa joined the staff of Harvey & Son, at T. Newenham Harvey's invitation, Harvey & Son was an important part of the life of our family, until father retired in the 1970's.

I myself worked in the office from 1947 to 1950, and learned the basics fairly thoroughly. I have described the roles of Grandpa, Father and cousin Frederick elsewhere, and have mentioned the various sides to the business – stockbroking, travel agency, insurance agency, house agency and the Waterford Working Men's Penny Bank. It was a good example of a small town "one-stop shop" with a variety of services. The house agency was not engaged in buying and selling properties, but looking after the fabric of, and collecting rents from, house property belonging to a number of substantial (and some smaller) landlords. Three or four tradesmen were employed full-time on house repairs. The only one I remember was Harry Giles – for some reason the name intrigued me.

Gladstone Street is a short street between Waterford Quay at one end and O'Connell St and George's St at the other. At the end of Gladstone St. facing north towards the river stands one of Waterford's finest buildings, with a superb oval cantilevered staircase, the Chamber of Commerce.

The front of Harvey & Son consisted of a doorway, with two shop windows (with screens for privacy) to its right hand side. On one side of No.12 was the Commercial Union Insurance office. A post office was on the other side and next to that Henry Gallwey & Son, bottlers and whiskey bonders, above which was the Waterford Club, where father very occasionally had lunch. Across the street was a newsagents (the Misses Cahill), and the Munster & Leinster Bank (later to become part of Allied Irish Banks). So "the office" was in a convenient location.

Inside the office was a short counter, behind which the cashier and book-keeper worked. During my time there, this was Michael Fitzgerald, a totally reliable, accurate and courteous person who was a real asset to the establishment. Prior to Michael the position was filled by another excellent person, Joseph Power. It was Joseph who, one day when Fred Chapman came in to the counter and asked whether there were any Jacobs on the premises because he would like to see one of them, replied "Yes, Mr. Chapman, there are three Jacobs here and one Joseph". Fred saw the joke and roared with laughter.

It was an inefficient building, with space for two rooms on each floor side by side in the front, but behind that it was narrower, with room only for stairways and landings and a single room on each floor at the back. There were four floors in all. The downstairs passageway led to a storeroom where bicycles were kept, a canoe made by cousin Frederick's son Christy was slung from the roof, and also various safes for keeping documents and cash. The first floor had father's office at the back, and Grandpa's at the front with, beside it, a small office for Joe Duggan who was typist and general factotum. Joe was a small man, with a gammy leg and a slightly malformed arm. He smoked a particularly foul pipe most of the time, and was very loyal to the firm and to father and Grandpa in particular.

Joe lived in Gracedieu, an old part of Waterford, in a one storeyed terrace house. Extraordinarily, nearly sixty years later, I discovered that a Dublin friend of mine, John Blake, had grown up in Waterford and had a best friend when he lived in Waterford in the 40's and 50's, who was a son of the above-mentioned Joe Duggan. John had then left Waterford, joined The Revenue, and later on, moved to Craig Gardner & Co (Auditors and Accountants). His first job with them was working on Goodbody & Webb's audit in 1971. When he retired thirty years later, he looked after my tax affairs as a private individual until 2007. I am sorry to say that father was not particularly generous in his employment of Joe Duggan.

When I started work in Harvey & Son I shared Grandpa's room, perching on a high stool at a high sloping desk (but I didn't have to use a quill pen).

The third storey consisted of a front room, a landing, and a small room at the back, the "lunch room". In the front room father had installed a bed settee during the war years, so that he could remain in Waterford overnight if he had an evening meeting at the Chamber of Commerce or elsewhere. Trains to Tramore did not run in the evenings then – there was a severe shortage of fuel. We had a simple lunch in the "lunch room" every day. It was Grandpa's invariable habit to get a fresh Hovis small pan loaf from Chapmans (a Quaker-owned grocery on the Quay), have a few slices of toast for lunch, and take the rest of the loaf home to Midvale in his leather Gladstone bag. Lunch time was a suitable intermission in the day's work to nip around to one of the nearby shops to get odd things. There were two department stores, Hearne's and Robertson Ledlie Ferguson. One of them had a central cashier with tightly stretched wires radiating out to the various counters.

When one gave one's money to the counter assistant it was put in a jam-jar sized container, a spring-loaded toggle would be pulled and the container would whiz along the wire to the centre. A receipt (and change if any) would be put in the container, which would be despatched back to the counter in the same manner. Peter Skelton in his "memories" mentions similar systems using hollow rolling balls on gently inclined raised "railways", and also relatively modern (for the times) pneumatic suction systems elsewhere.

Every week Ken White (mentioned elsewhere) brought fresh eggs in egg-boxes for Grandpa and father from his farm at Corloughan, Piltown.

The top floor was a "storeroom" – though it was really a dumping room, and thick with dust!

Ruminating on the changes in business methods during my life time I compare present day multi-million pound deals, completed electronically in an instant, with the way we did it in the 1940's. Father would write out a telegram to our agents in London, S.C. Maguire & Son, giving instructions to buy, say, 100 ICI (or Vickers or whatever), would then give me the telegram form, I would get the necessary cash from the cashier, I would cycle to the Post Office a mile down the Quay and hand in the telegram with cash, and return to the office. Two or three hours later a telegraph boy on his bicycle would arrive at the office, take the reply telegram reporting the transaction from the leather pouch on his belt and hand it over.

Of course if one wanted to telephone London, or anywhere more than a few miles from Waterford, one had to ring the Exchange, who would book the call, tell you approximately the delay (often an hour or more) and then ring back when the call had "come through". Even local calls were routed through the operator in the Telephone Exchange.

Running messages was part of my job. Slightly extra-curricular was collecting the week's takings from the Tuskar Lodging House for Father to lodge in the bank. This was an old Georgian house on Adelphi Quay that Waterford Quakers ran for the benefit of homeless men, and he was the Treasurer. It was not a very attractive place, and was unpleasantly smelly. Not surprisingly, it was very hard to get women who were willing to take on the job of looking after the men. It closed down not long afterwards.

Cousin Frederick's wife (who we called cousin Dorothea but everyone else called Queenie because her first name was Victoria) was very interested in paintings, and art generally, and she and Arnold Marsh were prime movers in the formation of the Waterford City Art Gallery. Cousin Frederick and Cousin Dorothea invited me to have an evening meal with them, on each of the two evenings a week that I attended Art School in the Waterford Technical School under Robert Burke. I enjoyed hearing words of wisdom from their extensive knowledge of art. After the evening sessions I normally cycled home to Tramore. If I had forgotten my bicycle lamp on a dark night, I navigated the wooded parts of the road by looking up and cycling beneath the gap in the trees above where the sky was marginally a lighter black than the trees themselves.

Of course all the firm's ledgers were kept by hand (cousin Frederick being a superb copperplate writer) and all calculations were done by hand, using books of tables when necessary. There was one big heavy adding machine which had a whole lot of press-down keys, and a handle at the side which one pulled down to complete the addition and record it on tape. Goodbody & Webb were Harvey & Son's stockbroking agents in Dublin, and S C Maguire & Son were its agents in London. Grandpa and father were members of The Provincial Brokers' Stock Exchange, which was subsumed into the larger Stock Exchanges in Britain and Ireland at a later date.

The Waterford Working Men's Penny Bank had been set up in the mid 1800's to cater for folk who wanted to save their small cash surpluses for a rainy day, or for Christmas, and this I think was before the Trustee Savings Bank was created. The bank never became very large, but was a real service, mainly to the less well-off, in Waterford. One of its features was the provision of "piggy banks" to depositors if they so wished. These were small steel "home safes" the size of a small book that could only be opened with a special key held at the office. One day when Grandpa was walking to the train with his Gladstone bag he heard a chiseler saying to a pal "Look at, there's Mr. Jacob taking all the money home in his bag".

Father had an enquiring mind and was a good communicator. He enjoyed chatting with clients about their particular interests, whether they were farmers, shop-keepers, solicitors or whatever, and whether their passion was steam engines, or pedigree cattle, or cromlechs and ogham stones, or the history of Waterford. He was proud to know Waterford man Peter O'Connor who won the Triple Jump Gold and the Long Jump Silver in the 1906 Olympics, thus earning the nick-name "the Long Jumper". Peter O'Connor was a solicitor, and if he had occasion to visit the Courthouse he would leap up the steps of the classical portico in one mighty bound.

Similarly he cherished his friendship with Tom Kiely from Carrick-on-Suir in Tipperary, who won the Olympic Medal for the Decathlon in 1904.

Harvey & Son was very much a Jacob family concern – you might almost say it was "part of the family".

Waterford Harbour and Bridge ("Old Timbertoes") over the River Suir, 1890's.

Waterford Quay and Clock Tower, early 1900s.

Dunmore East, sailing "Dunlin" 1948.

Chapter 10

Dunmore East 1944 - 1950

Before setting down my memories of Dunmore I will recount a potentially disastrous episode in which Father was involved in the early '40s, with Norman Baker, Dickie Beale, and Robert Jacob. They wanted to get ashore on the uninhabited Saltee Islands, primarily to see the great numbers and variety of seabirds there. They hired a petrol-engined fishing boat called the "Yankee Girl" in Dunmore, got to the Saltees, did what they wanted to do there, and set off to motor back to Dunmore, quite some miles away. Half way the engine spluttered and then died. One of them was quite knowledgeable about such things, and dismantled the appropriate parts, fixed the problem and re-assembled the engine. It still wouldn't start, no matter what they did. They were adrift on the high seas. No mobile phones in those days, and no radio on the boat. What to do? Two of them got into the dinghy, rowed miles to Dunmore and found the owner. A rescue expedition set out. When it finally reached the stricken vessel, the owner spotted the trouble. As part of the attempt to get the engine going the cover and leads were temporarily taken off the distributor. What they didn't know was that the owner had fitted a distributor from a different engine, and the firing order was different, so when they replaced the leads the way they thought they should it didn't work. The owner realised what had happened, corrected the leads, and the Yankee Girl motored home without a bother. Much relief on all sides. It could so easily have ended in tragedy. The sea is not always so forgiving.

Dunmore East evening sail, 1948.

Not specially connected with Dunmore but popping into my mind is the story of the "Secret Weapon". In 1944 Nazi Germany began launching un-manned rocket-propelled V-1 flying bombs across the Channel aimed at London. They flew low, and had various nick-names such as "Doodlebug" and "The Secret Weapon". Father had to pay a visit to London about that time, and on his arrival home he was carrying a parcel that contained something cylindrical, about fifteen inches long and eight inches in diameter. When he started to open the parcel, shiny aluminium became evident. Asked what on earth it was he whispered "Ssshhh… it's the Secret Weapon". It was in fact a "Sirram" Volcano Camp Kettle, with which most campers became familiar in the next few years. It has a cylindrical outer jacket with an inner conical sleeve, made of aluminium. A space between them forms a container for water, with a filler cap on the outside. The centre of the cone is open at top and bottom, and there is a detachable pan which sits beneath the contraption, in which you light a fire of newspaper, or sticks, or whatever is to hand, and you feed in additional fuel through the open top. The inner cone acts as a chimney, and before you know where you are the water in the jacket is boiling, whereupon you pour it out through the filler cap and make a smashing cup of tea in your billy-can. If there is no billy-can, you simply put the teaspoon (or newspaper twist) of tea leaves into the boiling water, through the filler cap, and the whole thing becomes a big teapot.

The first occasion on which The Secret Weapon was used was on an early morning train from Waterford to Wexford, when Father and some friends were setting out on one of their bird-watching expeditions to the Saltee Islands. The carriage was one of the old type, with no corridor – each compartment stretched from one side of the carriage to the other, and the windows were adjusted up or down with stout leather straps. The lads wanted a cup of tea so the Volcano was lit on the carriage floor, but the draught from the windows blew the smoke into everyone's eyes and panic nearly broke out – what if the whole carriage burst into flames! The doors on each side were opened wide to let the smoke out – fortunately the driver didn't notice smoke billowing from the carriage, but the experiment was not regarded as a huge success. The Volcano is now called the "Kelly Kettle", and it still makes the best cup of tea in the world.

THE "SECRET WEAPON"

By 1947 Weston and I had had good fun for some years sailing on Tramore Bay in our 10 foot dinghy Dreoilín, catching mackerel, gurnard etc., and we had learned a certain amount about sailing. About that time Father decided that it might be a good idea to participate in slightly more serious sailing (and racing) in Dunmore. Probably in conversation with Norman Baker and Dickie Beale he became aware that there was a bare hull of an Uffa Fox designed 15'6" dinghy available to purchase from Seamus Murphy who lived in Carrick-on-Suir. Seamus had started to build the boat some years previously but never finished it. I think Father used some money that had been left by our mother Kathleen in her Will for the benefit of Weston and me to buy it. The celebrated Uffa Fox designed the boat in the 1930's specifically for the needs of Dunmore, namely a dinghy with a good performance, robust enough to lie at moorings in Dunmore Harbour, and seaworthy enough to deal with the big swell and sometimes rough weather of the Atlantic Ocean in the mouth of Waterford Harbour. Major Lloyd, then Harbourmaster in Dunmore, had negotiated the design of the boat with Uffa Fox.

Most of the boats were built on the Ashcroft diagonal-ply principle. They had a straight stem, a V-shaped entry and front of the hull, flattening out to a broad stern so that the boat would plane (but only did so in fairly strong winds). They were Bermudian Sloops, with the bolt rope of the mainsail sliding up a groove in the mast, which was a relatively new innovation when the boat was designed. Norman Baker owned one called "Petrel", Dickie Beale owned "Penguin", Jack Egan had "Pochard" (beautifully built and finished by Major Lloyd himself), Len Hutchinson owned "Tern", and Tom Colfer had one too (the last two were clinker built, not moulded ply). Later on Robbie Jephson built one called "Skua".

The first year after I left school I spent quite a lot of time in the big room of Waterford Meeting House finishing off the hull that we had acquired, which we later christened "Dunlin". Bronze fittings were unobtainable, so we decided to get them made in the foundry of the Davis flour mill in Enniscorthy. The boats were half decked and it was necessary to make the deck, the oars, the mast, etc. In fact, the first mast that I made from Seamus Murphy's timber, soon snapped – I think the timber had become dozed in storage during the War years.

The timber for the new mast had to come from Dublin, but was too long for a lorry. By barge seemed the only way. Conveniently by then I had started working in Harvey & Son but was allowed to take quite a bit of time off to nip over to the Friends' Meeting House (which was about 50 yards around the corner) to work on Dunlin. Every winter Petrel, Penguin and Tern were kept in the Big Room in the Meeting House, and Dunlin joined them. We had a trolley on which, at the beginning of the season, we would roll the boats down to the edge of the river, push them down a convenient slipway, step the masts, and sail from there down the River Suir to Dunmore – quite an adventure, and a most attractive waterway. Then, at the end of the season, we would sail back up the river again. Naturally we chose a falling tide for the trip down river and a rising one for the trip back.

One of the regular crews for Norman Baker was Frank Neill an apprentice of Norman Baker's who was an accountant. During this period Len Hutchinson (of "Tern") married Rita who was a delightful person but sometimes a bit gullible. She had been painting Leonard's boat and after inspecting it the next day either Norman or Dick said to her "isn't it a pity that you put the paint on inside-out by mistake?" Poor Rita was distraught and wondered whether she should strip it all off and re-do it. After lots of laughter by the jokers she finally realised her leg was being pulled.

The first summer Weston and I sailed in Dunmore we camped in a tent beside the Circular Road round the back of Dunmore, and this suited us very well. A caravan was also parked there in which Riocard Farrell's daughter Valerie and her friend Nell de Bromhead were spending the summer. Weston was 17 and I was 15, and naturally we spent quite a lot of time with the two girls. One lovely starry night with a big moon the girls and I (Weston wasn't with us) went down to the harbour, hoisted the sails on our boat "Dunlin", and went for a magic sail. In retrospect it was a silly and dangerous thing to do, but at that age one doesn't think about such things. Not long afterwards the girls were forbidden to sleep in the caravan any more, and were kept under strict surveillance by their parents. I particularly enjoyed Valerie's company, and I think she enjoyed mine too – apparently she used toothpaste made by "Phillips", and when she went back to boarding school for the autumn term the other girls teased her and called her "Toothpaste". Some years later, Valerie had the good sense to marry Fred Morris, an aspiring young barrister, younger brother of Arthur Morris of "Symphony" mentioned in chapter 11. Fred did well, and retired recently as President of the High Court having reached the top of his profession.

Racing took place on the open sea, but nothing daunted us! The races were started from the lighthouse on the end of the pier. Captain Cherry acted as race officer and fired the gun. I think he was a retired army captain, not a seafarer.

Dunmore Harbour Lighthouse, with Hook Head light, in background.

Fishing for mackerel was a frequent occupation in those care-free days. On one occasion Robbie Jephson was out with an elderly and peppery George Ridgway. Robbie had caught a dogfish the size of a small shark which he didn't want, so he cut off the tail and threw it back into the water still alive. Old George Ridgway was furious and said something like "You bloody fool, that dogfish will go round and round like the Bismarck and frighten all the mackerel away". (The Bismarck, of course, was a German battleship whose steering gear had been wrecked in the North Atlantic by the Allies during the War and had gone round and round in circles before sinking).

The following year father borrowed Cousin Willie's caravan and parked it in Miss Harney's field, just beside the Rectory, and we stayed there. Sometimes we went out sailing early, caught a mackerel or two, brought them back to the caravan and fried them for breakfast. That's the way to eat them!

Before the caravan, we had used the "Palace" - a few dingy rooms created from the out-buildings of Len Hutchinson's mother's house, with some old bunks and rudimentary cooking equipment, but it was fun. Of course we cycled back home to Tramore quite frequently for supplies (it would have been all of ten miles). On one occasion I remember crawling under the wire netting fence of Miss Harney's orchard and picking up a whole lot of delicious windfall apples, and bringing them back to Tramore, where I kept them in the workshop until they were all eaten. I have always had a mildly guilty conscience about this. The Rector was Canon Jameson. His son Tommy, a tough, small, wiry, irreverent boy had been at Newtown School with me for a while some years previously. Miss Harney who owned the field also owned the bakery and grocery shop on the corner, near the Church of Ireland. Across the road from that was a lovely house looking out over the bay, owned by a Mr. Gibbon. Father, remembering that there was a type of monkey called the "Blue Tailed Gibbon", always referred to Mr. Gibbon as the "Blue Tailed Gibbon" which usually, but not always, produced a weak smile from the rest of us. Down the twisty road from Miss Harney's was Lawlor's Strand, but it was not particularly attractive as seaweed tended to build up on it, and a slightly unsavoury stream ran across it. Willie Lawlor's pub overlooked this strand.

About 1946, the Irish Dinghy Racing Association called a meeting in Lawlor's Pub where the proponents of a newly designed 14 foot dinghy as a national dinghy for Ireland were putting forward their case in opposition to the "Dunmore" class dinghy. Douglas Heard of Dublin, who was then the most distinguished sailor in Ireland, showed a film that had been made in Bermuda of Uffa Fox designed 14 foot dinghies sailing in ideal sparkling sunshine filled conditions. The renowned "Shorty" Trimmingham was one of the sailors. The film was in colour (fairly innovative in those days), and it all looked idyllic. Not surprisingly the IDRA decided to choose the 14 foot dinghy and not the "Dunmore" class. The "Fourteen" as it is now called was designed by George O'Brien Kennedy, later simply called Brian Kennedy. The fact that a substantial fleet of "Fourteens" are still sailing sixty years later and giving great enjoyment shows that they made the right decision.

Near to the Harbour was an old quarry, in which one or two holiday houses had been built, including a rather small and basic one designed by Norman Baker for his own use. We all called it The Bakery.

In those days the Waterford Harbour Sailing Clubhouse was simply a Nissen hut on the pier, between the Harbourmaster's house and the men's toilets. The latter consisted of a "long drop", with the sea water from the harbour sloshing in and out of a tunnel below the throne as the flushing mechanism. Not very sanitary!

Our boats were moored fore and aft with a pulley system. We had to climb down a chain, with links large enough to put our feet in to get aboard.

At this period there was a certain amount of herring fishing going on in Dunmore, and the fishermen all had stores along the side of the pier, but they were dark, damp, dank, and very smelly, most of them with stacks of crude wooden barrels outside to transport the herrings. There were always kittiwakes on their nests on the cliffs around the harbour. Their constant calling "kitti-wake, kitti-wake", which gave rise to their name, is one of my abiding memories of Dunmore. The backs of some of the dwelling houses on the main street were at the top of the cliff. One of these was occupied during the summer by Don Ferdinando d'Ardia Caracciola. On a summer's evening he often came out onto his balcony overlooking the harbour and sang Italian opera with a wonderful tenor voice that floated out over the water – another magic memory.

Once a year the Dunmore Regatta took place, mainly in the harbour, with rowing and sailing races, and also a "duck chase" when a big burly, strong, middle-aged, Dunmore man (Paddy Murphy I think) would don his swimsuit and would then be chased around the harbour by his "tormentors" in a rowing boat. No holds were barred, and he would dive in and swim across the harbour and climb out again before the rowing boat was able to get him – great excitement and shouting all round. There was also a "greasy pole" where contestants would try and reach the end of the pole without losing their grip and falling into the water.

On the road down to the pier there was a kipper plant for smoking and curing the herrings, but I don't remember it working in my time. On the main street of Dunmore there was a wonderful café, whose name I can't remember (Betty's?) run by a friendly soul who was always happy to produce a mixed grill for hungry young people.

Although sailing was the main attraction and occupation in Dunmore, other things did happen as well – tennis, and in particular swimming from the rocks and the many little coves and strands. Len Hutchinson was a keen swimmer. He was very short-sighted, wore thick lensed glasses, had only one leg but was game for anything. He had to wear his glasses when swimming, with a piece of string round the back of his neck so that he didn't lose them. When someone remarked to him how on earth did he manage to keep them on the bridge of his nose when he dived in and came up again he grinned and said "Well you see I settle them back on my nose again before I get to the surface".

Another person I remember from those days is Verona Hutchinson, a niece of Len, and indeed we occasionally swap memories of the old days by letter – Verona now lives in England.

Bishop Harvey of Waterford had two grown-up sons, Peter and Clem. Peter went on to become a distinguished cleric and Clem was an engineer. They had two boats which also wintered up-river, near Cheekpoint, not as far upstream as Waterford. One, the "Wasp", was yellow and the other was blue and called "The Gnat". They were very good sailors, and often won races.

A year or two before we started sailing in Dunmore, Norman Baker and Dickie Beale decided they would like to become members of the Irish Cruising Club. They took their boats down to (I think) Helvick Head, and then sailed up the coast to Dunmore so they could claim a sea passage of more than a certain number of miles. This was quite a daring thing to do, and I remember looking out over Tramore Bay from Summerville's upstairs window at about the time they expected to be passing, but we didn't see them – either we were too early or too late to catch sight of them.

Sadly, in a mighty summer storm, our boat Dunlin capsized on moorings in Dunmore Harbour, chewed her way through her mooring rope, was swept out to sea, and disappeared. Some days later we went over to the Co. Wexford coast of Waterford Harbour and found bits of her hull, showing how severely she had been pounded by the waves on the rocky shore. I was desperately sad at her loss, and remember shutting myself in my room at Summerville, utterly miserable, with tears rolling down my cheeks. We had not realised how fierce the storm was or that "Dunlin" was in danger, and had not travelled to Dunmore to make sure she was safe – though whether we could have saved her is a moot point. I still have a guilty conscience about it.

Councillor's Strand, Dunmore.

A Jacob Family
Tramore in the 1900s

*14 foot Dinghy Racing at Dunmore,
with Weston Jacob (inset).*

Chapter 11

Sailing

Weston's and my early days on the water were in the folding canoe given to us by Basil Jacob. Then, when I was about ten, father bought Dreoilín from Ivan Allen in Shanagarry – it was built by a Captain Roberts of Passage West. I have written about the canoe and Dreoilín elsewhere. Early on Basil took me sailing in Dun Laoghaire in his centre-board boat (like a Mermaid) called "Redwing". He also had a very handy little pram dinghy, with a sail, which he called the "wobby". Basil belonged to The National Yacht Club. The boatman there in those days, Billy, was exceedingly friendly and helpful.

I liked Basil's "wobby" and decided to build one. First I made a model, about nine inches long, but even doing that did not teach me that most of the planks had to be cut in an elongated C- or S-shape, out of a much wider plank. I only learned that from experience when I started building my own one in my late teens. I built this in the living room of the cottage father had bought from the estate of Mr. O'Connor beside Summerville, that is now called "Mansfield". She was about nine feet long, and I was delighted (and surprised) how well she turned out. Father and I carried her down to the pier one Sunday morning and she floated and handled perfectly. Partly because of her size and shape I decided to call her "Dabchick". This continued a tradition in our family - the name of each boat starting with a "D". I even made a sail for Dabchick out of a discarded sail from some other boat. Ultimately Dabchick was sold, I think to Jim Sexton. After the canoe, Dreoilín and Dabchick came "Dunlin", which I have chronicled in the chapter on Dunmore. Indeed, most of what I have to say about the sailing seasons 1947 to 1950 will be found in that chapter. This period included competitive meetings against Cobh Sailing Club at home and away in IDRA 14 foot dinghies.

C.S.J. BAILING OUT DREOILIN

A Jacob Family
Tramore in the 1900s

By that time there were a few "Fourteens" sailing in Dunmore including Arthur Morris's "Symphony", Red Colfer's "Brown Trout" and Pat Mosse's "Dipper". The first season that "Symphony" was in the water Arthur Morris asked me to sail it, with him as crew, in the Dunmore Regatta. It was blowing quite hard, so we reefed down, and lo and behold we won. Arthur was delighted. Sailing our Dunmore class dinghy "Dunlin" in a moderate breeze up one side and down the other side of the long Atlantic swell in the two mile wide mouth of Waterford Harbour was some of the most exhilarating sailing I have ever had.

In 1950, on my way back to Dublin after seven months in London on what would nowadays be called a "training course", I spent a week-end with Weston and four other young Dunmore sailors as a team sailing Fireflies in the Team racing Championships on the Marine Lake at West Kirby near Liverpool. The lake was only three feet deep, so it didn't matter capsizing!

When I arrived in Dublin in the autumn of 1950 I started in "digs" with Barbara Wigham, and I asked her could I build a Yachting World Cadet at her house, Edenvale. Bless her, she said "yes". The dining room had a wooden floor and was seldom used by the Wigham family, and that became my "boatyard". I set to and built the Cadet over that winter, subsequently selling it to Wicklow Harbour Sailing Club which had a small fleet of Cadets for its small members. A Jack Holt design, it was a fairly simple hard chine hull, with a pram bow, made of marine plywood, and turned out quite nicely. I remember ordering good sails from England, and spiriting them to Ireland without paying Import Duty. I am sure I shouldn't have done that! To carry on the tradition of a name beginning with "D", I christened her "Dithyramb". This is the word for an ecstatic hymn to Bacchus – there was no underlying reason for the word except that I rather liked it. Edenvale was a house of great character built beside the River Liffey on Conyngham Road, between the Phoenix Park and the River Liffey. The road was actually at the level of the roof of the house, so one descended a long flight of steps from a gate in the wall beside the footpath above. Dr. Joe Wigham was still alive at that time – he was a distinguished pathologist, and a Trinity College Professor. My first summer in Dublin I sailed whenever I could, crewing for Barbara in her Wag "Molly", for Dyko Morris in his 21-footer "Inisfallen", for Jimmy Mooney in his Dragon, etc.

Soon after coming to Dublin I started crewing fairly regularly for Johnny Hooper, who was then in his teens and already a superb helmsman. He sailed a Firefly and I went with him to the British Firefly Championships at Abersoch in North Wales. We camped in a tent. Johnny's boat, which was being transported from Dun Laoghaire, didn't arrive until half way through the week, so on one occasion I was asked to crew for one of the top English sailors, a girl called Peppy Lowles. At one stage I pulled the centre board up too quickly, the boat capsized, and we found ourselves swimming. She was furious, quite justifiably. Afterwards one of our party quipped that I was the first guy to have rolled Peppy Lowles over. I was frozen stiff from being in the water and when we got ashore Alf Delaney gave me a generous libation of gin, which I must say warmed me up.

A year or two later Johnny and I went to the British Firefly Championships again, in Plymouth this time, and stayed with a friend of Johnny's father, Wing Commander Grenfell, in Saltash. We neither distinguished nor disgraced ourselves on the water. However, one night we left the clubhouse after midnight, only to find that the day's last ferry across the river between Plymouth and Saltash was long gone. What to do? Well, overhead loomed Brunel's famous railway bridge over the river. So we climbed up onto it, and started across. To our horror, a train clattered onto the bridge behind us and we had to flatten ourselves against the railings, breathing a great big sigh of relief when the train eventually passed. Johnny and I often reminisce about those few minutes of danger more than half a century ago.

My next "digs" was with Mrs. Massey at 2 Rathfarnham Park and I spent all my spare time in the autumn, winter and spring of 1951/2 building an IDRA 14 foot dinghy in her garage (she was a widow and did not have a car). I used moulds lent to me by Donald Byrne who had, with Reggie Walsh, built one a year or two previously. The Moriarty family lived next door in No. 4 and I became friendly with Christopher, though he was a few years younger than I. The eldest daughter of the family, Cherry Moriarty, was a friend of Brigid Scanlan, who later became one of her bridesmaids. I married Brigid five years later, in 1956 (but not cause and effect). As they say, it's a small world!

When building a clinker built boat it is necessary to steam the ribs so that they will bend and conform to the fairly sharp curves of the inside of the boat. To achieve this I first bought a length of cast-iron down-pipe in a builders' providers. I was pushing it home on my bicycle and Henry Bell overtook me in his old Ford 8 motorcar. He stopped, opened up the windscreen of the old car, poked the down-pipe through it and very kindly transported it the rest of the way to No. 2 Rathfarnham Park for me! I then set up the pipe in Mrs. Massey's garden, stopped up one end of it, propped it in a gently sloping position, poured a few gallons of water into it and lit a fire under where the water was. I pretended I was Vulcan. When that was nicely boiling I put the long bits of timber for the ribs into the down-pipe, closed up the top, and boiled the ribs until they were pliable. Then I took them out, wearing gloves, and pushed them into position in the hull of the boat.

Once, on my return from a day's work at the office, Mrs. Massey accosted me and asked me did I realise that I had nearly been responsible for her house burning down. I thought this was an extraordinary thing to say, until she explained that the house was being painted, and the painter had been stripping the paint off the garage door with a blow-lamp. The flame had gone through a gap at the foot of the door and had set alight some of the shavings that I had stupidly left on the floor without sweeping them up the night before. Fortunately it was caught in time, with no harm done to the house, or more importantly, to my boat.

I had acquired most of the timber from T. & C. Martin, who were big timber importers at the time, and who produced some superb silver spruce for the planking and some good mahogany and oak for other parts.

Philip and Basil Jacob in "Redwing" 1940.

Basil Jacob's "Foam"

Charlie Sargent was the timber manager of T. & C. Martin. He was a skilled boatbuilder in his spare time, and had already built a number of dinghies. He was extremely helpful. I knew of four people that wanted to build 14 footers, Robbie Jephson, Colin Chapman and Leslie Crumpton (all of Waterford or Tramore) and myself. We decided that we would amalgamate our order for timber, so I organised that. I had hardly a penny to my name at the time, and Charlie Sargent asked for a reference to make sure he would be paid. I reckoned the total would be about £200. I gave the name of Jack Freeman, who was one of the partners in Goodbody & Webb where I worked, and was also, incidentally, the Chairman of the Provincial Bank of Ireland.

Stupidly I didn't ask him whether I could give his name as a reference. He approached me when he was asked for the reference, and asked did I really expect him to guarantee £2,000. Somehow an additional nought had been added to the original figure, by whom I don't know. Jack Freeman, being the sport he was, gave a favourable reference but warned me that I should never use somebody's name as a reference without their approval. I realised my transgression, and it was a lesson learned.

There was a problem making the mast, because it was too long for Mrs. Massey's garage. Very kindly, the Bewley family said I could use one of their storage sheds which was beside "The Barn" where Harold and Doris Johnson lived – Doris was, of course, a Bewley before she was married. I decided to get the best sails I could, so I ordered them from Ratsey & Lapthorne of Cowes. Jack Freeman generously paid for the sails as a 21st Birthday present to me. I decided to call the boat "Dryad" – the "D" was obligatory for 14 footers based in Dun Laoghaire, the boat was made of wood, and a dryad is a wood-nymph. Although I had finished the hull in 1952, the boat was not ready to sail, so I stored it for the winter at the Royal St. George Yacht Club and finished it in 1953. Soon after I began sailing Dryad, Douglas Heard, who was a very distinguished sailor and Commodore of the Royal St. George, gave me great encouragement by going out of his way to tell me how well he thought Dryad looked on the water.

Robin Montgomery was my first crew, after whom came various people - Nigel Barry, Brian Glynn, Joe Kelly (Joseph Lorenzo Kelly), David Wheeler and, for the longest and most successful period, Bill Pigot. One Saturday I was away and asked Joe to race the boat for me. To his huge embarrassment Joe got into difficulties and the mast broke, but it didn't take me very long to make a new one. Years later, when Bill Pigot bought his own "fourteen" I had various other crews, including Jane Haughton.

Paul Osterberg, whose father was a member of the Royal St. George Yacht Club and a distinguished sailor, proposed me for membership of the club in 1953, and I am now the fifth longest standing member. I had tremendous fun sailing Dryad for over twenty years, and finally sold her in 1975.

I particularly enjoyed the occasional trip across the bay from Dun Laoghaire to Clontarf or Sutton or Howth, meeting Laurie McClelland, Michael Appleby, Jackie O'Reilly, Liam "Guinea" McGonigal, the Sargents, Chandlers and many others.

My eyes were opened to the real world in a particular race during a Howth Regatta. One of the most successful helmsmen in our class, but a fiercely competitive one, deliberately left out a buoy thus shortening the course for him. I was the only person to see this. When we got ashore afterwards I said to him "I suppose you're not signing a declaration card that you obeyed all the rules?" to which he replied "Of course I'm going to sign it – you were the only person that saw me". I am glad to say that kind of thing happened very seldom.

"Guinea" McGonigal was another natural sailor - I remember one season when he hadn't been sailing at all, he took his boat out of his garage, shoved it in the water, stuck the mast in, sailed the race and came in first by a mile.

Jennifer Guinness is a few years younger than I am, and comes from a sailing family. As a girl she had a small sailing dinghy in Dun Laoghaire which she often pottered around in – it had striped sails (blue and pink I think) and we all called it the "Pyjama Boat".

David Wheeler and I always worked on Saturday mornings in those days. We would have lunch together and then sail in the afternoon race. One day he had soup, main course and pudding, and then decided to have soup again. The result was he fell fast asleep in the middle of the race, stretched out on the bottom of the boat. Fortunately there wasn't much wind, he acted as ballast in the right place, and I think we came in first. David had a great regard for Johnny Walker, one of the best sailors in the Bay, and always referred to him as "the man with the beautiful wife" (and he was quite right too). We had a small supply of joss sticks which, on a virtually windless day, we would light, and watch what way the smoke blew so that we would know how to trim the sails. Every year the 14 Footers had a picnic on Dalkey Island and I have a wonderful photograph of Tansey Millar aged about 2 cradling a gin bottle at the picnic.

By the time I started sailing Dryad Douglas Heard and Jimmy Mooney had both moved on into larger boats, but Harry O'Flanagan (No.8), Peter Kennedy (No.2), Donal Byrne (No.6) and Jennifer Millar and Tom Hudson (No.1 - "Error") were still in our fleet.

Toby Millar, Jennifer's father, a delightful character and then owner of a Dublin Bay 17-footer (gaff-rigged with a top-sail) is memorable for arriving at the club one day, already late for the start, after a wedding. He had clearly indulged himself rather too well, as he boarded his boat in his morning suit. He then managed to hoist the top-sail upside-down, much to everyone's amusement. I can't remember whether he finished the race or not. For one period Keith Collie and I shared ownership of two dinghies, my Dryad and his Sgadán. As his was a 12 Footer and there were no races for them any longer, he and I took the helm of Dryad in alternate races - I crewed for him and he crewed for me. After that I had a similar arrangement with Michael Browett, but that came to a very sad end when Michael was tragically drowned swimming at Derrynane in Kerry, leaving a young widow who was expecting their first child.

In 1957 David Wheeler and I brought Dryad to Crosshaven for the Dinghy Championships. We finished third, but the week was specially memorable because we were camping and I had put our provisions in the sail bag with Dryad's sails, only to

Sailing

*Front view of Basil Jacob's wooden sailing boat "Foam"
and himself top left in the 1940's, and bottom right in 1979.*

find when we arrived that the lid had come off a Bovril jar and the sails (and some other things) were soaked in Bovril. It took hours to wash it all out, but the aroma and colouring remained for a long time! Brigid, who was expecting Owen at the time, stayed with Joe and Jean Healy at "Orchard Corner" – the Healys and the Scanlans had been very good friends for many years. Although Dryad did reasonably well, I then had to compete in an 18 Footer to confirm my skill as a helmsman, but I failed dismally with an absolutely hopeless performance.

The next time that Dryad competed in the National Championships was in Baltimore in 1964 where, with Bill Pigot as crew, we won. He truly was a superb crew. By far my most enjoyable dinghy sailing was when Bill was crewing. He also was a good helmsman, though slightly unpredictable. He gave a demonstration of his ability sailing single-handed out on the trapeze, with a tiller extension, when we were in Baltimore. Sometimes he would take the helm, with me crewing for him. One day, in Dun Laoghaire harbour, with a strong breeze, he was at the helm, we were going dead down-wind towards the Melampus buoy, I was facing forward, ready to let the centre board down, and suddenly the boat swerved off course. I shouted to Bill "What are you doing?" No reply. I looked round and there was Bill in the water 50 yards behind – his toe had missed the toe-strap, and he had fallen overboard. With that, the boat capsized. One season, with Bill crewing, Dryad won 24 out of 36 races, and won the Regatta trophy as well.

During the 1950's sailing and The Royal St. George Yacht Club were an important part of my life – I was on the Sailing Committee and I was Secretary of the Regatta Committee one year, the first year that over 200 boats took part. Dr. Rory O'Hanlon was by that time Commodore, a big, genial, able man and a good sailor who was one of the pioneer cruising members of the George, as well as racing regularly. He had a dreadful stutter, and on one occasion he told the Sailing Committee that we should get a new motor boat for ferrying people to their moorings and "t-t-t-t-tart up the punt and s-s-s-s-sell it" much to our amusement.

The space that is now the changing rooms and club room under the main floor of the Club was then the boat house and was used for winter storage of boats where we sandpapered and varnished them ready for the new season. Non-members changed in a dark, dank dungeon under the pavement. Some of us enthusiastic young members improved matters a little by turning what was an open space under the arches into the non-members' changing room, which sufficed for some years. During this period A.H. Masser, (an active sailing member) and Sir Basil Goulding organised a complete re-vamp and re-decoration of the inside of the Club that began to bring its rooms out of the Edwardian era, and brought new life into the Club.

In 1965 we acquired a holiday cottage beside the sea in Cashel, Connemara. Soon after, I decided to build a "Mirror" dinghy to use there, so I got the kit and worked away in our garage at Avondale Road. It is a brilliantly designed boat and not at all difficult to build.

There is one part of the process which involved lifting the hull into the kitchen, warming up the kitchen, and applying fibreglass over the taping along the seams both inside and outside the hull. We decided to paint it yellow, and on the tin it said "Dolphin Yellow", so what could be more natural than to call the boat "Dolphin". It has given a great deal of pleasure and is still in commission.

We also had a ten foot fibreglass punt called "Doodle" and a Seagull outboard motor at the cottage, but I felt a larger boat was needed and in conversation with Donald Robb, the chief engineer of the seaweed factory in Kilkieran, it was suggested that I should get a traditional Galway Bay fishing boat. Not a full sized hooker, but a Gleoiteog (pronounced Glow-chug), which is a sailing boat with a foresail, jib and a large gaff rigged mainsail, the stout wooden hull being tarred black and sails "barked" a rich brown colour. A skilled and talented boat builder from Rosmuc called Colm Breathnach came with me to Lettermore and Gorumna scouting for a suitable hull and we found one – a 23' 6" hull with a classic shape. Colm then repaired and rejuvenated the boat in his shed in Camus. He understood boat building perfectly – he could fashion a complicated knee or other piece by eye, and it fitted perfectly first time. We installed an 8 horsepower single cylinder SABB marine diesel engine and called the boat "Duibhéan", (pronounced Dove-ain) which is Irish for cormorant. Literally translated it means "Black Bird". Only afterwards did I realise that a cormorant, of course, spends a lot of its time under water, which is not a very good thing for a sailing boat to do!

Shortly after I got the boat a local and I were looking down into it from the quayside in Cashel, and I was saying how I planned to cast some slabs of concrete to put in between the ribs as ballast. The local chatted away and gradually got round to saying that the locals usually just used rocks from the seashore as ballast. I afterwards realised that it was his natural tactful and kind way of telling me not to be so silly as to put cast concrete in – that would inevitably trap moisture and cause rot. With loose bits of rock any water that got into the boat would slosh around and there would be plenty of ventilation between the rocks as well. I got new terylene sails, and had to make a new mast (out of a telegraph pole) when the old mast fell out on the quayside and broke in two. Duibhéan was laid up over winter near Mick Nee's house for some years, at first with a tarpaulin cover and then with no cover. She was repaired at different times by Paraic Davis of Roundstone and Colm Breathnach of Rosmuc. In later years she was over-wintered at Wallace's Quay and looked after by Joe Lee, but he let her sink more than once (she needed regular pumping out) and this was not good for the engine - it was never the same again. The last time we had to get the engine taken out it was lifted out by the same truck that collects cut seaweed for the seaweed factory and uses a hydraulic grab. Ultimately she was sold to a man in Kenmare. She was lifted out of the water by a JCB, using slings, at Glynsk, and then taken to Co. Cork by lorry.

Eventually I tired of getting soaked to the skin racing dinghies in Dun Laoghaire, and sold Dryad in 1975 to Fred Yoakley, who later sold her to Erica Mason and Jill McCullough, and then I lost track of her until quite recently. She has been carefully restored and is now owned by Martin Judge who lives in Lacken beside Blessington Lake. He won't be racing her, but will sail her from time to time. He just wanted to own a "classic" old style wooden clinker built boat!

In 1976 Robert Mollard invited me to be one of the crew of five sailing his Swan 34 in the round Britain and Ireland non-stop race. It was about 1,850 miles, and took almost two weeks. Robert Mollard, the skipper, included Michael Bourke, Jarlath Mullen and me among of the crew. It was an unforgettable experience, but I would never do it again! For the first three days some of our competitors remained in sight both ahead and astern, but after that we didn't see any of them until after the finish.

We were sailing into the blue, or thrashing through stormy seas, on our own, almost all the time out of sight of land. We had a special celebration when passing Muckle Flugga, the northern-most island of the Shetlands, before turning south down the North Sea. Days later, about as far south as Norfolk, dead reckoning seemed to show we were many miles offshore. Because of thick fog, I was checking signals from radio beacons, and detected what I thought was Cromer, the famous life boat station which saved many shipwrecked sailors from the Haisborough Sands, but I was told we couldn't possibly be that near to land. Minutes later to our horror, we passed by a big buoy which showed that we were indeed sailing right over the sandbank. Fortunately it was high tide, and there was a strong tide ripping past the buoy. We quickly changed course in order to get clear. I wonder to this day whether the rest of the crew realised what a dangerous position we had been in – saved by the grace of providence. Some days later in the English Channel we ran into thick fog again for some days. We were in the busiest shipping channel in the world, and had to rely on ships passing by to spot us on their radar. It was all too easy to imagine an enormous tanker failing to spot our little yacht, and running us down.

When we were off the south coast, in thick fog and not at all sure where we were, we motored for a mile or two at right-angles to our course (which was allowed in the rules) to get out of the main shipping lane and were then boarded by some Royal Navy personnel from a frigate which had suddenly loomed up beside us in the fog. They came on board and I am sure they suspected that we were carrying drugs or illegal immigrants, but they soon realised that we were *bona fide* and left us. They kindly volunteered that we were "exactly three miles due south of Brighton Pier".

For a couple of days we sailed on through the fog with very light wind, and often heard the thump, thump, thump of the engines of enormous tankers approaching too near for comfort. More than once in the middle of the night we were roused from our bunks, went on deck, and had to put on our life jackets - afraid we were about to be run down. Eventually we landed in Portsmouth, having safely completed the course (but coming in near the tail-end of the fleet).

I rang home and was informed that Uncle Bernard (Jacob) had died in Saffron Walden, so I put on my shore clothes, shaved off my beard, and went straight to the funeral, in Essex.

After that I was taken on as a crew for regular twice weekly racing from Dun Laoghaire with Keith Collie in his excellent small cruiser racer (a Trapper 300) called "Daybreak". Keith's wife Alice was a regular crew member, and on one occasion learned that it was my birthday, so when I got on board what was there on the cabin table but a birthday cake with candles – very thoughtful! Blair Halliday was the other regular crew. Some years later I moved to my brother-in-law Pierce Butler's Puppeteer "Flycatcher", then when Pierce moved up to an Impala called "Aeolus" and eventually his Sigma 33 "Moonshine" I remained one of his crew, along with Ronnie Moloney, Jill Fleming, Pierce's son Hugh (an outstanding crew), Andrew his son-in-law, sometimes Penny Bleakley, and various others. I eventually bowed out in 2004.

I was part of the crew of Aeolus when it raced in Baltimore Regatta one year, and in Pierce's absence I was asked to take the helm for one race which went out round the Fastnet Rock lighthouse and back through Roaring Water Bay. There was an uncomfortably strong and gusty wind, I was not in good form, I sailed the boat extraordinarily badly, and committed a foul early in the race but kept going, with the intention of sailing outside the finishing line. The final straw was when a navigation buoy near the finish swerved across our course unexpectedly in the current, and our spinnaker got caught on it and ripped to pieces in front of all the crowd watching the end of the race. I think that was probably the turning point of my enjoyment of racing, though I did continue for a few years more before giving up.

In 1988 I left "the office" for the last time (not retirement – just change of occupation!). Ron Cudmore, one of my colleagues at the office, suggested I might like to borrow his 35 Foot Ketch "Morgana" and sail most of the way round Ireland. This was really very kind of him, and I jumped at the opportunity. He sailed the boat as far as Schull in West Cork and then our son Charles, Robin Tamplin and I took over. Within the first few hours the jib fell to pieces, but fortunately we were near Crookhaven and moored there. I hitched a lift with Hugh Coveney to Cork, and went straight to Harry Cudmore's house – Harry was Ron's father. Mary Cudmore took the jib to McWilliams for repair and put me up over night. Harry very kindly then drove me back down to Crookhaven with the repaired sail in his new small Lancia. He was delighted with what appeared to be great fuel efficiency, about 100 miles per gallon, until he realised that the milometer was calibrated in kilometres and not miles!

The following three weeks, sailing up the west coast of Ireland, across the north coast and down the east coast to Dun Laoghaire was the most enjoyable sailing I have ever done in a keel boat. To wake up on board, at anchor in a little cove or harbour like Derrynane or Inishbofin, then put up the sails and have a wonderful day's sailing, and to anchor that evening in another delightful spot, day after day, was magic. We changed crew a couple of times. Charles and Robin got off and David Rowe, Keith Collie and Norman Wilkinson came on at Roundstone, then Keith and David went ashore in Burtonport and Robin Tamplin and Graham Naughton came on for the last stretch. I will probably chronicle this "holiday" in more detail elsewhere.

A Jacob Family
Tramore in the 1900s

Edwin Jacob and baby Ann Jacob.

Chapter 12

Memories of Edwin and Jessie Jacob
Jenny (Jacob) O'Sullivan

I have very fond memories of Edwin B. and Jessie E. Jacob - to me they were simply Grandpa and Granny. They had a lovely cosy house with a large fireplace and a bellows to get the fire started, and the kitchen with a long wooden table which Winnie scrubbed without fail every night. I looked forward to Monday nights. As Dad and Mum were at choir practice I stayed with Grandpa and Granny. Grandpa would have me sitting on his knee and read stories or read from a book. Granny would help me with my homework and in particular my spellings.

When Mirza and Fritz, who were refugees of World War 2, came to stay they had a beautiful black dog who unfortunately died and I remember clearly the dog being buried in the garden where there was a lovely hedge arch overhanging. In the summer when Elizabeth and Rosemary came to visit we would all head off to the seaside village of Bonmahon.

The most outstanding memory I have of Granny was on the occasion when Mum took a 'bad turn" with her heart and Dad asked me to go to Grandpa's house to phone for the Doctor (we had no phone at the time). I dutifully ran up the road, it was just getting dark at the time, and I knocked loudly on the door which was quickly answered by Granny in her night attire, a satin long nightdress, and she had let her hair down which was long and white. I got such a fright I was barely able to get out the message that Mum needed the Doctor. Anyway it all ended well and Mum made a full recovery.

When our cousins Ann, Lynne and Leslie came over from Saffron Walden with Uncle Bernard and Auntie Sally, we always played games in the garden and Grandpa would help with hide and seek and place parcels in various parts of the garden for us to find. They were lovely Grandparents and my abiding memories personally are on my Birthday the fuss that was made, and the excitement when Weston and Philip were coming home for Christmas.

Bonmahon Beach Waterford

A Jacob Family
Tramore in the 1900s

Bernard Jacob.

Sally Jacob.

Bernard and Sally's Wedding, at Waterford Meeting House, 1936.

Chapter 13

EBJ, JEJ, Bernard and Sally

(These are some recollections of our grandparents, Edwin and Jessie Jacob, and of our parents, Bernard and Sally, written by Ann in consultation with Lynne and Lesley)

Midvale, Summerville, and Tramore – what vivid memories they hold for me, strengthened no doubt by the fact that they are the first places I can remember. In 1939, when I was two, my parents were on holiday with me in Tramore staying with Granny and Grandpa Jacob (as we called them) at Midvale when the war broke out. As it was thought that London and its environs would be heavily bombed, my parents were persuaded to leave me over there for a while, and I lived firstly with Granny and Grandpa and then with Chas and Stella until I was three and a half, when they came to collect me and bring me back to England, by which time Lynne was nine months old.

Midvale had a wide hall with a beautiful mosaic tiled floor in cream, terracotta, brown and black (which I understand from the present owners is still there). The sitting room, with large square bay window, blue carpet and sofa (a colour Granny loved) had a dark marble fireplace with a high mantelpiece on which stood vases and bowls in a very specific shade of deep rich blue, known to us always as "granny blue", and also a blue and white bowl with willow pattern on the outside, which was often used to serve stewed loganberries. It is difficult to know which was the more delicious – the taste of the loganberries, grown by Grandpa and served with carrageen jelly (a white milk jelly, made with seaweed) or the visual impact of the rich reddish-purple juice and fruit in the blue and white bowl, somehow so reminiscent of Granny.

There was a large garden, mostly cultivated by Grandpa, which was divided into different areas. The front lawn and gravel drive was separated from the vegetable and fruit garden by a grass walk with rose arches along. Above the kitchen garden, near the house, was a lawn almost completely enclosed by a tall clipped cupressus hedge, with its spicy dusty smell, that provided privacy for relaxing and sunbathing. Grandpa was a wonderful gardener. The ground was enriched with seaweed collected from The Cove nearby and produced not only vegetables and fruit (especially loganberries!) but also sweet peas in abundance, in rich mixed colours, picked and set in the hall or sitting room in one of the "granny blue" vases, scenting the whole room. In addition he kept bees, tending to them garbed in his bee-hat and veil. This love of gardening was inherited by all his children and at least my father (and probably the others too) also inherited a love of bee-keeping.

Grandpa perhaps appeared a bit austere and formal, and certain routines like mealtimes and his dinner being on the table at the right time were important. But he was much more loving and imaginative with children than he might have seemed. One of my very early memories, when I can only have been about two and a half (I was still sleeping in a cot in their bedroom) is of him letting me tie his tie (which he must have taught me how to do) before he went off to the office in the morning. I remember him taking me for walks too, holding my hand as I walked along a grass-topped wall at the edge of what was then a field, but is now the supermarket by the cross roads down to The Cove. And who could forget his love of words, rhymes and "sayings"? "How do you spell Habakkuk? An H and an A and a B and an A and a K and a K and a UK", "Boy Gun, Toy Fun, Gun Bust, Boy Dust" or "Boy Wire, Electric Fire, Blue Flashes, Boy Ashes".

And I am sure all the grandchildren loved as much as we did receiving at Christmas and birthdays a thick envelope containing a half-crown (sometimes even two half-crowns) embedded in a circle cut out of a thick piece of cardboard, and wrapped in a note from him so that the Post Office would not detect that actual cash was being sent through the post (not permitted!). The letter would be addressed in his distinctive copperplate writing (and much more recently it was so nostalgic to find his writing on the flyleaf of several of the Bibles in Tramore Meeting House, dating from his time as Clerk of the Meeting I suppose).

Granny was a very sagacious person and in many ways much in advance of her time, for she brought up all four of her children, both boys and girls, to be equally domesticated and my father certainly exemplified this, for he played a very large part in our domestic life and upbringing as children (which was a very radical thing for a man). For me especially a measure of her wisdom is that while she was caring for me, although I have no memories of the time before living in Ireland, I was never under any impression that she, or indeed Stella, was my mother. I was always aware that my parents were in England, loved me, and were coming back, and I was kept in touch with them and aware of what was happening. As a result it was a very happy time for me living both at Midvale and with Chas and Stella at Summerville, and a hugely influential part of my life. This has understandably given me a much closer feeling of identity with Ireland than either of my sisters, and a feeling of being "at home" there as well as in England.

As I spent some of my early time in Tramore also living with Chas and Stella at Summerville, perhaps it is permissible to record some of my clearest memories from then, and from later holidays. The smell of the escallonia hedges bordering the path to the house when it rained. The nasturtiums in jewel colours outside the French Windows of the sitting room – Stella used to put the seed-pods in salad sometimes. Stella's involvement with Newtown School and her choir, and her trilling "Three Little Maids from School are we" around the house. And Stella sitting me on the bottom stair to sit quietly if I was naughty (I never remember her smacking me). The Garden Room, which Chas had had built to accommodate the extra number in the home when the Maguire children came to stay, like me to remain safe from the war. A big feature of The Garden Room was the gramophone with large amplifying horn and picture of the HMV dog on the side, telling of the love of music Chas shared with Stella.

Little Ann
about 1940.

Bernard Jacob
about 1907, aged 1½ years.

Holidays in Tramore 1945.
Lesley Jacob, Philip Jacob, Peter Skelton, Ann Jacob, Jennifer Jacob, Lynne Jacob.

A Jacob Family
Tramore in the 1900s

Weston and Philip's patience about entertaining and playing games with me when I was little – they were my heroes! Later, when Jenny came into the family, having another cousin there, and Stella's pleasure in her arrival.

After I returned to England early in 1941, soon after which Lesley was born, holidays that we had until 1947 were mostly spent with Granny and Grandpa at Midvale, and sometimes at Summerville. Both Granny and Stella must have been extremely tolerant and accepting to have a family with several children coming to stay for two or three weeks at a time! I have no recollection of Grandpa coming over to stay with us in England, though he may well have done, but Granny used to visit and I remember her coming over to help when Lesley was born, and when I had an upset stomach giving me her unfailing panacea (and a very effective one) - stewed apple! As rationing was in force for most of this time she helped us sometimes by sending or bringing things that were difficult to obtain in England. I remember parcels with flattened packs of Irish butter in them, which miraculously survived the postal system. Customs controls limited what could be brought into England but Granny, the most honest of people, had not appeared to think it was a dishonest evasion of Customs to travel over on one occasion with a swathe of flannel for mother wrapped around her body under her clothes! On another occasion she provided large travelling rugs, which were then transformed into dressing gowns for my parents and worn for many years thereafter (and mother's was passed on to me when I went to boarding school).

Granny was a person with a great concern to help others and was friends with people from all walks of life. But she could be quite critical, sometimes irrationally. For instance she used to cut the pictures of people she did not like out of the Radio Times! I understand her brother Lance did too, so maybe it was a Baker family trait.

Our parents Bernard (later known to most people as Barney) and Sally (Graham) Jacob had both attended Newtown School, but at different times, as he was ten years older that she. Sally was only 16 when they met at a summer camp run every year by his family, and friends who were known to her brother. She told me he used to come to try and see her while she was still at school, which she sometimes found a bit awkward as it rather cramped her style! Nevertheless they were engaged when she was eighteen and married when she was twenty, at Waterford Friends Meeting House. She once told me that they had only spent a total of one month together at the time they were married. They, and especially father, were full of fun and loved jokes and "japes", and he was a great raconteur. Indeed we still revisit his stories and jokes over 30 years after his death. He told us one story of when he was in one of his early teaching jobs in England at a school in the midlands, where the staff all hated the headmaster, who was very "status conscious" and unpleasant. He (this headmaster), who lived in the school, had spent a great deal of time and effort having a piece of the school ground levelled and smoothed to create a tennis court for his own use. When it had been sown with grass seed father and some of his staff cronies went secretly in the middle of the night and sowed the whole court with carrots, turnips, swedes etc.

Bernard Jacob on a Rudge Motorcycle, 1919.

"Reading a story"
Lynne, Bernard, Leslie, Sally, and Ann Jacob, 1946.

The headmaster never could understand what had happened to his beautiful tennis court. Sally was not above a "jape" either. When they were engaged she came over to visit him in Saffron Walden and while on the train she dressed up as a bent old woman. No-one else alighted from the train when he came to meet her, so instead of his beautiful fiancée all he saw was an old crone!

Father was physically very fit when young and taught PE, games, swimming and geography throughout the whole senior school at Friends' School in Saffron Walden, though sadly he later developed Parkinson's Disease and was ill for many years. He had a wonderful tenor voice and sang a great deal at home, at the school, for some occasions locally, and indeed whenever the opportunity arose. I was told recently by a former pupil of his that in the last geography lesson of term if they pressed him he would sing to the class instead of teaching. When he and my mother were on honeymoon in Achill he was singing in the lounge of the hotel and my mother was told by another guest, who was a singer herself, that he really should have his voice trained, but he never did. He also played the penny whistle very well, although that activity did not seem to last into his later life – however, I remember it very well. Another thing typical of him was that he could spout off streams of imaginary words without thinking – these neologisms I later learned were commonly linked with the development of Parkinson's Disease, but to us they were amazing and we liked to "possess" them. Often they were related to real words, "Farpling" or "fippling about" for instance meant messing about, and "pyjancipers" for pyjamas, but many of them were purely imaginary, ("lyprendig hopsirollit is one that comes to mind). Quite apart from this he had a love of words in general, and was extremely well read. He and mother were both very much "word people" and he engendered it in us, often playing spelling games with us when we were young and he always made it seem like fun. We are all very good at spelling as a result!

The factors leading to father's later development of Parkinson's caused him, throughout his life, to suffer from sleepiness any time from about six o'clock onwards. As I have indicated earlier, he was very much involved in our upbringing, and on occasions when he was putting us to bed mother would come upstairs and find him asleep on the bed, and us quietly playing. Lesley once dripped water on him when he was thus asleep and he woke with a start, shouting "I'm on fire, I'm on fire!" When I was away at Boarding School he wrote to me regularly, often when he was taking "prep" and I could always tell the point at which he had dozed off because the writing would trail off into a squiggle down the side of the page, and then become normal again further down when he came to (or was woken by noise from the pupils).

Although he fell asleep in the evenings he always rose very early. He would often spend an hour or two on his allotment before coming in to wake us up, or go up to school and mark exercise books there. He was very often the one to get us up in the morning, preceded by a cup of tea and piece of bread to stop us quarrelling (with hunger!). Early morning tea was known as "twinklum twanklum" and its arrival was preceded by the sound from the kitchen of the very specific way he stirred the tea.

Saffron Walden.

Saffron Walden Friends' School.

A Jacob Family
Tramore in the 1900s

Sally Jacob

Mother also had a great sense of fun and as a pair they were extremely sociable and hospitable and we always had people coming to the house or coming to stay. We never were required to call visitors by formal names, always by their first names. She was in many ways the organiser of the family and was strongly committed to our education – not in a slavish way, but to offer us the best opportunities from our schooling. She worked hard in all sorts of ways to enable Lynne and me to go to a school very like Newtown in its ethos, where her own experience had been so happy and formative, as she believed so strongly in its philosophy. She herself had left university before taking her degree in order to get married, but being the tenacious person she was she later, once we had grown up, decided to complete her degree and did so externally, at the same time as caring for father, graduating in 1963. Yes, she was a very tenacious person! In addition, she was always very much involved in local activities, both political and cultural.

We are especially grateful to mother for her concern for health and diet. We were vegetarian (which was much more unusual in those days) and during the war years, though not particularly a lover of cooking, she made sure she knew about foods combining to provide proper protein in our diet. She achieved this by using a number of items not "on ration" such as nut butters and creams, soya flour, and a number of vegetarian products containing such things. Additionally, aided by father's allotment products, we had plenty of vegetables and fruit, as well as our own honey. Her belief in natural remedies influenced her approach to any ailments we had, although not to the exclusion of orthodox medicine if necessary. As a result, we have all had not only very good health, but a valuable knowledge of, and interest in, healthy food and cooking.

Ireland always remained very much in Sally's heart, even though she lived in England from the time she was married. She had learned Irish at School and when about 18 (I think) she spent a period of time living with a family on the Blasket Islands to perfect her Irish. This was an experience she simply loved, however poor the life was. She had I think lived with the family of the king of the island, and had known Peig Sayers, the storyteller. Some forty years later, after father died, she amazed me by still being able to hold a conversation with some Irish speakers in a pub in Kerry!

We were lucky to have had such a very fortunate childhood and to have had many of the influences which have come down through the family from our grandparents (and mother was very close to Granny) and enhanced by our parents.

EBJ, JEJ, Bernard and Sally

Bernard, Dorothy, and Charles on the "Rabbit Burrows" in the early 1920's, with the Back Strand and Tramore in the background.

A Jacob Family
Tramore in the 1900s

At Midvale August 1942, after Dorothy and Kenneth's marriage.
L to R
Back: Grandpa Clay, Granny Clay, Kenneth Clay, Dorothy (Jacob) Clay, Sally, Weston, Lynne, Philip, Bernard.
Front: Marguerite Skelton, Jessie, Lesley, Edwin, Stella, Ann, Charles.

Chapter 14

Dorothy(Jacob) Clay and Family
(Written in 2003)

My sister, Elizabeth and I, Rosemary, are the two daughters of Dorothy Elizabeth Clay and Kenneth Clay. At the time of writing, autumn 2003, it is a decade since Dorothy died; Kenneth had died three years earlier. Now that I look back at our lives together, I am aware that we had a very privileged childhood. At the time we took it for granted, it was all we knew. Our parents created such a loving, safe place for us to grow up, in particular this was Dorothy's doing, as she gave up her teaching job while we were young to devote her time to our up bringing.

Dorothy Jacob (as she was then), and Kenneth met when they were both teaching at Friends' School Lisburn, Northern Ireland, in 1940. Kenneth was quite new at the school and was rather the centre of attention among the young single members of staff. There was to be a village dance one evening and this was to be quite an event. Dorothy loved dancing and was greatly looking forward to it. Unfortunately, during the day of the dance, Dorothy tripped and twisted her ankle, and was unable to go. Kenneth had never liked dancing and had probably not intended to go in the first place, but he suggested, to make up for Dorothy's disappointment, they could go to the cinema together. This they did, and so started the romance.

They were married in 1942 on August 5th in Tramore, where Dorothy's sister Marguerite was Matron of Honour and Alfred Bewley was the Bestman. Dorothy's two brothers Charles and Bernard were there with their wives, Stella and Sally. Marguerite's husband Jack and the nieces and nephews, all helped in the celebrations. Both sets of parents were also present. After the wedding they left for their Honeymoon by bicycle with a small bouquet of flowers attached to each of their handlebars, to show that they were just married!

They started their married life living at Lisburn School Gate Lodge, where they lived until Kenneth was appointed head master of Brummana High School in Lebanon. They both started off by teaching there, Kenneth in the senior school, and Dorothy in the junior department.

Dorothy was in her early forties, when first I was born in 1947, and Elizabeth in 1949. By then she was already half way through her life. These memoirs are of the Clay family from that time on. I shall refer to Dorothy as mother and Kenneth as father from now on.

I was born in Lebanon during the time mother and father were working there, mother had had several miscarriages before this successful pregnancy. There was a good deal of celebration after my birth, even though all the Arab staff and visitors said to mother that it was a shame she had a little girl, better luck next time!

Dorothy Clay with Rosemary (aged 9 weeks) and Jessie Jacob, at Brummana, Lebanon, 1948.

Brummana School, Lebanon, 1948.

A telegram was received from Uncle Bun and Auntie Sally saying "girls are best." They had of course three girls themselves, Ann, Lynne, and Lesley. Granny Jacob came over to Lebanon for several months, before and after my birth, to help with her latest grandchild.

Beruit Lebanon, Bab-Idris Street, 1948.

Our little family returned to England in 1948, we moved to Chelmsford where Elizabeth was born and father taught at the technical college, then to Sibford, where father taught at the Friends School. Both of these were short-term positions, because I was only three when we moved to Chellaston near Derby. This house became our home for the next fourteen years, all of our happy childhood.

We were on holiday in North Wales with Granny and Grandpa Clay, when father went off on his bike to cycle to Derby to look for a house for us. He had just been appointed Lecturer in French, Spanish and British Constitution at Derby College for Further Education, this was a position which he held until his retirement. He had a selection of houses to view, and make a short list from before mother went to make the final decision.

The most important thing to mother when we moved to Derby was that the house should have a garden. Obviously, it also had to have adequate living accommodation, and be close to a school, and bus route (we did not have a car at this time. In fact father did not learn to drive until Granny Clay came to live with us in 1963). But above all, it must have a garden. So father returned to Wales with his short-list, and mother went to make the final choice. The house she chose was just outside the village of Chellaston, four miles south of Derby, it was on a bus route, and the local primary school was only a short walk away, and it had a garden. It was a good one right from the start, but mother made it her own, it was an extension to the house, a garden to be lived in. Mother had been brought up at Midvale in Tramore Co. Waterford, where the garden was very special; she must have had a love for gardening since she was a child there.

Chellaston Village near Derby.

The back garden could be roughly divided into three, starting from the house, the first section was laid to lawn with flower beds and a rockery down the right hand side, three mature apple trees in the lawn with flower borders around them. To the left there was a large area of fruit bushes, raspberries, red and black currants and gooseberries. There was a path that led between the lawn and the soft fruit bushes that turned at right angles. Mother built a pergola here and trained climbing roses into a beautiful rose arch, as a division between the lawn and the vegetable area. Elizabeth and I had our own little garden; we each had a den made under and between the bushes and a large sandpit to play in. All of these could be seen from the kitchen window. Further down the garden were rows of vegetables, and a very special plum tree which mother grew from a stone. The plum must have been eaten on some significant occasion because this tree was looked after and loved more carefully than all other plants, trees or shrubs. Eventually it was even moved to a special spot in our garden at the next house, where it continued to grow and fruit well. In 2003 a sapling from this tree bore a bumper crop of fruit in Elizabeth's garden in Borrowash.

The third section of garden we referred to as Mrs Scrubies, I'm not sure why, but the previous owners had kept hens here, and there was still an old henhouse which was great for playing hide and seek. This area was roughly divided into two, one half growing potatoes and the other half more soft fruit bushes, including a cultivated blackberry bush, which produced the most wonderfully big juicy blackberries the like of which I have never tasted since.

So by the end of the summer, mother was always busy with preserving, bottling and making chutneys from all the ripe fruit. Elizabeth and I began to help in this "hive of industry" as soon as we grew old enough. Chutney making had to take place on a day when father had an evening class at college, because he could not stand the smell of boiling vinegar. These days were the only ones I can remember him not cycling home for lunch.

The front garden was much smaller than the back garden. However, it did have two large trees which shielded the house from the road. One was a lime, and the other a copper beech, both excellent for climbing! There was a rhododendron bush to one side and all sorts of other bushes such as teasels, honesty and hydrangea, which mother used to grow and then dry, so that they could be used for dried flower arrangements in the winter. Elizabeth and I did a lot of growing up in this garden, including learning to ride our bikes, and roller skate.

Mother loved the garden which she had created, and was always happy to be able to be out working or relaxing in it. Whenever possible we would eat our meals outside. One in particular that I remember was a meal with Auntie Marguerite and Cousin Bernard, they had come to stay with us, and go to watch the cricket test match at Trent Bridge. Weston and Hilda also spent that day with us, Weston was Uncle Chas's oldest son. They lived in Manchester at that time and came to Chellaston on their motor bike. It was a very happy family gathering. Years later, mother and John my husband, used to spend hours discussing gardening, flowers, bushes and how best to plan the garden at *our* first house which we bought in 1972. It was one of the things mother and John had in common.

Both of our parents were teachers, mother was a real natural with small children; she had all the necessary skills and patience required. When we were small Elizabeth and I benefited from these, as mother decided to stay at home with us and devote her time to our development. She always had time for us, and encouraged us to develop and discover our own talents. At first she concentrated on pre-school activities, learning to read and write, simple arithmetic, drawing and painting which gave us a good start at school. Later she helped us with all kinds of art and craftwork; we used to make plaster-moulded ornaments, seashell ornaments and calendars which we would give to relations at Christmas. We also learned to sew, knit and cook while still quite young. We spent evenings doing these things, probably because we did not have a television until much later. Even in those days it was unusual not to have a television. At the time, I resented the fact that I did not know some of the programs my peers were talking about at school, but later I realised that the extra time spent with my parents had been more valuable.

A Jacob Family
Tramore in the 1900s

Dorothy Jacob
May 1910, aged 3¾ years.

Dorothy Jacob 1938.
Changed very little!

Dorothy (Jacob) Clay,
on her Wedding Day, August 1942.

Dorothy Clay.
Hardly changed at all!

Mother always thought keeping in touch with the family was very important, in this I don't just mean our family of four, I mean the extended family. She would communicate by letter with both sets of Grandparents weekly and also very regularly with Marguerite, Chas and Barney. She also had a close relationship with her first cousin Doreen, they used to go away on coach tours together, while Doreen was working at Ashgate Maternity hospital near Chesterfield. One famous trip that they took together was to Germany and Austria, where they saw the Passion plays at Oberammergau. Doreen was a frequent visitor to our home. When she retired she moved to a little flat, very close to our Vernon Street house.

Before mother was married she had been quite involved with the care of her nephews, Weston and Philip who were both quite young when their mother, Chas's first wife, died. I remember stories of camping trips and visits to the circus, she always remained close to them. Many years later she and father visited Weston and Hilda and their family in Canada, this was after Weston had been diagnosed with cancer. I know that they were very pleased that they made that trip.

Derby Meeting, and The Society of Friends in general, played a very important part in the Clay family lives. Father would cycle, and mother would take Elizabeth and me on the bus, from Chellaston to Derby to the Meeting House every Sunday morning. It was a ritual, there was never any question about it, it just always happened. Meeting for Worship lasted for one hour, and when we were young, we would spend part of that time in Sunday school. Mother would take her turn in teaching the children. Each year she produced a Christmas play, which the Sunday school children performed, for the rest of Derby Friends. These were very imaginative productions, which she wrote, cast, produced and costumed, showing her terrific talent for "managing to get the best out of people." Mother had always been a Quaker; she was brought up in a Quaker family.

Father was not brought up a Quaker, although he did attend two Quaker schools in his teenage years, Great Ayton and then Bootham, both in Yorkshire, where he was brought up. Then in his late teens, he was Student Master at Friends' School, Saffron Walden, for a year, before he went to Leeds University, where he got first class honours in his French Degree. The following year he took an Education Diploma. In 1939 he became a Doctor in Political Science, after studying in Geneva.

At some time during his education, he did join the Society of Friends, and become a Quaker. His parents also joined later and became very active members of Rawdon meeting. Rawdon is near Leeds where they lived.

Father was a life long pacifist, and on leaving Geneva during wartime, he became a conscientious objector. He was given a conditional exemption from military service because of his beliefs, and so began his teaching career. Father's mother, Granny Clay, thought he should have been a Foreign Diplomat and who knows, if it had not been wartime, he might have had a different career. He certainly had the intellect and knowledge of different languages.

Kenneth Clay, on his Wedding Day.

Father loved to cycle. He used his bike every day; he came home each lunchtime from Derby, during term time. Thus doing about twenty miles each day, at weekends he would use it for meeting or monthly meeting, in Chesterfield, Mansfield or Nottingham. I cannot remember a single occasion when father did not use his bike, even in the middle of winter in the snow, ice or fog. Partly he was saving money, but he also really enjoyed riding his bike. In the first few years of teaching at Derby, he would take a group of students away to France or Spain. They would cycle all the way and of course, practice their French as well.

When studying in Geneva, he used his bike to cycle home to England, to visit his parents in Yorkshire. One year he had been home for Christmas, and was cycling back through the snow covered Alps, on New Years Eve, especially so that he could be the first person to cross the Swiss Border in the New Year (1937).

Mother also enjoyed cycling, and they had many happy rides together, later Elizabeth used to ride on the little red saddle in front of father, and I had a seat on the back of mothers bike. We sometimes went to Meeting like that. I remember trips into Derbyshire, for picnics in Dovedale and going blackberry picking. It was fun. As soon as we were old enough, Elizabeth and I had our own bikes. Then we would ride two a breast, with mother and father beside us. On one occasion early on, we were approaching a roundabout near the Meeting House, father shouted, "turn right!" but the sign on the roundabout said "keep left" Elizabeth rode straight into it!

Now that I look back, I realise that we did not have any spare money, when we were very young. The mortgage on the house with only father's salary was difficult to manage. So it was to save money that we used our bikes so much. On other occasions, we would walk to the next bus stop, because it was a cheaper fare stage, thus saving a few pennies.

Mother would make our birthday and Christmas presents, with much love and care. In particular I remember one year, she made a whole school set for our dolls and teddies, including maths books, writing and spelling books, each covered in different paper and stitched together. Each book had the dolls name on it. The reading books were made from used stamp books! She must have been planning it for months, to have so many stamp books ready. We were thrilled with this present, I do not think any bought toy could have given us such pleasure, or kept us occupied for so many happy hours.

Elizabeth and Rosemary Clay.

Dorothy and her daughters.

A Jacob Family
Tramore in the 1900s

*Marguerite and Jack Skelton, Dorothy and Elizabeth Clay,
Charles and Jessie Jacob, Kenneth and Rosemary Clay.*

Kenneth Clay, Dorothy Clay, Bernard Skelton.

The year Elizabeth was five and I was seven, we were told by mother to expect two joint surprises, one on each of our birthdays. My birthday came and the surprise was a beautifully decorated Christmas tree, with our first set of electric fairy lights. We were thrilled with this first surprise, but the one we got on Elizabeth's birthday was even better. It was a little ginger kitten, we gave him the name Jazar, which means carrot in Arabic, but sounds much nicer than carrot. Jazar very soon became part of the family; he was an extremely friendly and placid cat with a lovely nature. All our neighbours were fond of him too, and were happy to look after him whenever we were away.

Because our birthdays were so close together, with Christmas in between, we used to have a small party at home, when Granny and Grandpa Clay were staying with us. They came every year to spend Christmas, and would arrive in time for my birthday on the 23rd, and stay until after Elizabeth's on the 28th. We all went to Meeting at Christmas, and usually, they would be there to watch us in the play that mother produced. Mother loved singing, and tried to included a song or hymn in her play. She often used to say that she would like more singing at the Meeting House. Her singing voice was lovely. Eventually she joined a choir, at Derby Cathedral and got a lot of enjoyment from that. Once I remember her starting to sing a hymn, at the Meeting House, expecting others to join in, but it was rather an unusual one, and nobody else joined in, so she sang the whole thing as a solo.

Then in the summer we would have another party, this was usually a picnic, in a field just out side the village of Chellaston. It took a lot of organising, because all the food, jelly, cake, sandwiches, drinks etc. PLUS the games, had to be transported there by bike. Mother used to plan treasure hunts and nature quizzes, I remember these parties as being very "different" and our friends loved them as much as we did.

We always managed to have a holiday, even before we had the caravan. While Granny and Grandpa Jacob were still living in Tramore, we spent our summer holidays there, at Midvale and then Summerville. I have a few recollections of these early holidays, such as beehives on the lawn at Midvale. Walking down to the harbour where I learnt to swim, being rewarded by a silver halfcrown from Grandpa for swimming 30 strokes. Buying fresh mackerel from the quay, and Granny cooking it for us for breakfast. Cousin Jenny letting us play with her toys, and reading us stories.

One year, I think it must have been our Grandparents 50th wedding anniversary, because most of our aunts uncles and cousins were gathered at Midvale, we went for a walk, to a remote beach. It meant crossing a field, which had a bull in residence in it. I remember uncle Bun leading us all to safety, holding a stick in front of him and reciting the Lords Prayer. On that same holiday, Elizabeth went up to a dog that had been left guarding its owner's belongings, on the beach. She tried to coax it away, to play with her but with no success, so she pulled its tail. The dog turned round and bit Elizabeth; she had to have stitches above her eye. The thing I have never understood, is how this incident put *me* off dogs for life, but *not* Elizabeth!

A Jacob Family
Tramore in the 1900s

The Clay Caravan.

The Clay Family at the Beach.
Kenneth, Rosemary, Elizabeth, and Dorothy.

Father was usually very careful with money; he enjoyed saving, and later in life, investing his savings. So, when, one day he came home from college at lunch time, and announced that he had bought a caravan, this seemed some how out of character! Maybe he had been mulling it over in his mind for some time, I don't know, but this was definitely the first any of us had heard about it. The caravan was not a smart one, in fact it had been home-made, by one of father's colleagues, who now wanted to "upgrade" and to sell his old one. For us it was brilliant, we had many wonderful holidays and weekends away in that caravan, during the next few years. We did have a problem in moving it about though, as father did not drive at this time, so we had to rely on friends towing it for us. We had quite a good arrangement in the end; father offered the driver a free stay for his family, in the caravan, for each move he helped us with. During the winter the caravan was parked in Derbyshire. At first it was kept in a beautiful spot, on a farm near the village of Fenny Bentley, close to Dovedale. It was quite an expedition to get to Fenny Bentley, by bus from Chellaston. Mother, Elizabeth and I would set off after school on Friday afternoon, with everything we needed, including food, for the weekend. We had to change busses twice and then a long, up hill walk with all our baggage to the caravan. Father came on his bike straight from college. We loved our weekends at the caravan, and it was definitely worth the effort to get there.

The caravan was moved to the seaside for the summer holiday. Father set off on his bike for a few days, to find a site for the caravan. The first year he went to the East Coast, he found a site at Saltfleetby in Lincolnshire. It seemed to be a very good spot, with just a row of sand dunes between the site and the sea. However, what father did not realise, was that the tide only came in like this, close to the dunes, once a month, when the moon was new.

For the rest of the time there was a great area of mud flats between the sea on the horizon, and the coast, not ideal for a beach holiday! This was our only failure during our years of caravaning holidays. We spent six weeks there that year, and went on lots of day trips by train to such places as Skegness, Grimsby, Mablethorpe and Cleethorpes, none of which were very nice!

After that, each year we went to Trearddur Bay, on Holy Island Anglesey, in North Wales. This was always very successful; it was a beautiful place. We used to spend two weeks there, and then go over to Ireland, using the ferry from Holyhead to Dun Laoghaire, near Dublin. Here we visited Auntie Marguerite and Uncle Jack and other friends and relations. Later Elizabeth and I went over by ourselves. Auntie Marguerite took us to the Dublin Horse Show, which was tremendously exciting! It must have been a welcome break for our parents too.

One year, probably our last, father, Elizabeth and I cycled to the caravan at Trearddur Bay. Previously father had always cycled, but we had gone by train, with mother and all the luggage. This time mother had to travel on her own, with all the bags and cases, needed by a family of four, for a six week holiday!

There were thirteen bags, bundles and cases in all, she had to taxi to Derby station, change trains at Crewe and Chester and taxi again from Holyhead to the caravan. Mother did not complain about having to do this, she may well have decided that it was worth it, to have three days peace and quiet without us. There used to be a photograph of her, in the middle of all the bags, but over the years it has been mislaid.

This journey was the longest we had done by bike. A few weeks before we were due to go, father decided we should have a practice run. We went into the Peak District, for a three-night preparation trip. It was great fun and we managed very well, staying each night in YHA's. So when the time came, we set off for North Wales. The first day was mostly main roads, and we stayed our first night with father's cousin Margaret in Stoke-on-Trent. The next day was a lovely ride to Chester, the third night was at Colwyn Bay, a beautiful ride and finally over the Menai Strait to Anglesey, and on to Trearddur Bay. We then enjoyed a relaxing holiday before our return journey. On the way back we rode up through Snowdonia, instead of the coastal route, and stayed at Betws-y-Coed, Llangollen and Stoke-on-Trent and back home. I remember more about the journey there and back, than I do about the holiday that year.

At the end of that year we were advised that the caravan should not be moved again, so it was towed to its final site in Brailsford, which is about eight miles from Derby, towards Ashbourne. Much closer than the previous winter site. We did continue to use it occasionally, but by this time Elizabeth and I were both away at school, so we would go in the Easter holidays and take our friends. Eventually, in 1996, John and a college friend made use of it for a few weeks when they were unable to find a flat to rent, while studying at Derby College of Art.

Mother was a very imaginative and creative craftswoman, something I think I have inherited from her. When we were small, she would make all our clothes, sometimes converting a garment she or father had finished with, or sometimes using a remnant from the excellent fabric stalls on Derby market. I remember embroidered jackets, satin party dresses with velvet sashes, sundresses, towelling beach robes and school skirts. The skirts were made from flannel trousers. Elizabeth and I would usually have matching or co-ordinating outfits to wear for any special occasion.

Both of our parents were skilled knitters, mother taught father how to knit during the war years, he became excellent at it, he was not very practical with his hands generally, but he did enjoy knitting, especially if the pattern he was following was complicated and written in French! Later, when we were staying in the caravan, we all used to knit squares, and join them together, into blankets to send to the refugees via Oxfam. All through our childhood and probably later, mother and father would always have knitting on the go.

One year, mother enrolled at a soft toy making class, and this was the start of another creative hobby. She made lots of toys, dolls, teddies, rabbits and many other animals, mostly using fur fabric from Derby market. Whenever there was a new member of the family, or a friend had a baby, mother would put her creative expertise to work.

My older two sons had special toys, made by their Granny, but by the time Nick was born, mother was no longer able to do such fine work, so I made him a teddy using one of mother's patterns. She did knit Nick a cot blanket, which I think was the last piece of knitting she did.

Another craft hobby that mother became very involved in, was stone polishing. This was probably her last *new* hobby, but it did give her and others a lot of enjoyment, for several years. First she had to collect interesting stones, and then they were polished in a drum shaped machine, in batches. Each batch took three weeks of churning in the machine, in a muddy substance, to be ready for use. When they were ready, the transformation was amazing, an insignificant pebble would turn out almost "jewel like." Mother, then used the polished stones to make all kinds of gifts and ornaments, such as jewellery, earrings, brooches, chokers and necklaces. She would also fill an interesting shaped bottle with polished stones and use it as a lamp base; once again using her imagination. Whenever mother and father were away on holiday in the car, mother was always on the look out for different coloured stones for her craftwork. Some holidays were specifically planned around a particular beach where mother knew she could collect unusual stones!

Music was always important in our home. Mother played the piano and loved to sing. Father enjoyed listening to classical music, and he was very knowledgeable about it. Both would love listening to a concert on the radio, so we were brought up to the lunchtime concert on radio 3. In fact, the radio was always tuned into radio 3 for the music, except when there was a cricket test match on, then, we all had to listen to ball by ball commentary on the cricket.

Mother and Elizabeth tolerated it; I became really interested in it, and still follow English cricket now. Cricket was something John and father shared an interest in too. Father never played, but John and our three boys do. I am glad that father was able to watch Ben and Tom play for their school, it brought him a lot of enjoyment. He would have loved to see our youngest son Nick play, now at the age of sixteen he plays for the county (Cornwall) and also for Tintagel 1st XI, as a wicket keeper and batsman. This season, 2003, he was awarded the "Player of the Year" award.

As well as being musical and a good crafts-woman, mother was also very well read. She enjoyed reading both classical novels and contemporary writings. She was also keen on all kinds of Natural History books. She loved poetry, and had had a few of her own short stories and poetry published. At one stage when Elizabeth and I were away at school, she did a series of readings of her own Prayers on Radio Derby. She was always modest about her own achievements, but she really was a clever and talented person in such a wide variety of ways.

Both mother and father did a lot of voluntary work with in the community; mother was a marriage guidance councillor for many years. Father was a Samaritan and also did a lot for Amnesty and UNICEF. Also they both served on numerous Quaker committees, in Derby and London.

I went away to school in Saffron Walden at the age of eleven, and Elizabeth followed two years later. Both our parents had been educated at Quaker boarding schools, and so they decided this was best for us too. It must have been a struggle financially, although mother was teaching again by this time. It was a wrench for us to leave the family at that age, and our close relationship with our parents changed. But I suppose that was growing up! The wrench was made easier for us, by having Barney and Sally in Saffron Walden, Barney was teaching at the school when I started there. Cousin Lesley was in the sixth form; this was very helpful for me at the beginning. Mother's cousin Dorothea also lives in Saffron Walden. First with her father, Uncle Lance, and then after he died, Auntie Win (Granny Jacob's sister), shared Dorothea's house. Elizabeth and I used to go there for tea on Saturdays. Last year, 2002, Elizabeth and I stayed with Dorothea when we were in Saffron Walden for Old Scholars weekend.

I think being away from home helped us to become more independent, and although I did love being there in the end, I personally would have done better academically, if I had been watched over by my parents. Elizabeth would certainly have done well if we had not had our terrible car accident before she took her GCE's in 1966. In the end she took her exams at a later stage, and did do well.

The winter of 1963 was a very severe one. The snow and ice did not thaw between Christmas and Easter. During this time Granny Jacob and Grandpa Clay both died. Grandpa Clay's death was very sudden and unexpected. Granny Clay was already in a very confused state and could not understand what had happened. Father had promised Grandpa, that if Grandpa died before Granny he would look after Granny.

Therefore Granny came to Chellaston, to live with us. This was a very difficult time for the whole family, and in particular mother, as she was the main carer. Granny never grasped that her husband had died, and used to spend the nights wandering around searching for him. She had been a lovely lady, but at this time she was very awkward and difficult to look after. Mother was the most caring person, but even her patience was tested by Granny. I think that this time was the only time in my life, that I ever saw mother really bad tempered and exasperated, but even then she got over it quickly. She was so understanding and resilient. One day, after a particularly difficult night with Granny, mother made Elizabeth and me promise, that if ever she or father were to get into this condition, we would not try to look after them, in either of our families. I must say having made that promise, did make it easier on our consciences almost thirty years later when, exactly the same thing happened, father died suddenly and left mother absolutely confused and in a half world of forgetfulness and mental confusion.

During the time Granny Clay lived with us, father decided to learn to drive. The main reason being that Granny was used to being taken out in the car. Father felt that it might help her settle, to be given a change of scenery. He did not find it easy to pass his driving test but eventually he did and after that there was no stopping him! Father came to love driving almost as much as he had loved cycling.

Mother and father had enormous pleasure from their car. It gave them a new kind of freedom that added greatly to the quality of their life from then on. They had holidays in Scotland, Wales, Norfolk, Cornwall, Ireland and France using the car.

It was fortunate that father learnt to drive when he did, as his health deteriorated for a few years, after Granny Clay had died. He was a year or two away from retirement, and was not enjoying teaching any more. He had some kind of a breakdown, and spent the summer in the Retreat in York. During this time Mother, Elizabeth and I moved from Chellaston to our new home in Vernon Street, Derby. The house had belonged to a fellow member of Derby Meeting, Joyce Blake. She had taken up the head-ship at The Mount school in York, and wanted her elderly mother to move with her. But there was also an aunt, who shared the house with Joyce and her mother. Mrs Blake was reluctant to leave the aunt alone. Many years previously, Mother had expressed a liking for this house in Vernon Street, and had told father that if she was ever going to leave the Chellaston house, it would be to live somewhere like the Blake's house.

It was therefore arranged that we should move there, and the aunt would remain in the up stairs flat; which she did until she died. This house was larger than the old one, and very convenient for the centre of Derby. It had a nice garden, but it was not big enough for mother, so she took on an allotment and continued to enjoy her gardening. She got a teaching job at the local junior school. Father came home from the Retreat, in time to return to college in September. I had left Saffron Walden and had started a Dress Design Course at Derby College of Art. I could walk there from Vernon Street.

Undoubtedly, the worst thing to happen for all our family was the car accident that Elizabeth and I had in January 1966. I was driving Elizabeth back to Saffron Walden after the Christmas Holiday, when a lorry came straight out in front of us from the central reservation. We did not stand a chance of stopping. Elizabeth, in the passenger seat, bore the brunt of the collision. This was in the days before safety straps, and she flew through the windscreen and back into her seat, severely damaging her head in the process. I was relatively unhurt thanks to a collapsible steering wheel. Elizabeth was in a critical condition, with a serious head injury, six broken ribs, punctured left lung, and many cuts on her face. She was given "a fighting chance." She was unconscious for three weeks, in intensive care. During the first week mother and father were called to the hospital on three occasions because Elizabeth's condition had deteriorated. But each time she was slightly better, by the time they arrived. She was having so much trouble breathing that she was given a tracheotomy that eased the breathing, but it gave her another nasty scar. I was able to visit after the first week. We then took turns in visiting, believing that it would help her to regain consciousness if we kept talking to her.

Elizabeth is a fighter, and against all odds she came through. She regained consciousness after three weeks, and then began the long process of rehabilitation. She stayed in hospital for six weeks, and then the long period of recovery continued at home. Friends and family were vital to us, without their support this tragedy might have been even harder to bear.

Mother had already had to be so strong for us, prior to the accident, while father had been incapacitated. Now many people thought father might not be able to cope with what had happened to Elizabeth. But in some strange kind of way, father got instantly better, and the great faith both my parents had, got them through this terrible ordeal and enabled them to help me through it too. Elizabeth herself was wonderful, cheerful and happy. In hospital the other patients had called her "their little ray of sunshine!" This sums her up - always trying to make the best of things.

This is not to say that she was always happy, there were times when she was frustrated, at not being able to do things that she knew she used to be able to do, and she was worried by her appearance. She had several plastic surgery operations in the months that followed the accident, which helped her to feel more like herself. She returned to Saffron Walden for half the year, and then, went on to do a typing course at Derby Technical College. She took her O and A levels and did particularly well in French. She took after father in this respect.

For a couple of years after this she went to France with a Derby family as an au-pair where she did very well, and her French continued to improve. In 1971 she went to Paris to work at their Quaker head quarters. This connection with French Friends still continues today.

During the summer after the accident, mother and father celebrated their 25th wedding anniversary. We were all over in Dublin because Cousin Janet and Tim were getting married and we all went to their wedding. We stayed on in Dublin after their wedding, and enjoyed a family get together in the function room at Phoenix Park, Dublin Zoo, in honour of mother and father's Silver wedding anniversary.

The four of us then had a three-week holiday in Ireland, during which time we visited friends and family from Waterford to Lisburn. A very fitting way to spend the anniversary holiday, this time though we went by car and not bike!

I was half way through my Diploma course at Derby College of Art, (I had made the dresses that mother, and Elizabeth and I wore to Janet's wedding.) I had started to go out with John Lawson, who I later married in 1970. John was also at the college of Art, doing a photography course, at which he excelled. After graduating, he went to work in London, first as an assistant photographer, but after a couple of years became a self employed photographer in advertising, a very good business to be in during the next two decades.

I followed to London, to do my last year of training, a teachers certificate, at Westminster College. Then in 1969 I got a teaching position at Hammersmith and West London College. I taught Fashion and Textiles within the art department. My subjects were dress design and making, and embroidery and other related craft subjects. I held this position for the next eleven years, but reduced to half time when our first child was born.

Our wedding took place at Saint Joseph's Roman Catholic Church. John and his family are Catholics. After the ceremony everyone transferred to Derby Meeting House for a Friends Meeting for Worship. Uncle Chas stood up at the start, to explain a Meeting for Worship to all gathered, I remember it being a very warm and moving meeting and memorable wedding celebration. The Catholic side of our family still comment on it.

John and I moved to a flat near Hampton Court, in Surrey for the first two years of marriage. In 1972 we bought our first house, in Kingston-upon-Thames. It was a three bedroomed semi with no bathroom, and just an outside toilet! But it had great potential and a good-sized garden. Mother and father were our first visitors and they persuaded us to have an extension built, instead of our original plan of converting one of the bedrooms into a bathroom. We took two years of hard graft to make this house into a home, but in the end it was lovely. Our older two sons, Benjamin and Thomas, were both born while we lived here, so we were very glad we had taken the parents advice and kept three bedrooms. Mother and father were proud Grandparents, mother had a little photo album called "Granny's boasting book" full of the most recent photos of the boys, and would take it out of her bag at the slightest suggestion that someone was interested.

They made a point of visiting for birthday parties, until the boys became too boisterous! Both parents were on committees, which met once a month at Friends House in Euston Road, London. They would come and stay with us, for a few nights and attend their meetings, and see the development in their grandchildren each month. An excellent arrangement for all concerned. Mother and father were elderly but fortunately in good health, and able to enjoy taking the boys to the park and for walks by the river.

They commented on the boys being different from their girls, probably because the football had to go every where with them! Mother spent time with John planning our garden, they both enjoyed that. We lived in Kingston for ten years, by which time the house was getting too small for us. We moved to Esher, three miles further out of London, in 1982 when the boys were seven and five. Mother and father continued to visit us monthly.

Elizabeth and Dave Davies were married on a snowy Saturday in March 1972. The wedding was at the Quaker Meeting House in Derby, Elizabeth's dress was a traditional Quaker dress in grey silk with matching bonnet. She looked great, and it was a very original idea. Mother, Elizabeth and I, made the outfit. It was quite a challenge, especially as Elizabeth was living in France, until shortly before the wedding, so with me in London and Mother in Derby we did have a few problems to overcome, but it was all fine on the day. The Marriage did have to be delayed slightly however, because the coach bringing Dave's family from Llandudno in Wales had got stuck in the snow! They managed to get there a bit late, and the rest of the day went very well. Elizabeth and Dave bought a very nice house in a quiet road in Borrowash a few miles out of Derby and convenient for Dave, who worked for Rolls Royce. They still live in this house today and Dave still has the same job, although it is no longer Rolls Royce.

A Jacob Family
Tramore in the 1900s

One summer, before Ben and Tom had started school, we went on holiday to Scotland. This was a suggestion made by mother and father. They had been to stay on The Isle of Mull and thought it would be a great place for us to go with our young boys. We stayed in a small family run hotel there, and were very impressed by everything we saw. The friendliness of the owners, the home cooked food, the imaginative menus and wine list. They were a couple from Yorkshire, who had given up their jobs down south, to run a hotel. We thought that we could do this, and would enjoy doing it too.

About sixteen years later when John had had enough of photography, advertising and the daily drive into London, we did just that, bought a Hotel and started to run it ourselves. The difference being, we chose Cornwall instead of Scotland. It is a shame that mother and father had died before we did it, but we have always thought that they would have approved, and in a way, because of their recommendation all those years before, it has felt as though we have been given their blessing. At the time of writing this, we have been running The Atlantic View Hotel for seven seasons, each year has been busier and more successful than the year before and we are both thoroughly enjoying it.

The year that John and I moved to Esher was mother and father's Ruby wedding anniversary. We had a celebration weekend soon after we moved in. Elizabeth and Dave did quite a bit of fostering children, at that time they had Stephanie and John staying with them, so they all came along, and of course mother and father, making ten of us altogether. The weather was perfect and we were able to be in our lovely garden. This was the first of many family get togethers that we held in our house and garden.

This house was in a good condition but not as we wanted it, so we spent the next four years renovating it. It was big enough to be liveable in at the same time. It was more difficult to do work of this kind with two young children, than it had been in Kingston, before they were born. However the finished result was very pleasing.

I stopped teaching when we moved to Esher, and went into a soft furnishing business with John's sister Michele. We made high class silk and lace cushions and bedspreads and sold them through Interior Design Shops, in many small towns in Southeast England. The business thrived during the 1980's. It fitted in well with looking after the children. I loved working at home, and Michele and I worked well together. I continued with this until we moved to Cornwall, in 1996, and Michele is still doing it now, on her own.

Now with both daughters married our parents decided that the house in Vernon Street was too big, and it was time to look for somewhere smaller. Dave said he would look round for them. It didn't take long for him to find a very nice bungalow in Ockbrook, which is the next village to Borrowash, where Elizabeth and Dave lived. The bungalow was called Glenlyn; it was on a corner site, so it had garden all round. This suited perfectly and it was all arranged very quickly. Mother and father made this last move in 1978. They were very happy there.

The garden was a good, but manageable size, with plenty to keep mother busy. Very soon, mother converted two lawns into vegetable patches and created a beautiful herbaceous border and rockery, so that there was always something colourful to see, whatever the season was. There were a number of mature damson trees, and mother continued jam making and bottling while she was still able to.

Village life suited them both; they entered into it whole-heartedly. Father joined the amateur dramatic society, and mother the WI, they held coffee mornings and sales of work to raise money for various village issues. They did meals on wheels for the elderly-many of whom were younger than they were! The first few years at Glenlyn were certainly very good ones, both parents were beginning to feel their age but they were still very active, and involved in such a variety of activities, and enjoying their retirement.

At about this time, mother and father, started a new type of holiday! They would pack their tent, inflatable mattress, picnic equipment etc. into the car, and set off for France, where they spent several weeks touring and visiting French Friends. They became very involved with this, and started to attend French Yearly Meeting, and represent British Friends there. It became a very important part of their lives. They made lots of new friends and continued to visit them annually until the driving became too much for father. In his last year of life, they went once more, this time with Elizabeth and she drove. French Friends were very pleased about this. Elizabeth has continued to attend each year, I am sure our parents would be happy to know this. This was also the start of Elizabeth's connection with the French Friend Adeline, and subsequently all the involvement in the ongoing project in Senegal, helping with the desalination of seawater, to enable the crops to begin to grow again. Once again Elizabeth is making good use of her French.

Some years while the parents were away, cousin Peter and his wife Mary and their first child, Lucy used to come and stay in Glenlyn. This would serve two purposes, they would look after the house, garden and cat while having a holiday themselves. A good arrangement for all concerned.

Every trip to France included a one or two night stay with us, in Surrey in each direction. Our third son, Nicholas, was born while mother and father were in France in 1987, so it was with great excitement that they arrived back from France that year, wondering if their new grandchild had arrived yet. I can still see, in my mind, the look of expectation in their faces as I opened the front door to them! Of course, they were delighted to meet him. Mother and father were now no longer on their committees, so visits became less frequent, father was finding the drive to and from Derby too long by himself. Elizabeth came with them on several occasions, and she did most of the driving. Mother's mind was beginning to fail, she knew she liked seeing us, but was not sure who we were, a very sad time, especially for father.

Father died very suddenly, one week before his seventy sixth birthday, in 1990, at the same age as his father. They both died of heart failure, and they both left their wives in a state of total bewilderment. Mother never really grasped what had happened.

Elizabeth was working at a residential home for the elderly, called Victoria Lodge, she had arranged for mother to spend the day there to give father a rest. Elizabeth went round to Glenlyn to visit father and found that he had died, while eating the lunch he had prepared for himself. Mother never returned to Glenlyn, we were very fortunate in that we were able to get a room for her at Victoria Lodge. She continued to live there until she died in October 1993. The confused state of mother's mind must have made it easier for her to cope with the loss of her husband, but for Elizabeth and me, it seemed as if we had lost both our parents at once.

Three weeks later, at father's memorial Meeting for Worship, at Derby Meeting House, mother was there, smiling and welcoming everyone, pleased to see so many familiar faces, but not realising why everyone was there. It seemed fitting to think of this Meeting as being the end of both of their lives on this earth. We were content, that for the next few years, until mother's death, she was warm, well fed, and looked after, until she could join father again in the next world. Elizabeth saw mother often, both because she worked at Victoria Lodge and she regularly visited. I went whenever it was possible. But mother did not know who we were.

Now, ten years later, I prefer to remember mother as she was before the deterioration of her mind. A wonderfully kind, helpful, caring person who had time and a good word for everyone. A thoroughly good person, almost always smiling and cheerful, I am proud that she was my mother, and hope that some of her goodness has rubbed off on me!

When John and I moved to Cornwall, Nick was nine and so moved schools, from Thames Ditton to Tintagel. He had one year and one term at Tintagel Junior School, before transferring to secondary school in Camelford. All this worked out well, and he fitted in and was successful at both schools. Ben and Tom were already involved in their own lives when we moved, and so did not move to Cornwall with us, but visit as often as they can.

Ben is now 28 and is living and working in Wandsworth, Southwest London. He works for Plowden and Smith, an Art Restoration and Exhibition Company. He has been involved with several very interesting projects including repairing the Parchment Parliamentary Scrolls, and the wrought iron Hereford Screen, which is displayed at the Victoria and Albert Museum. He has done repair work at Windsor Castle and Hampton Court. Last year he went to Dubai to set up a pearl exhibition and next month he is going to help move a Buddha exhibition from the British Museum to a Museum in New York.

He is a very creative and practical person; he plays the piano and the guitar. He is in a band that plays regularly in Wandsworth, and sometimes elsewhere. He studied Musical Instrument Technology at Leeds College of Music, and graduated in 1999. He has made several guitars for himself and others.

Tom, who is now 26 is living and working in Norway. He and his girlfriend, Elin, moved there eighteen months ago. Elin comes from a beautiful little village called Son, on the banks of the Oslo Fjord. They are renting a flat at present, but are hopefully, going to buy their own place, in the near future. They are both working in different restaurants over looking the Fjord. We visited them there earlier this year and it is a very beautiful spot.

When Tom finished at school, he got a bar job; in the first place, this was just for a year, before applying for university. However, he really enjoyed the work, and he had not really enjoyed studying for his A levels, so when it was suggested that he should take a management course while working in the bar, he jumped at the opportunity. He did very well, and got several promotions within the company, all of which helped him to get his present position as manager of the Olive Restaurant and bar in Son.

Nick is 16, and took his GCSE's last summer. He did very well in passing 9, four with grade A. He left school and has started an A level course at Truro College. It is a very good college with excellent facilities, which make the daily bus journey, of one and a half hours each way, worth while.

As I have mentioned earlier, Nick is a keen cricketer, this is something we are delighted about, as when he was eight, he had Perthes disease in his left hip. It looked for a while that he would never play any sport. But, with an excellent consultant and surgeon, and a great deal of determination from Nick, he has made a complete recovery.

He makes the most of living by the coast, and spends spare time surfing at our local beach, Trebarwith Strand. He has recently become interested in photography, and has taken some beautiful shots of the beach, cliffs and rock pools, showing that he has a real talent, and takes after his father.

John and I run the Hotel ourselves, with some part-time help. We are open from March until October each year. It is very hard, but rewarding work, which we both enjoy. We do manage to appreciate the beautiful spot that we live in, and enjoy cliff walks, the wild moor, and wandering on the beach. We never tire of the quite fantastic coastline of North Cornwall.

Bernard Jacob, Marguerite Skelton, Dorothy Clay, Charles Jacob, 1970.
(The four children of Edwin and Jessie Jacob, of Tramore)

Chapter 15

Clay Family Memories
Elizabeth (Clay) Davies

**(Elizabeth is Dorothy (Jacob) Clay
and Kenneth Clay's younger daughter, written in 2004)**

Throughout Rosemary and Elizabeth's lives, the love and support of family and friends have surrounded them. Sadly I (Elizabeth) can remember next to nothing about my Jacob grandparents, Edwin and Jessie. I remember them as kindly people. Their names, also other family members' names were frequently mentioned in our everyday conversation. As was Marianne's. In fact, Marianne is no relation, but was someone who has stayed with different members of the family. Shortly before I was born, at the end of 1949, she lived with Dorothy, Kenneth and Rosemary; she stayed on for a while after I had been born, to help.

Some of my first memories are of us eating breakfast, and for each meal, Dorothy, Rosemary and I would use our own individual spoons, with our own initials engraved, and followed by "EBJ". I still regularly eat from mine. I think that we, the entire "Jacob clan," were all either at Midvale or Summerville in the mid 50s (would this have been to celebrate JEJ & EBJ's wedding anniversary?) when everyone was offered honeycomb honey, straight from Grandpa's beehives. It tasted delicious. Some of us would go down to the beach in the early morning and there would usually have been a good catch of fish brought in by the local fishermen. I remember shoals of silvery fish on the quayside. I think that it must have been then that Jenny taught us to sing "what ever will be, will be".

Weston and Hilda came to visit us in Chellaston on Weston's motorbike. He kindly gave Rosemary and me a short excursion on the back of his bike. At one time, they lived in North Wales, quite near to a large amusement arcade.

We had our caravan towed to Trearddur Bay for several summers and one time, whilst we were there, Rosemary and I were invited to spend the day at Weston and Hilda's. While there, we were both able to spend some time going on rides etc. We had a lovely time.

Whilst in Trearddur Bay, we would all also catch the mail boat to Dun Laoghaire to spend a few days with the Skelton family. I became unwell once, and Bernard kindly read to me, meaning that the adults could go out for the evening. A great excitement one year was, that Marguerite had managed to purchase some tickets for the Dublin horse show for herself, Rosemary and myself, enabling us to watch when the horses were jumping. I think that at that time, I was particularly interested in horses so it was a special treat to go to see so many.

A Jacob Family
Tramore in the 1900s

Rosemary Clay, Hilda Jacob, Elizabeth Clay, Weston Jacob, about 1953.

Rosemary and Elizabeth Clay.

Rosemary and I both went to Friends' School, Saffron Walden, Essex. At that time, Uncle Bernard (Jacob) was a teacher there, teaching geography and games. He was a popular teacher. Dorothea Baker lived nearby with Uncle Lance and Auntie Win. Uncle La was already frail and he died soon afterwards but Auntie Win continued to be in good health for several years and I used to pop in to see her most Wednesdays on my return to school after the road traffic accident.

As Rosemary mentioned, we were involved in a road traffic accident on 12-01-1966. At the time when the two vehicles collided, I, sitting in the front seat, was talking to Jeannie who was in the back. My head went through the windscreen. I was unconscious for some time. As my left lung has been punctured by one or more of the six ribs, which became fractured on impact; to aid my breathing I was connected to a machine, which inflated my lung. In those days, this procedure involved making an incision in the trachea, also making a small incision to allow fluid to drain out of the damaged lung into a receptacle. As one of the incisions was directly in the trachea, I was fed through a tube inserted via my nose into my stomach. If I had been fed through my mouth, the food would all have escaped into the machine before entering my stomach. Apparently, on regaining consciousness, one of the first things I did was to remove this tube from my nose.

A lot of people; family, extended family, friends and fellow patients all helped the staff in encouraging me to communicate. Because I had been lying down for over 3 weeks, the muscles in my legs had lost their strength; leaving me very wobbly when I stood unaided. I would be conveyed in a wheelchair to the physiotherapy department for some exercises in the physiotherapy block. (I referred to this as fizzledee therapy). As this involved leaving the heated main hospital block to go into the cold fresh air outside, I would be well wrapped up in a red hospital blanket. It would always be the same charming man called George who wheeled me. Once in the dept., I would be encouraged to use the climbing bars. I progressed to managing to climb up and down four or five rungs each time as far as I can remember, the strength was returning to my muscles. Of course, this must also have helped with my balance. I must have been very restless whilst still in bed one time, as, for my protection, the staff placed some sort of netting over the top of my bed. I did my very best to escape out through the end railings, but sadly my head was too large to fit through! All of the rest of me had fitted through, but my head could not.

I think that it was in the physio department where there would be simple lego type puzzles for patients to use. In the ward, several other patients and I became friends and would pass the time of day. One girl about the same age as I was, showed me how to apply make up and let me use some of hers. There was a charming elderly woman whose bed was just at the end of the ward before reaching the toilets. She was very good in calming me down when I became upset. Part of my brain realised that I was in unfamiliar surrounds, and I was very anxious to return home.

A Jacob Family
Tramore in the 1900s

Auntie Win Baker of Halstead.

*87 Head Street Halstead, (extreme left),
where Uncle Ted and Auntie Win (Baker) lived.*

Quite where home was, I was unsure of, but I wanted to go there. Once we had both been discharged, father kindly drove me over to see her. It was suggested that I might enjoy doing a bit of knitting if there were some knitting needles available. Mother provided an extremely large pair, with some "knitting cotton". Mother would cast on 30 stitches and I would knit "squares". I could remember that 30 stitches = a knitted square. In fact, Mother was able to use these oblongs, which were made in hospital, as dishcloths until they gave out. All of us also regularly knitted wool squares, Dorothy and Kenneth more often than Rosemary and I, to be made up into blankets for Oxfam.

In those days, the wards were long with a central corridor between the rows of beds. There would be several wheelchairs positioned in the centre of the ward for general use. I remember that on one occasion, I got into one of the wheelchairs for fun and propelled myself around the ward. I may only have done this once, as it was not really recommended, but in a way it was a plus sign for me, as it showed that I had figured this out for myself.

Once back home, immediately on our arrival, Jazar, our lovely ginger pussycat who would then have been aged about 11, came running down stairs with his tail held up and purring. Although I am sure that it was more mother whom he was greeting, it made a very nice homecoming for all of us.

To begin with, Rosemary kindly shared her bedroom with me. Her bedroom was downstairs and mine was upstairs. At that time, I think that climbing a fairly steep flight of stairs would have been too difficult for me to have negotiated. My mental age and vocabulary at this time was that of a very young child. Back in familiar surroundings, and with mother's good cooking, I continued to improve.

That year, Whitsuntide was beautifully warm and we were able to spend a few days in the caravan now stationed in Brailsford. Janet Skelton visited us there. Shortly after this, Jenny was visiting friends of hers nearby and kindly called to say "hello" and was able to spend the afternoon with us. Weston also called in to our house on his way back home from Russia. As he was spending the night, we were able to move my bed back upstairs for him to use, and when he left, we thought it would be good if I moved back to my room again.

There was a branch of Derby College of Further Education very very close to Vernon Street so I was able to resume English, French and Maths starting in the spring of 1966. (April/May only a few weeks out of education in all). I can remember that there was some almond blossom coming out quite near to the college. I was able to study there until the end of the summer term and returned to FSSW for the autumn term. The following year, I was able to sit O Levels and I took fewer subjects. Because I was taking medication I was allowed an extra half-hour for each exam. (Although I am no longer taking medication this extra time still holds good this is being written in 2004).

Peter and Mary Skelton lived quite close to Saffron Walden at that time and they invited me to spend the weekend at their home. Mary and I spent a lot of time putting paint on walls and, in my case, on myself and on the painting clothes, which Mary had kindly provided me with. Much later on, when Dave, Stephanie and John, (2 children whom we were fostering at that time) and I were on holiday in Cornwall, Mary and Peter with their two Lucy and Mark lived nearby and we met and had a lovely time down on the beach. There were a vast number of jellyfish scattered about on the beach. I got the chance to get to know Ann & Bernard Skelton and their family later on when they kindly invited me to spend a few days in their home.

Dorothy and Kenneth would travel round France, calling in on Friends. Kenneth had studied at the university in Geneva when quite young, and there were several Friends who remembered him from when he worshipped amongst them then. One year, the two people who were working at the International Quaker Centre in Paris, were Odette and Tony Clay. Dorothy & Kenneth always wrote a letter to Friends on their return home and this time, they included Odette and Tony on their list. Tony replied, adding as a PS, "do you know of any person who would like to be a cleaning lady during the day and hostess at night at the International Quaker Centre, as the current person was to retire at the end of that year and they would like to find a replacement..." At that time, Dave and I had recently become engaged and when I mentioned to him that this was a job opportunity, which appealed to me, he suggested that if I wanted to go to Paris for a year, now would be a good time. I already had A Level French and spent a very happy year there.

Philip has always been a keen sailor, sailing regularly and he was very good at calling into see Dorothy and Kenneth. One time, when D & K had moved to Ockbrook, near to where Dave and I lived with our dog, Ross, Philip, Ross and I walked down to a country park approx 1 mile away, a good bit of the way round and back home again. He and Brigid have always been very helpful in offering accommodation on several occasions and with Philip's knowledge of sailing etc, he helped me to understand several technical terms which I was unsure of when I was trying to translate a text from French into English. This relates to L'Association TARA, a project which I am very interested in in S. Senegal, where through simple river water filtration, they have been able to make certain areas of land viable again, thereby enabling people to have areas of land where they can once more cultivate crops etc.

A bit later on, I spent a few weeks of my holiday in France, travelling via Southampton and Ann Jacob kindly let me spend the night in her house.

Right from the time when I was able to breathe unaided in 1966, my breathing had sounded more and more noisy. This was embarrassing but was never painful. In 1995, almost 30 years after the road traffic accident, I went to Birmingham for an operation. What the surgeon did was to remove and discard the damaged small section of my windpipe. He then resutured the trachea and my breathing returned to normal.

Ann, Lynne and Lesley Jacob, have been able to spend weekends with their mother Sally in Saffron Walden, taking it in turns. Dorothea lives nearby and there is usually a family meal at Sally's each weekend. I have been able to return to there on several occasions since I was at school there, usually staying with Dorothea, and this has given me the opportunity to get to know everyone a lot better. *(Sadly, Sally died in 2008, since these words were written - PRJ).*

When Dorothy, Kenneth and I were able to travel up to Yorkshire, we were able to call in on Janet Jerram and her family. I think that Conor, Sam and Millie would all still have been at school so we would have been able to see them all briefly before heading home.

The loving support extended by family and friends is very much appreciated.

Weston Jacob and Hilda Shaw Wedding, 1953.

A Jacob Family

Tramore in the 1900s

*Marguerite Moss Jacob,
1921, Aged 10 years.*

Chapter 16

Marguerite (Jacob) Skelton
4/7/1910 – 30/10/2000
(Written by Janet (Skelton) Jerram in 2005)

My mother Marguerite Moss Jacob was born in Tramore Co. Waterford in July 1910 and was the youngest child of Edwin and Jessie Jacob. She had two brothers – Charles and Bernard and a sister Dorothy but my mother always referred to them as Chas, Bun and Pol (short for Polly). They lived in a semi-detached house called Midvale on the outskirts of the seaside town of Tramore. What I have written about my mother's life is based on what I remember her telling me and may not be entirely accurate!

Marguerite's Education

Marguerite had an unusual childhood because her mother educated her at home until she was 10. I think she was rather isolated because Bun and Pol were very close and Chas, being about 8 years her senior seemed rather remote. I am not sure why the decision was taken to teach her at home because her siblings all went to school and I don't think it was for health reasons because Marguerite was very robust. My grandmother used a correspondence course to educate her, sending off completed exercises and written work to be marked using a system which was popular with families living in the colonies at the time.

When Marguerite was 10 a major decision was taken in her life – this was to send her off to boarding school in the Gower Peninsula in South Wales. The little school was called Borva House, had about 18 girls there and Marguerite loved it. All the pupils were very friendly and cared for one another and were given a lot of freedom. They were allowed to swim and play on the beach with very little supervision. Despite the rather Spartan conditions at Borva Marguerite blossomed and remained there for 4 years, travelling back to Tramore by steamer for the holidays. She described excellent school holidays with Charles, Bernard and Dorothy and other Young Friends when they went cycling and camping in the Comeragh Mountains and had great hilarity trying to pitch a tent in a roaring gale.

Marguerite's next 3 years of education were spent at The Mount School, York. Compared to Borva House The Mount seemed very restrictive and strict with some odd rules. Both inside and outside schoolgirls had to walk in twos, always with the same partner. If for some reason your partner was absent (which Marguerite's often was) you were not allowed to join another pair and had to walk around by yourself. It was because of this rule that Marguerite started playing the viola. She noticed that the school orchestra had to be seated before assembly, so she decided that if she could play in the orchestra, marching into the hall each morning could be avoided.

(Despite this crafty plotting she disliked playing the instrument and never progressed musically!) Although her experience at The Mount was not a particularly happy one Marguerite made some close friends there and remained in contact with them for the rest of her life. She also spoke warmly of the Quaker families in York who invited girls out for tea on Sundays, providing a welcome break from school. A group of boys and girls from Waterford used to travel together at the beginning and end of each term to the two Quaker schools in York (The Mount and Bootham) and it must have been a very long journey involving a boat and several trains each way.

Higher education for girls was quite unusual in those days but when she left The Mount Marguerite was encouraged by her parents to go to Westhill College in Sellyoak, Birmingham. Here she studied to become a Sunday school teacher (a fact she kept very quiet about when she had children) and also undertook a course in early Personnel Management. I think she was in Westhill for 2 years and either during or after her course she did a survey into Sunday schools which involved travelling to various parts of England by train. She then did a period of work at Clark's shoe company in Street, Somerset before returning to Ireland.

Adulthood

Now newly qualified, Marguerite started work in Jacob's biscuit company in Dublin where she provided support for the factory girls – a sort of welfare worker. Jacob's was a Quaker firm owned by a very distant cousin of her father's. She lived in digs in Monkstown and then in Upper Mount Street and her social life revolved around Young Friends and a walking group called The Holiday Fellowship. It was through these activities that she met my father John Skelton (known as Jack).

Jack worked in a Dublin insurance company and lived with his sister Emily and his widowed mother in Cowper Road, Rathmines. He was also a Quaker and he and Marguerite married in Tramore Meeting House in 1939. We have a newspaper cutting which refers to the wedding and "the many and costly gifts" received by the happy couple! They spent their honeymoon in Co. Kerry (in January!) and started their life together living with Jack's mother and sister. They remained happily married for 60 years.

Family Life

Their first child Peter (my older brother) was born a year later and he was 2 when Jack and Marguerite moved into their own home. They were able to buy this house at 15 Vergemount Park, Clonskeagh, Dublin because Marguerite's father Edwin inherited money from a cousin which he generously divided between his four children. "Cousin Annie" was legendary among my brothers and myself as the provider of the family silver which my grandfather also divided up amongst his family. I was born in 1943, followed by my brother Bernard 2 years later and the Skelton family had a stable and happy life in 15 Vergemount Park.

Marguerite (Jacob) Skelton

*Marguerite Jacob (later Skelton)
in the Summerhouse at Midvale 1913.*

*Peter and Janet Skelton 1945.
(Note the likeness in the photo left).*

*Marguerite Jacob
aged 28, 1938.*

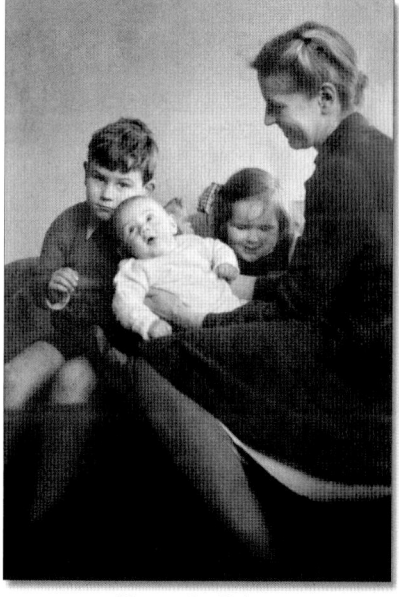

*Marguerite Skelton,
with Peter, Bernard, and Janet, 1940's*

All three of us went to Rathgar Junior School, a small Quaker school which was progressive for its time. For example each pupil had a small plot of garden in which to plant seeds – mine was situated under a tree and I don't remember anything flowering! We had nature walks, a play each Christmas, a band mainly consisting of triangles, drums and tambourines and a sports day in the summer term. It was a totally non-competitive school and I remember the shock of discovering there were such things as weekly tests and end of term exams when I moved on to my secondary school. This was Alexandra College for girls and Peter and Bernard went to St. Andrew's College for boys. We were all day pupils.

Marguerite gave up work when she married, as was the practice of the time and was always around as we grew up. She used to take us on outings during the holidays – often by train to the seaside where she taught us to swim despite hating cold water. We sometimes went to Howth Head on the tram where we had a picnic, or scrambling about on The Scalp near Enniskerry. A high light of the year, for me anyway, was having a half-day off school to go with her and Bernard to the Spring Show in Ballsbridge. Marguerite read aloud to us every night – usually a Little Grey Rabbit book followed by a chapter from one of the Swallows and Amazons books by Arthur Ransome. Her fame at reading spread among the other children who lived in Vergemount Park and they were allowed to come and listen as long as they behaved themselves. My friend Elizabeth has told me that being barred from the reading for a week made a deep impression on her!

As well as looking after her family Marguerite became involved in various types of voluntary work. Being a confirmed teetotaller, she joined and later became Secretary of the Women's' Christian Total Abstinence Union and we still have a large (probably Victorian) poster describing the evils of alcohol which came from the W.C.T.A.U. Although we sometimes teased her about this, she stuck to her strong principles and at least once a month went very early in the morning to the Dublin cattle market where the W.C.T.A.U. ran a coffee stall. Here they provided hot drinks, sandwiches etc., for the cattle drovers to offer an alternative to going to the pubs which used to open early on market day. She was also on the committee of the Liberty Crèche, which was a day nursery in the city centre, providing care for children whose mothers had to work. True to her practical nature Marguerite used to go and help the paid staff and I remember being roped in with this, which I enjoyed. On one occasion a friend and myself put on a puppet show for the children and I did a written project at school about the history of the Crèche.

Jacob Relations

During our childhood were visited regularly by Jacob relations. Uncle Bernard and Auntie Sally Jacob came to stay from Saffron Walden and Uncle Bernard always had a cribbage board in his pocket so that we could play cribbage together, which we did with great enthusiasm. Auntie Dorothy (known as Pol) and Uncle Kenneth Clay and their daughters Rosemary and Elizabeth came from Derby. Pol was extremely good at handicrafts and used to arrive with all the materials to make a soft toy or a piece of jewellery and spent hours teaching me how to do this. Cousin Doreen stayed on her way to Tramore where she had a cottage. One of her interests was cricket and she met the West Indian Cricket team because a nursing colleague of hers was the sister of Frank Worrall, the captain. Cousin Basil Jacob was a regular visitor for Sunday lunch so we knew him well. He was a bachelor of regular habits and on Saturdays always cooked himself a joint of roast beef, which he ate cold every day until next Saturday when he started all over again. We would see Uncle Chas and Auntie Stella when we visited Granny and Grandpa in Midvale because they lived just round the corner in Summerville with their daughter Jenny who was the same age as me.

Visits to Midvale

I have very happy memories of visiting Midvale where we spent summer holidays, travelling there by train from Dublin. We used to chant the names of the stations as we got near to our destination – "Thomastown" "Ballyhale" "Mullinavat" "Kilmacow" "Waterford"! Midvale seemed to have an enormous garden and we played on the grass walk in a little truck known as "the Ree Cart". We would pull each other up and down in the cart – I think Peter did most of the pulling and Bernard and I were passengers. Grandpa was usually working in the garden or dealing with a swarm from one of his many hives of bees and we often came home with a section of honey.

Granny and Grandpa were both very kind and gentle and made us very welcome at Midvale but Grandpas' deafness made communication rather difficult. I remember one unfortunate occasion when he was sitting quietly in the front room while Bernard and I were fooling around and we accidentally knocked a screen over which cut his head! After the initial shock he forgave us but my mother was mortified. He was very thoughtful and used to send us money each Christmas – a coin carefully inserted in a piece of cardboard – and he rewarded all his grandchildren with 30 old pence (half a crown) when they could swim 30 strokes unaided. I managed my 30 strokes while on holiday in Tramore and Uncle Bernard counted them.

Once while staying at Midvale Marguerite, my brother Bernard and I set off on foot for a walk to the sea. I remember it seemed a very long way and we finally settled ourselves down to play by the seashore when Marguerite spotted a large mine floating in the water and gently bumping against the rocks! She hastily packed everything up again and led us complaining back to Midvale.

I think the highlight of our visits to Tramore was Granny and Grandpas' Golden Wedding when all the family (except my father and cousin Philip) gathered to celebrate. This happy occasion epitomised the feeling of love and welcome we experienced at Midvale.

A Jacob Family
Tramore in the 1900s

Peter Skelton on Tramore Pier.

Chapter 17

Memories of Tramore
Peter Skelton
(Written in 2005)

Getting There

My memories of my grandparents' house Midvale, at Tramore near Waterford are somewhat fragmentary as I only spent short holidays there while I was growing up in the forties and early fifties. But one thing I do remember very clearly is how long it took to get there. We went by train of course, from Kingsbridge station in Dublin (now called Heuston) and it seemed to take the better part of a day. Mother always made sure we got to the station in plenty of time to be sure of catching the train, and to find good seats. This was sensible of her (she was) as trains then were few and far between, and always very crowded, but I do remember once being allowed on to the footplate of the famous "Maeve" or one of her sisters which was waiting on another platform with a Cork express; it appeared huge to me compared to the more modest engine on the Waterford train. They were all steam engines of course in those days, and the carriages were all of the old pattern with side corridor and doors to each compartment with windows which let down with a leather strap – draughty but you could lean out if Mother would let you. (The ideal was to get a compartment to ourselves, but this was most unlikely when there was only one train a day). When the train did finally leave it went reasonably fast at first and passed a few stations without stopping but once past Kildare, and even more when we left the main line at Port Laoise as the Waterford line did in those days, it went slower and slower and stopped everywhere for a chat. There would be groups of old men at each station who had come just to see the train come in and pass the time with driver and guard.

Steam Train of the era.

Peter Skelton, 1944, aged 4 3/4 years.

Even though the schedules were generous the trains would lose time due to the poor fuel available during and after the emergency, and got later and later. On one homeward journey I remember being stopped for hours at Port Laoise due to lack of steam pressure. As we obviously weren't going anywhere, Mother let me out onto the platform and when I asked the driver why we had stopped, he said the fire had gone out and he had to re-light it! I must have been about six at the time. As we got nearer to Waterford we children would chant the names of the stations "Ballyhale, Mullinavat, Kilmacow, Waterford" but it never made them come any quicker. And when we finally approached Waterford itself we would look out for "Jumbo" a very small engine which was sometimes to be seen shunting in the yard. Even when we reached Waterford the journey was not over. We still had to get to Tramore, and the Waterford and Tramore Railway went from a completely different station on the other side of town at Waterford Manor. On at least one journey, we went from one station to the other in Waterford, perched on an elderly jaunting car of the kind nowadays only to be found in Killarney for the tourists. The Waterford and Tramore was a funny little line only seven miles long and totally separate from the rest of the system, with ancient carriages whose windows and doors only opened on one side – the platform side – and with one small engine in steam. From Tramore station it was then quite a long walk up the very steep hill past the church, turn left at the top onto the Dungarvan road and there finally was Midvale a few hundred yards along on the right, set back from the road.

Skelton Family Tramore 1951.

Midvale

I can't remember a lot of detail about Midvale (I cannot for the life of me remember what colour the wallpaper was or what pictures if any, were on the walls for example), but my impression is that it was very comfortably furnished, without ostentation or too much luxury, as befitted a Quaker home. When I was small it seemed enormous to me. It was in fact a fairly large late Victorian or early Edwardian semi-detached house, with a long gravel drive and turning area in front which Grandpa raked regularly. The hall was long and narrow with red and black floor tiles, smelt of polish, and felt very cool on a summer day. I suppose there were coat racks, umbrella stands and so on, but the main thing I remember is the absolutely archaic telephone on the hall cupboard; it must have dated from the twenties at least if not earlier, a wooden cube with a handle sticking out at the side and an old fashioned handset on a cradle above. To make a call you turned the handle several times, and the operator down at the post office answered if you were lucky and put you through to the number you wanted. This intrigued me greatly. The number was Tramore 36. Apart from the hall, the whole ground floor front of the house was taken up with a large sitting room with a high ceiling and a red curtain over the door to keep out draughts (there was of course no central heating in those days). It was made larger by the bay windows and the low windowsills were just the right height for children to climb out over, with the help of a white garden seat outside.

We did this a lot, it was much more fun than going out through the front door. There were lots of bookshelves on the inside walls[1] – in fact the house was full of books which I of course inspected avidly but found little to interest me. There were very few books for children - any books which might have belonged to my mother, her brothers or sister when they were young, had long since disappeared. Grandpa had evidently been interested in railways as a young man as I found several books about them (some quite technical e.g. "The Working and Management of an English Railway") all dating from the 1890's. He very kindly gave me two or three of them when I was older and I kept them until very recently. Otherwise I remember lots of bound volumes of "Punch" (I didn't understand the jokes, which notoriously weren't very funny anyway), and a great many books about religion.

Behind the sitting room through the connecting door was the dining room. This felt smaller than the sitting room – when we were all seated round the big table it seemed rather a squash. I can't remember much about the food except eating Grandpa's honey with soda bread, and stewed loganberries from the garden in blue and white china bowls. Also some strange American breakfast cereals, which I have never seen since (this was just after the war) which came in boxes with masks or aeroplanes on the back, which we cut out and played with.

We kept out of the kitchen (which had an electric cooker as well as an old fashioned range); there was a large cool pantry/larder as well at the back of the house, full of mysterious jars. Outside in the yard at the back was the old hand pump, which had supplied water from a well before mains water came along. It still worked, but Grandpa had put a wooden bung in the spout and run a pipe from the pump to a cistern sunk in the ground beside the summerhouse round the corner, from which he drew water for the garden. We would pump the handle like mad, and then run round and if we were lucky would see water emerging mysteriously into the tank.

There wasn't much garden at the back of the house (which looked onto a field in those days), but a large garden at the side running back down to the road, separated from the drive by a white painted metal fence. Grandpa was a keen gardener and grew lots of vegetables and flowers. He also kept bees, which we kept well away from. In the summerhouse he kept a sort of box on wheels with pulling rope, which he presumably used to take watering cans and other heavy objects round the garden. We seized gleefully on this and used to give each other rides up and down the long strip of lawn; for some reason best known to ourselves we christened it the "Recart". It can't have done the lawn any good at all. There was also a grassed enclosure completely surrounded by a thick tall hedge. This was a suntrap, and mother told me how once when she was young she fell asleep out there on a rug, woke up with a bad case of sunstroke (half her face was purple, she said) and had to spend days in bed recovering.

Granny and Grandpa

My grandfather Edwin B. Jacob [1868-1958] was in his seventies and eighties when I knew him, and had become very deaf. Because of this deafness I found it quite hard to talk to him; he really disliked the primitive hearing aids available in those days and flatly refused to wear one. I remember him as a quiet kindly and generous man, tall and well built. He was born in Cork, and as a young man had been apprenticed a teacher at the Friends School at Wigton in Cumberland. By coincidence, among his pupils was a certain Johnston Skelton from Maryport, and much later their respective offspring were to meet in Dublin and marry (at Tramore Meeting House) in January 1939. When he was trained Grandpa returned to Ireland and taught at Newtown, the Friends School in Waterford. However in the eighteen nineties he ceased to be a teacher and became a stockbroker when he was offered the chance to join and take over Harvey and Son, the family business in Waterford. He also ran the Waterford Working Men's Penny Bank to encourage thrift among the populace – a very Quakerly thing to do.

At about the same time as he changed careers, he married Jessie E. Baker who had come from England to be a governess to a Quaker family. They lived at Percy Terrace near Newtown School in Waterford at first, but by the time my mother was born in 1910 they had moved out to live at Midvale in Tramore.

He continued to go in to the office well into his eighties and I can remember him setting off with a carnation in his buttonhole (grown himself of course) to walk down to the station in the morning[2]. When younger he had cycled to work, and according to mother always took a bottle of milk and some bread in the basket; by the time he reached Waterford the motion had churned the cream at the top of the milk to butter which he then spread on the bread - typical Jacob thrift! By the early 1950's however he was only going in two mornings a week, and Uncle Chas who by then was running the business was having to find little jobs around the office for him to do.

He was as I have said generous to his family. He bought my parents house at Vergemount Park for them in 1941 (saying, so I was told by mother, that he would prefer that his money did some good before he was dead rather than after). When he heard that I had started a stamp collection he gave me a quite rare set of Provisional Government of Ireland overprints from his own collection, which became the centrepiece of mine. And we all had our silver "Grandpa spoons", and when we each had learned to swim and could manage 30 strokes unaided he would send us a half crown coin (two shillings and sixpence) through the post. The Jacob family of course had been Quakers ever since Richard Jacob came from Devon to Ireland in the seventeenth century, and Grandpa was very much a Quaker – a "weighty friend" – and held various offices in the Society including Clerk of Dublin Yearly Meeting[3], and Clerk of Munster Quarterly Meeting.

He was one of a delegation of Friends appointed by London and Dublin Yearly Meetings who went to Buckingham Palace to congratulate Edward VIII on his accession, along with deputations from other Free Churches. He left an account of this visit, and a copy is now safely in the archive at Friends House Library – all I remember from reading it is that they spent a long time waiting in line, and his comment that the king "looked tired".

Granny [Jessie E. Jacob nee Baker, 1879-1963] was by all accounts a rather more forceful personality, small and of strong principles. She was English, was born at Halstead in Essex and still retained something of what I presume was an Essex country accent. Strangely, I don't remember her very clearly when they lived at Midvale, but rather towards the end of her life, after Grandpa had died and she came to stay at Vergemount Park for a while – at that stage she mostly lived with Uncle Chas and Aunt Stella in Waterford, but paid regular visits to the rest of her children in turn. By then she was around eighty and very much feeling her age, but would talk to me and remember the country walks around Halstead, which she had taken as a girl. She used to say that when it was first suggested to her that she should go to Ireland as a governess she felt as if she would be going to the other side of the world, it seemed so remote. It is hard to realise how much the world has shrunk in a hundred years or so.

A Jacob Family
Tramore in the 1900s

Janet and Peter Skelton 1943.

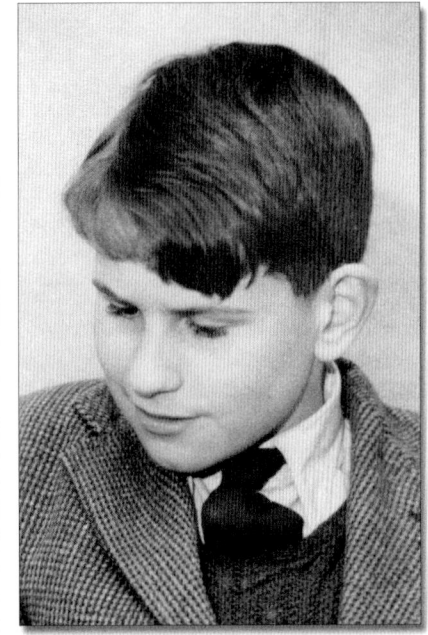

Peter Skelton.

Peter Skelton receiving a book prize.

Peter and Jack Skelton.

What we did on our Holidays

When we were on holiday at Midvale we didn't go very often to the big beach for which Tramore is famous (and which it is named after), as it was quite a long walk down into the town. Mostly we went down past Summerville (where Uncle Chas and Aunt Stella lived) to the Cove, which was a little former fishing harbour near Midvale, where we could build sandcastles etc, to our hearts content, climb on the rocks, explore rock pools and paddle or swim in safety. Through I'm told that once Mother was down there sitting on the rocks with Janet and Bernard (I wasn't there) and discovered an unexploded mine from the war bobbing around in the sea. She reacted with admirable calmness, moving the children away without frightening them (Janet says they were in fact rather cross as they had just settled down to play and couldn't see why they had to move).

We did other things of course. We walked along the Doneraile, a cliff path from Tramore Hill to the Cove, and we walked out to the Metal Man – the big brick pillar on the headland overlooking the bay, which looks like a lighthouse but instead of a lamp on top has a large iron statue of a nineteenth century sailor pointing out to sea to warn seamen off the rocks[4]. We went down to the station and took the train into Waterford where we climbed Reginald's Tower, visited Grandpa in his office, and went shopping. I particularly remember one drapers shop on the Quay. It didn't have tills or cash registers or even pneumatic tubes like the department stores in Dublin, but when you made your purchase the shop assistant put the money with the bill into a hollow wooden sphere the size of a cricket ball and sent it to the cashiers office across the shop rolling along a little railway track suspended from the ceiling. After a few minutes wait it came rolling back with the receipt and change inside – the system must have dated from Victorian times. Then we returned to Tramore, and once at the station the engine driver allowed me to stand on the footplate while the engine ran around the train, which was very exciting.

Christmas in Midvale

Mostly we visited Midvale in the summer, but one year, 1948 I think, we spent Christmas there. Granny had gone out to the Lebanon to Brumanna where Uncle Kenneth and Aunt Dorothy were teaching at the Friends School; the birth of my cousin Rosemary was imminent and Granny had gone to be with Aunt Dorothy, leaving Grandpa on his own. We went down to spend Christmas with him. On Christmas Eve we decorated the sitting room with a big Christmas tree and coloured paper streamers. According to Mother this was the first time there had ever been Christmas decorations at Midvale, as Granny didn't hold with them – the old Quaker way was not to make a fuss about particular festivals – but Mother insisted, Grandpa didn't seem to mind a bit and the big room certainly looked marvellous. We had our stockings, presents, dinner and so on just as we would have had at Vergemount Park. On St. Stephens Day (Boxing Day to the ignorant English!) we went to see Uncle Chas and Aunt Stella who were staying at their holiday cottage in the Comeraghs, and this was the only time I ever saw genuine Wren Boys. Mother had told us how they used to dress up and go around from house to house in Tramore on Stephens Day when she was a girl, with the body of a wren on a thorn branch, singing a special song[5] and asking for food, drink and/or money. I suppose this was a distant echo of an ancient pagan ritual, and by the 1940's it no longer happened in towns or cities (it was felt to be uncivilised; anyway catching and killing a wren must have been difficult; carol singing would have been much easier). But the old practice just about survived in the mountains. Actually the "boys" were rather a disappointment as they didn't seem to know the words of the song at all – I imagine they were very drunk.

Bonmahon

In 1950 and 1951 we didn't stay at Midvale, but stopped off on our way to and from summer holidays at Bonmahon which is a village a bit further along the coast from Tramore. An enormously generous Friend in Dublin called Harold Johnson had a Ford van which he had converted into an estate car, and he very kindly loaned it to us both times so we drove down via the Glen of the Downs instead of taking the train – a very long drive on the roads of those days which had not yet been straightened or widened. The holiday cottage at Bonmahon belonged to a Jacob cousin (Cousin Frederick[6]) and other family members had also stayed there, including Aunt Dorothy and Uncle Kenneth – Mother was very tickled to be greeted by a neighbour; "My haven't you lost weight!" and had to explain that she wasn't Mrs Clay but her younger sister.

The cottage was in the middle of a terrace on the Dungarvan Road at the edge of the village, and on the side of a slope so that it had two storeys at the front and three at the back, and you went downstairs to the kitchen. It was very basically furnished – I remember I slept on a lilo (airbed for the uninitiated) on the floor – and in 1950 Bonmahon had no electricity and the cottage was lit by oil lamps. They glowed with a beautiful warm light. By 1951 the Rural Electrification Programme had reached the village; from our point of view the great thing about this was that the shop cum pub[7] near the beach where we bought our orangeade now also sold ice cream. The beach itself was fine, sandy and un-crowded and of course we spent a lot of the holiday there, building sandcastles, swimming and so on. It wasn't particularly safe for swimming as there was quite a strong tidal current and undertow and at least once when the sea was rough I got into difficulties and Father had to come in and pull me out. There were a few other families there and we played with the children while our parents talked. One day a small boy watched fascinated as Father (who rolled his own with a Rizla machine in those days) went through the ritual of taking out tobacco, putting it in the roller, inserting the paper and finally producing the cigarette. Very seriously the little boy then asked, "Now will you make a match". I can't remember the family's name, but I'm sure Father said the father was a well known athlete, Pat O'Callaghan, who had won an Olympic Gold medal for hammer throwing early in the century.

But we also explored the countryside around in the van – there is a photo of us all at Lismore Castle to prove it. The running family joke was that we must never ever meet the Dungarvan Bus coming the other way, as the roads were so narrow. I don't know if we ever did meet it, but we did go to Dungarvan, on market day. The main street was full of cattle, very noisy and smelly, and one day the Circus came to Bonmahon and we went to see the show. It was a very small circus – you could tell by the fact that one of the main acts featured on the posters was "Quackers the Amazing Talking Duck" and about six people did everything from taking tickets, playing in the band, and clowning to acrobatics, but we enjoyed it.

The "Jacob Jamboree", and My Last Stay at Midvale

I believe the last time I stayed at Midvale was in the summer of 1952, when I was 12. Mother had taken Janet and Bernard down, and Father and I joined them a week later. He had taken me to England, where I had had a marvellous time – one of the best weeks of my life, and much more enjoyable than the scout camp in Northern Ireland I also went to that year – at the Sibford Summer School at the Friends School at Sibford Ferris near Banbury. It took me several days before I stopped talking about all the things we did and people I had met, and to recover from the rigours of the journey[8].

One event at Midvale which occurred during that holiday and which I must mention is the "Jacob Jamboree". This is what we called a notable gathering of almost the entire Jacob clan to celebrate Granny and Grandpa's Golden Wedding Anniversary. Practically every descendent of theirs was there – as far as I am aware the only absentees were my father and my cousin Philip.[9] Cousin Weston was certainly there with his fiancée Hilda, along with all my aunts, uncles and other first cousins. A family group photograph was taken outside the front window to record the occasion, and a meal was had. As usual I can't recall what we ate, but do clearly remember the enormous amount of washing up, which we all helped with afterwards! Goodness knows how everyone was accommodated, even using Summerville as well as Midvale.

Finale

Granny and Grandpa continued to live at Midvale for another couple of years, but the house was evidently getting too large for them. I think I also heard from Mother that Granny fell out with the next door neighbours but I have no idea whether that is true or not. However that may be, Uncle Chas and Aunt Stella had a new house built in Waterford in 1956 which they went to live in, while Granny and Grandpa moved to Summerville which was much smaller (though it did have one of the steepest flights of stairs of any house I have ever seen, so I imagine they must have stayed downstairs). Unfortunately as Grandpa got older he began to show signs of dementia and also to fall – and he was a big man, too big and heavy for Granny to lift easily. Uncle Chas tried to find a male nurse to help but could find nobody suitable (they all drank).

A Jacob Family
Tramore in the 1900s

In the end he had to arrange for Grandpa to go into Bloomfield, the Quaker private mental hospital in Dublin. Granny took lodgings in Upper Leeson Street a short walk away from the hospital and visited him every day. Mother also visited regularly, but I did not, to my shame. I now wish I had. He died in Bloomfield in 1958 at the age of 91. We all drove down to Waterford behind the hearse for the funeral at Waterford Meeting House and the Friends Burial Ground at Newtown where he was buried among several other Jacobs. They stopped the traffic for us in Kilkenny and in other towns as we went through, and all the passers by took off their hats and/or crossed themselves as a mark of respect as we drove by which I found very moving. Granny lived for another 5 years, mostly in Waterford, and died there in 1963. Again, we went down for the funeral.

Grandpa's and then Granny's funerals were almost the last time I ever visited Waterford. Soon afterwards in 1963 I moved to England to seek my fortune, and only returned once to Waterford some twenty years later when with Mary, Lucy and Mark, I attended the European Friends Family Gathering at Newtown School. On the last day, when it was all over, father and mother came down from Dublin to see us. We picked them up at the station at lunch time (trains in Ireland were a bit quicker by the eighties!) and drove out to Tramore.

There we spent a pleasant afternoon at the Cove sitting in the sun and reminiscing. Of course we drove past Midvale – and most mysteriously it had shrunk!

Peter J. Skelton, written for Mary, Lucy, Mark and Esme.

Note: *This has been largely based on my memories, both of my own experiences and of conversations with my parents and other relatives. My sister Janet and my cousin Philip Jacob have also provided valuable information. My memory is notoriously fallible, as I have discovered several times while writing this, but I have tried to be as accurate as I can.*

Footnotes:
(1) *My guess would be "William Penn making his treaty with the Red Indians" and "Christ the Light of the World" as these were very popular in Quaker homes in my grandparents' time, but this is only a guess.*
(2) *They always rang a bell at Tramore station five minutes before a train was due to depart, so if you were still at the top of the hill when it sounded you knew you were probably too late. They rang similar bells at one or two other Irish stations in those days – I remember hearing one at Mullingar in 1953.*
(3) *Nowadays called Ireland Yearly Meeting, while London YM is called Britain YM.*
(4) *According to Mother he is saying "Keep out, keep out, keep out from me, For these are the Rocks of Misery"!*

(5) *"The Wran the Wran the King of all birds, on Stephenses day was caught in the furze", "Dreoilín dreoilín where's your nest? – 'tis under the trees that I love best – 'tis under the holly and ivy tree, where all the birds do follow me"* and *"Mr Jacob's a wealthy man, 'tis to his house we brought the Wran. With pockets of money and buckets of beer, we wish yez all a Happy New Year"*. That is all I can remember of the Wran Boy song as Mother sang it. *"Dreoilín"* is Gaelic for wren.

(6) Thomas Frederick Harvey Jacob, a partner in Harvey & Son. He probably did not actually own the cottage, but rented it. I cannot remember ever having met him, and am not sure of his exact relationship to me – first or second cousin twice removed I imagine.

(7) I believe it was called Little Fitzgeralds, to distinguish it from Big Fitzgeralds, a larger establishment up the road. Once we treated ourselves to Sunday lunch at Big Fitzgeralds. I've no idea what the food was like but clearly remember all the house martins' nests under the eaves in the yard with the birds flying in and out in the sunshine.

(8) This was my second trip with father to England, and the journey was memorable in its own right. Father had planned for us to stay on board the Mailboat overnight as you usually could in those days, and travel on the first train next morning, changing at Chester and reaching Banbury at lunchtime. But we were greeted by the dread sign *"No sleeping on board after arrival"*, and so were unceremoniously turfed off the boat at midnight to take the *"Irish Mail"*. The ticket inspector said firmly *"Banbury? Change at Rugby"*, and we did. I don't know if he really thought there was a connection, or if he was a good London Midland man determined to keep passengers away from the Western Region at any cost, but the result was that we found ourselves on the platform at Rugby Midland at about four in the morning, where the staff were very surprised to see us and denied that any connection to Banbury existed. After consulting timetables they discovered that there was an early morning train to Banbury – from Rugby Central. Of course there was no transport of any kind between the stations at that time of the morning. So, as day broke, we lugged our suitcases what seemed like miles through the deserted streets of Rugby. We did catch the train, a typical cross-country one of the time, small, slow, and virtually empty which finally reached Banbury around breakfast time. Father took me to Sibford on the bus, rather than hang around Banbury all morning. I was very tired and feeling apprehensive about turning up so much earlier than expected, but I needn't have worried. I was made very welcome, was swimming inside a quarter of an hour, and as I said, I had a wonderful time for the whole week. The journey back overnight to Waterford via Fishguard was uneventful, just very tiring.

(9) Father, and my cousin Philip, were not at the Jamboree as they were at the big Friends World Conference in Oxford early in August 1952. I had assumed Father attended the World Conference while I was at Sibford, but now I believe he must have turned around and gone back to England for the conference almost immediately after returning me from the summer school.

A Jacob Family
Tramore in the 1900s

*Jack and Marguerite Skelton (née Jacob),
on their Wedding Day.*

Chapter 18

Jack Skelton
(Note by P. J. Skelton 2005)

John Mark Skelton, was born in Dublin in 1906, the youngest son of **Johnston Skelton** (1869-1934) and **Sarah J. Skelton nee Hogg** (d.1942). In January 1939 at Tramore Friends Meeting House, he married **Marguerite Moss Jacob** (1910-2000), the youngest daughter of **Edwin B. Jacob** (1868-1958) and **Jessie E. Jacob nee Baker** (1879-1963) of Tramore, Co. Waterford. They had three children: **Peter John**, (b.1939) **Janet Elizabeth** (n.1943), and **Bernard Ashton** (b.1945). After their marriage they lived at first with his mother and sister at 75 Cowper Road, Dublin, but in 1941 moved to the house that was to be their home for over 50 years at 15 Vergemount Park, Clonskeagh, Dublin.

In his memoir he is characteristically modest about the extent of his reading and interests – he was very widely read in history, philosophy, religion and politics, and had a passion for classical music. He was a much loved and valued member of Churchtown PM in Dublin, where he was an Elder. His ministry in meeting for worship was always thoughtful; he could see and bring out connections between apparently unrelated previous items of ministry, and thus move the meeting forward. He served the Society of Friends in many ways, notably as Assistant Clerk of Ireland Yearly Meeting from 1947-1949, and Clerk from 1950-1953.

He worked for the Sun Insurance Co., and its Irish subsidiary, the Patriotic Assurance Co. until his retirement, and was well regarded in the Dublin business community. He rose to be acting Branch Manager, and had to oversee the amalgamation of the two branches and move to a new office, when the Sun and the Alliance companies merged in the 1960's. Shortly after this he retired at the age of 62, and almost immediately suffered a serious heart attack. He made a full recovery and lived another 30 years with the loving support of his wife. They spent the last two years of their life together in New Lodge, the Quaker Nursing Home in Donnybrook, Dublin. He died on 9th April 1999 aged 92 at St. Vincent's Hospital following another heart attack.

Tramcar of the era.

Tramcars at Terenure Crossroads.

Memories of Youthful Days
John M. Skelton
(Written in 1986)

I was born on 17th September 1906 at 64 Upper Beechwood Avenue, Ranelagh. Beechwood Avenue looks much the same today as I remember it except that the big Catholic Church at the top was only being built and at that time there was a small corrugated iron building. Also the street lamps were gas not electric and I remember a man lighting them with a gas flame on the end of a long pole. My earliest datable recollection is being with my father somewhere in town and asking why there were flags and being told the king was dead so this must have been 1910 when I was four. I may say that mother expressed doubt that this was a genuine memory as she did also of my being in a pram in Oakley Road. There is no doubt however, that I recall the visit of King George and Queen Mary in 1913. We went down to Leeson Street near the end of Appian Way and when the procession came, I was lifted up on to a garden wall to see the soldiers and the royalty in open carriages. It may be that this memory is clear not just because I was older, but because when I went home I was playing with a toy boat and nearly put my eye out, by falling on the mast. I recall lying on a sofa in semi darkness until a doctor came and presumably said I was not seriously injured.

This brings to mind the fact that when young, I was accident-prone. When playing with my sisters in Palmerston Park, hide and seek in a shrubbery I ran my head onto a spiky sawn branch and have a dent in my skull to this day. Also trying to emulate them in stepping from one seat to another in a summerhouse I fell and broke my wrist. Much later at a scout camp I fell off a wall and dislocated my elbow. These accidents may mean that I was not naturally well coordinated but they may have been on account of my sight. It was only when I was almost 14 that it was noticed that I was shortsighted since when I have worn glasses.

I suppose I was five that is in 1911, when I went to Sandford National School to the infant's class. I have no very strong recollections about my school days and I think I was a pretty easygoing child who took things as they came. When I moved up from infants to first form, we had lessons in the parochial hall which was part of the school building and we played in the main playground and I remember feeling very small on the first day in the crowd of big boys and girls. However, I cannot have been too overawed as one of the big girls said, I was like a rabbit rushing about! The infants and lower forms were taught by Miss Colgan and Miss Elliot who were quite well liked but from 4th onward we were under Mr. Hobson of whom we were a bit afraid, as he was sometimes free with his cane. He was from Tyrone, and I have wondered if he was connected with the Quaker Hobsons, but I think not. I made some friends at Sandford but this was mostly later when the scout troop was started. Round about this time my brother Hubert went to Brookfield School, Moira, Co. Down, so he was away from home except for holidays. As he died when I was only twelve, I never really got to know him.

From an early age we went on Sunday morning to Rathmines Meeting. It was held in 83a Rathmines Road, which was one of a terrace of houses behind the shops where the Swan shopping centre now is. It was a three storey and basement house with steps up to the front door. The two rooms on the right of the hall had been made into one as the meeting room and the front room upstairs was used for Sunday school and the cloakrooms were at the end of the hall. The rest of the house was occupied by the caretaker. According to a list of members for 1913 there were about 50 adults and 25 children. Of these, the only ones I know to be still here, are Marjorie Boyd (Hill), Winifred Burne (Bewley), Eirene Douglas (Gilpin), Stanley Halliday, and Doris Jones (Alesbury and then Copithorne).

I may be wrong, but I don't think father or mother usually went to meetings, and that we went with Grandma. There was an evening meeting at which I believe there was a prepared address, but I have no recollection of attending this. Apart from my grandmother, we were classed attendees and although we went to Sunday School in the afternoon, I went to such things as Band of Hope meetings occasionally, my full involvement in the Society of Friends only began in my late teens.

In those days, as well as the usual bread and milk deliveries, people came round selling vegetables, fish, coal, etc, or offering to clean windows or do other jobs, and newsboys went about selling papers. The latter only penetrated as far as Beechwood Avenue if there was a "stop press", i.e. a special edition including an important piece of news which had just come in. More was charged for a "stop press" than for the ordinary edition and father would usually say that it was not worth buying. But I remember one evening he bought one and came back saying "An Austrian Prince has been shot". I do not suppose any of the adults thought this very important, and certainly they did not know that this was the start of a world war that was to bring great changes to our family.

At first life went on much as usual, although food and other goods became scarcer and I suppose business became difficult, but until 1916 nothing happened to affect deeply a child like myself. We had no relatives in the army, and although we heard about and some times saw wounded soldiers the war seemed far away from Dublin.

On Easter Monday 1916, which was a lovely fine day, our family went on a picnic, leaving Grandma at home. Father, Hubert and I think Lucy went on bicycles, and Mother, Emily and I went by tram to Terenure, and then on by the steam tram to Tallaght. We went to somewhere on the Dodder near Bohernabreena, but I do not remember much about the picnic or the walk, which was quite a distance for a boy not yet ten. I know that when we got back to Tallaght there was a troop of boy scouts waiting for the tram. This was the Portobello troop composed of the sons of British soldiers in Portobello barracks.

When we got to Terenure we were surprised to find the city trams outside the depot and people standing about talking. Father and Hubert, who had waited for us, told us that there had been a rebellion with some shooting in the city, and that all transport was stopped. Father decided to cycle as far as Aungier Street if this was possible, so that he could put up the shutters on Skelton's shop in case there was rioting and looting. The rest of us walked home, and I am sure mother was worried at the thought of father going towards town. The last we saw of the scout troop was as they marched down Terenure Road with their flag flying. I believe they got home safely.

When father got home he told us that the rebels had occupied Jacob's biscuit factory just opposite the shop, which was undamaged. He had got the shutters up. He had been told that the insurgents had occupied the G.P.O and also Stephens Green, and other places in the city, but that fighting had died down.

It must have been towards the end of Easter week that mother decided to go to the bakery in Ballsbridge to get bread. I imagine deliveries of bread had ceased, and that supplies had run out in the local shops. Hubert and I think Lucy came on their bicycles, and I walked with mother. When we got to Ballsbridge we saw a lot of soldiers who had just arrived from Kingstown sitting or standing by the side of the road. Their rifles were stacked beside them and ladies were giving them tea etc. These were not the first troops to arrive, and we heard that the first arrivals had had severe fighting at Mount Street Bridge, but that all was quiet there now.

British troops patrol Dublin streets.

After we had got the bread, Hubert and Lucy took the loaves home on their bicycles and I was left with mother. We walked down Pembroke Road and over Baggot Street Bridge and down Lower Baggot Street. From the bridge on we saw fewer people, and eventually we got to the corner of Merrion Row and Stephens Green. I saw a dead horse and an overturned cart in the road. I heard two shots in the distance, and saw what seemed to be an ambulance going down Grafton Street, but otherwise there was not a person in sight. As we peered cautiously round the corner, we heard a shout "Get back" and looking up saw a soldier on the roof of the Shelbourne Hotel with a gun pointing at us! So needless to say we set off home at once. It may seem incredible that mother would bring a small boy into the city, but she may have been told the fighting had ceased. I read somewhere that the rebels in the College of Surgeons, Stephens Green, were the last to surrender.

The only other incident I remember about the rising is going up to the footbridge at the top of Beechwood Avenue and seeing in the distance a tricolour flying on top of Jacobs factory. This must have been on Tuesday.

Easter Rising devastation Dublin 1916.

In 1917 a scout troop was started in Sandford parish and some of my school chums persuaded me to join. This began an association with Sandford troop and church, which lasted until 1932. It interests me to recall that helping with the preliminary organisation of the new troop, was a man called Yeomans who had been scoutmaster of the Portobello troop mentioned above, which had collapsed as the soldiers and families had been moved from Dublin. In our first year we had a camp near Trim of which almost all that I remember is that the site had a lot of long wet grass, that we knew nothing about camping and that my brother Hubert though not a member came to help the scoutmaster. Hubert had left Brookfield School and soon got a job with the North British Insurance Company.

The big thing for our family at this time was not that the war was slowly coming to an end, but a drastic change in our circumstances. A dispute occurred between my father and his brother Robert. What caused this I am not sure, but it seems probable that war conditions, such as shortage of cloth, made the tailoring business unprofitable. Although I never heard him say so, my father may have regarded himself as partner in the firm where as he was strictly only an employee, and in that case, how was he to be treated if he became redundant? An important point was that the house we lived in was not my father's but Robert's. In whatever way the matter was settled, we had to leave Beechwood Avenue, and my father felt that he had been badly treated. So far as I know, he never spoke to Robert again.

We moved to 9 Ranelagh Avenue and although this house had more rooms than our previous one, it was in a poorer neighbourhood and in poorer condition. Father had a temporary job with the Ordnance Department's clothing store but this ended as the war did. To relieve the financial pressure, my Aunt Cis took Lucy to live in London with her and Daisy Coles. All this was a great sorrow to my parents but a much greater tragedy hit them.

The influenza epidemic of 1918 killed millions throughout the world, more in fact than died in the war. Many died in Ireland and indeed my Aunt Sarah Duan, her son Mark and daughter Sarah all died within days. My brother Hubert having apparently recovered from influenza, it turned to meningitis and he died at the end of 1918 just before his 18th birthday. This was a blow from which I feel my father never recovered and which mother only survived because of her greater inner strength.

Although father knew the tailoring business, he had not been trained in measuring and cutting, this having all been done by Uncle Robert. He approached his brother-in-law Mark Duan who was quite well to do and he helped father to get the necessary training so that he could set up as a tailor, and he did so working in one of our rooms at home. For a time he did all right as for a while after the war ended clothing was scarce and dear and people wanted old suits turned or repaired or a coat made up from their cloth. But this did not last as the big firms got back into business. Father got employment first with a well-known firm O'Connor's and later with a Jewish firm in the wholesale trade. But the strain was too much and eventually he had a mental collapse, made an ineffectual attack on mother and an attempt to kill himself and ended in the mental hospital at Grangegorman. But this is to anticipate and I must now back track to the period immediately after the war.

In 1920 for the first time, I went out of Ireland. There was in that year the first international scout jamboree, although I was not one of the party of Irish scouts, who took part. My aunts invited me to stay with them, so that I could attend the displays which were at Olympia. I can't remember anything about the journey or who brought me, but I do recall the visits with Lucy to Olympia and seeing all the usual sights such as the Tower with the crown jewels and St. Paul's where I climbed as far as one can go and peered out from inside the ball. Something I would not do now if paid a fortune!

Another happening about this time, was an unexpected visit from my cousin Johnston Skelton of Maryport who was a marine engineer, and whose ship had come to Dublin for the first time. He was much older than Emily and I being married with a son, but we were enthralled by his stories about escaping trouble in a Russian port where the civil war was still raging or coping with drunken sailors and with his description of distant places such as Japan and New Zealand.

As a result of this visit, father had closer contact with his Maryport relatives and it turned out that a family connection was married to an engineer named Carser who was on a small ship, the Glenageary, which came to Dublin with coal for the Gas Company, sometimes from Maryport. So it was arranged, with the connivance of the captain that I should go over, stay a week with Uncle John, and come back on the next voyage. This was a great adventure. 1921 was a very hot dry summer and going over the sea was so calm that after dark there was phosphorescence on the bow wave, some thing I have not seen since. I saw porpoises for the first time, and coming back, I was up on the bridge chatting with the steersman most of the night and seeing the lights as we passed the Isle of Man. And I had a supper of fried herring and was not a bit seasick. Wonderful. At Maryport I met uncles, aunts and cousins, whom I recall as mostly fat, very friendly ,who fed me enormous quantities of food. I never met any of them again.

Cross channel steamer 1920's.

The Custom House Dublin, burns during Irish Civil War 1922.

*Ferrymen row across the River Liffey, Dublin,
as the Custom House burns in background.*

A Jacob Family
Tramore in the 1900s

There was of course no free secondary education in my time and my parents could not really afford to send me to a secondary school as apart from school fees there were many extras such as uniform, gear for football and cricket etc. So I stayed at Sandford until I was fourteen and a half, after which I went for a year to a vocational school at Ringsend. The thinking behind this is not clear, as I do not think I had the necessary qualities to make a mechanic or craftsman. I learnt things like mechanical drawing, woodworking, metalwork, met a lot of decent chaps but did not make any close friends.

After a year of this, one of my pals suggested that I should apply for a job which he was vacating, for a better one in a newspaper office. The post was with grain merchants, Peake and Drury, Astons Quay, and as well as the partners there was only a lady typist. I was just an office boy going on errands to other firms, buying stamps, making up post etc. What I liked best was being sent to get a sample of grain. This meant finding the consignment in some warehouse or railway siding, opening a sack, putting the hand well into the grain so that the sample was from the centre and not the top, then putting the handful into a linen bag and bringing it back to the boss. My wage was 7/6 per week, increased after three months to 10/- of which I gave half to my mother. So my business career started, but it was a dead end job and I answered advertisements in the papers for better ones, principally at insurance offices. After a number of unsuccessful attempts I had an interview, was accepted, and in March 1923 I started in the Motor Union Insurance Co. Ltd., Suffolk Street, Dublin. This was a real job at last and as soon as the autumn came I started evening classes at the Rathmines school of Commerce in the course for associateship of the Chartered Insurance Institute.

I don't remember much political discussion in our home, but of course one could not ignore what is now known as the War of Independence leading to the Treaty, and the setting up of the Free State followed by a Civil War. There were not many incidents near Ranelagh as far as I can recall, though there were many lorries filled with armed soldiers or auxiliary police dashing about. These by the way were covered with wire netting in case a grenade was thrown at them. There were also searches of houses and for a time a curfew so one could not go out without a permit. Only a few incidents stay in my mind. An early one is seeing Countess Markievicz being escorted by an enthusiastic crowd to a house in Belgrave Road, after she had been released from jail in England. She made a speech from a window, and I recall her aristocratic accent and how she said she was glad to see "Ireland thoroughly rebel at last". Another is seeing a house in Oakley Road where I think some of the Pearse family lived, badly wrecked after a search and people standing around muttering. Later a house in the same road was wrecked by a bomb perhaps as a reprisal. But the most vivid recollection is being in a shop in Camden Street to buy provisions, when there was a loud explosion followed by rifle shots and a crowd of people rushed into the shop and threw themselves on the floor. It transpired that a grenade had been thrown and the soldiers replied but of course the bomber got away. When I came out I saw windows shattered further down the street but so far as I know, no one was hurt.

Later in 1922 I remember I went with an advance party to prepare a campsite for our (scout) troop in the Isle of Man. We were in ordinary clothes with our uniforms etc. in kitbags, and when we met at Sandford Church, we found that there was no traffic being allowed into the city over the canal bridges, as there was trouble with the "Irregulars". So we went in two cars to the Ringsend Bridge over the Dodder, where we were able to get down steps onto the Quay, and walk back with our gear to the berth of the Isle of Man steamer.

Another Civil War incident, which must have been between the last mentioned and my starting at Peake and Drury's, was almost the end of fighting in Dublin. I went down to see what was happening and got as far as Westmoreland Street, where a number of people were in doorways and looking across O'Connell Bridge. There was a lot of smoke so it was difficult to see what was happening though I saw some St John Ambulance men crouching beside the O'Connell statute.

There were occasional shots and then a long silence. Some one said they saw a white flag and a few people started to walk slowly onto the bridge. At that there was a shot and they rushed back to their doorways. I may say I stayed put. Just then a lorry-load of Free State troops arrived from College Green and ordered us away. I slipped into Fleet Street, and from there to Aston's Quay, as I wanted to see what was happening at the Four Courts which I had heard was on fire, and that the Republicans had surrendered. But suddenly I heard a shout and on looking up a side lane I found a machine gun pointed at me so I beat a hasty retreat home.

Spectators watch the Custom House burn.

The mention above of going to the Isle of Man recalls a very vivid incident, which occurred at that camp. Acting as assistant scoutmaster was a Mr. Biggs. He had been a lieutenant in the Great War, and had been invalided home from France badly shell-shocked. Whether as a result of this or not, he had a very bad stutter especially when excited, though strangely enough he could recite dramatic monologues without difficulty. One evening at camp a game was being played and it got a bit wild and the scoutmaster felt it was getting out of hand and said it was supper and bedtime. So we were all in the mess tent drinking cocoa when Biggs suddenly collapsed in some sort of fit. We were some distance from a town and a messenger was sent to get a doctor. Meanwhile we brought a camp bed to the mess tent, lifted Biggs into it, sent the younger scouts to bed and the Scoutmaster myself and another senior watched over Biggs. Suddenly he started to talk and we had to hold him to prevent him getting out of the bed. He was reliving the episode in France and it was so vivid, one could almost see what was happening. He was urging, in very choice language, his men to hurry and it was obvious they were withdrawing to new positions. Suddenly he shouted, "They are sending over minnies". Minnies I believe was the slang term for German mortar bombs. Then with a cry he fell back on the bed and one could feel that the "Minnie" had exploded nearby.

In 1922 coming back from Ringsend one day I met a party of the Irish Army marching into Beggar's Bush barracks to take over and soon we had all the paraphernalia of a new state, new flags, stamps, police etc. I welcomed all this although many, perhaps most, Protestants did not, and recently I have wondered why this was so. My father was English, the books I read as a boy were English, and I had been to a Protestant school and yet I felt myself Irish and was glad to be a citizen of an Irish state. I think this may have been due to our being Quakers and therefore not believers in empire and the glorification of military prowess and also I think that although she did not talk politics Mother may, when she was young, have been a nationalist in the days of Parnell.

As I have mentioned at this time I was more and more involved with the Sandford scout troop, which grew to become one of the largest and most successful in Dublin. The Rector, Canon Harvey, invited me to attend a special Holy Communion service which he organised for young people and only laughed when I pointed out that I was not baptised, let alone confirmed. At one stage he even suggested that I should become a clergyman!

My involvement with Sandford Church meant that I had less and less connection with Friends and I might have drifted away altogether if it had not been for the starting of Friends Badminton Club. Emily and I were invited to join and did so. We played in Meath Place in one of the oldest meetinghouses dating from the 17th century but then used mostly for the charitable work of Dublin Friends Mission. I remember one night when play had gone on very late, I was walking down the Coombe when a guard seeing my bag said "Out on a call Doctor"? I may say I was pretty poor at badminton and never got beyond the lowest team, but I got to know my contemporaries in Friends and made many lasting friendships. I also started to attend the Young Friends group, which at this period was flourishing, largely due to the fact that it had the essential thing needed for a successful group, namely an energetic efficient secretary in Ethel Pim.

In 1926, the Young Friends held the first of a series of annual Easter weekend gatherings, at Glenmalure. I attended many of these and became drawn further into Friends; in fact, on one occasion I was a Young Friends representative to London YM. At that time Friends were much concerned with India and Gandhi's non-violent campaign, and the YM was addressed by Rabindranath Tagore and Friends House was so full, that we young ones had to sit on the floor. Tagore looked a real figure of a mystic poet, in a blue robe with long hair, beard and glowing eyes. He spoke with a musical voice and we were very uplifted but I confess that after the length of time I cannot remember what he said!

All this meant that I became firmly convinced that so far as religion was concerned I was a Quaker. Also I began to feel that I had got all I was going to get out of scouting and had nothing much to put in, so in 1932 I was glad to retire from being scoutmaster and hand over to a better man. But I must say that I had got a lot of fun out of the scouts, going to various camps in Wales; to jamborees at Wembley and Birkenhead and to a Rover Moot at Kandersteg in Switzerland, my first time on the continent. Nowadays going to the continent is commonplace, and anyway we have already seen it all on television, but in 1930 it was a tremendous thrill to go by mountain railway high up on the Jungfrau and see snow peaks all round and a glacier in the valley and everywhere to feel the hot sunshine and the pure air.

The people too looked healthy and sunburnt although it was somewhat humiliating when toiling up to a pass to be over-taken by two youngsters aged about ten. Before I leave the scouts, I must mention Fred Willis the curate at Sandford and scoutmaster for some time. He was a good man with a sense of humour and I liked him. I used to go and see him sometimes at his lodgings and I remember him talking to me about Shakespeare and encouraging my interest in literature. I may say that I have always been fond of reading and this has helped to make up to some extent for the deficiencies in my education but my reading has been too haphazard and undisciplined.

I must now return to my career with the Motor Union Insurance Co. This was quite a small company, which had been started by the Automobile Association and did mostly motor insurance. The staff in Dublin was about twelve. The manager was a man named Blair whom I did not like, but I had little to do with him. He was out a lot of the time driving a yellow sports car, and was said to be carrying on with a dashing widow who had a white sports car, and who sometimes visited Blair in the office. I recall a dramatic occasion when the widow was in the manager's office and Mrs Blair arrived unexpectedly. The staff kept their heads down to their work, but out of the corners of our eyes we could see excited shadows on the muffed glass screen!

The Chief Clerk was a decent man but too fond of the bottle, and the rest of the staff were pleasant to work with. One I must mention is Claude Wall who was about my own age. He was very musical, and I went with him to the Gaiety Theatre during the visits of the Carl Rosa Opera Company. There I heard many operas such as La Boheme and Carmen, Pagliacchi and Madame Butterfly and even Wagner's Siegfried. We sat in the gallery on hard wooden seats without backs rising in tiers and the price was 6d. There was a tradition of singing in the gallery during the intervals although this was dying out. If you saw someone whom you knew could sing reasonably well you called out "a song from Mr. So-and-so" and if others took this up he would oblige and would be applauded. If the orchestra came back to their place before the singer had finished, the conductor would wait, but as soon as the song ended someone would say "opera please" and there would be dead silence.

There was a story that John McCormick first came to notice singing in the Gaiety gods, but there was no one of his class when I was there. Claude was also keen on mountain walking, and I remember on a bank holiday walking with him over Djouce, Maulin and War Hill to Lough Bray, where we had tea, and then over the Featherbed to Rathfarnham. Claude who was a devout Catholic, entered a monastery as a novice but found it was not his vocation, so came out and re-entered the insurance industry. I sometimes see him at concerts.

I got on well with the staff in the offices, and I also did well in the first two examinations of the insurance course. On the staff was a Miss Coote and one day she said that I would have better prospects if I was in one of the large companies. She said that her father had been the manager of the Dublin branch of the Sun Insurance Company for many years and that she knew the current manager Mr. Smith. She suggested that she should mention my name to Mr. Smith, and I of course agreed, with the result that I was interviewed and in December 1926 I joined the Sun and remained there until I retired in 1968. This was I feel a fortunate move as not long after I left the Motor Union, there was a scandal with some sackings, and I could have got some of the stigma even if I was not involved. Also the Sun is now part of one of the strongest insurance organisations and can afford to treat its pensioners well, which is no small consideration in these times.

In the period following World War I, a great interest was the advent of radio or as we called it "the wireless". It seems extraordinary now to recall going to Sandford parochial hall to listen to a demonstration of a wireless by Mr. Dixon of Dixon & Hempenstall, who was one of the first to import these new newfangled instruments. Wireless exercised the sort of fascination over the young as computers do today and we made sets, swapped parts and magazines. Somehow I got a pair of headphones and I made first a crystal set, and then a one valve set, and I would sit up past normal bedtime trying to get foreign stations. I would have liked to have been employed in the technical side of radio, but this was not really a practical ambition. Another excitement of the period was of course the development of aviation.

I first flew at a scout camp in Wales when a pilot with a three seater open biplane came to a nearby field, and gave short flips for 5/-, just up round the neighbouring fields and down again. Sometime later Sherwood Glynn whom I knew from Young Friends and had just got his licence as an amateur pilot, asked me if I would like to come up with him. So greatly daring, I went with him on a Sunday to Baldonnel airfield, and he took me up in an open two-seater biplane and we flew down to Co. Kildare, circled the Curragh and came back to make a perfect landing. My first commercial flight was in Germany in 1933 on a short flight from Frankfurt to Cologne.

German Airfield 1930's.

From about 1928 there was a great depression in industry, which lasted almost until the Second World War. This caused hardship in the industrial countries with massive unemployment. Even in our office, increases in salary became very few and small although we never had an actual cut in salary, as happened in some offices. But there was some compensation in the fact that some prices were cut. For instance in 1932 when shipping companies were desperately trying to get passenger, I went on a cruise with Geoff Trapnell, and Ivan Webb, from London to Tangier, Barcelona, Algiers, Gibraltar, and back to London for £16. In 1933 I went to Germany, and as I remember the boat and rail fare from Dublin to Cologne and back was about £7. Later I went to Germany again, this time to go in a canoe from Trier on the Moselle and Rhine to Cologne, and to Austria and to Czechoslovakia.

There were of course many amusing incidents on these trips, but I will only mention one. On the Austrian trip we went in Geoff Trapnell's, or rather his parent's, car. This was an ordinary Ford and he said had only one defect. Occasionally the clutch would jam, in which case one had to rock the car back and forth, and the pedal would jump back. This did not happen until we were at the Brenner Pass going on a short run into Italy. Having ended formalities we got into the car when the clutch jammed. Jumped out, rocked car, clutch out, back in car and away. I will never forget the look on the faces of the Italian frontier guards. One knew they were thinking that these mad Irish men had come well over 1,000 miles in a car, which had to be pushed to get it to start!

The inter war period was overshadowed by the rise of Fascism and in particular of the Nazis. In Ireland it was not paid very much attention, in fact I think many people thought Fascists a good thing. Through the Society of Friends we knew a little of what was happening, and this was reinforced for me by my continental trips when I saw the kind of anti-Semitic posters displayed, and also felt that some people were not anxious to talk to strangers about political matters. Later of course I met refugees in Ireland but this was after the period I am now considering.

In 1934 my father died. Since he had gone to hospital some years before, mother had gone to see him every week. This can not have been easy, as sometimes he was very shut in on himself and the conditions in the hospital in those days were far from good. But I never heard her complain, father's breakdown must have been a terrible blow. She was a good woman. After this, Emily and I with the help of a mortgage were able to buy a house in Cowper Road in Rathmines and we moved in there with mother.

Sometime in the 1930's, Emily joined the Holiday Fellowship walking club and persuaded me to join too. The club organised walks on Saturday afternoons ending at a tea place and after tea we would walk to the nearest bus or train for home. Some of the club joined the newly formed Youth Hostel Association (An Oige) and we had weekend outings staying at hostels. All this meant that I made a new circle of friends. Another result was that I got into amateur acting. Ernest a member of HF was producer of plays for the dramatic society of the Presbyterian Church at Parnell Square and I was in two of their plays including a dramatisation of "Pride and Prejudice" in which I was Mr. Collins! I was also in the An Oige Dramatic Society in two plays. At a later stage I was in a left-wing society, called New Theatre Group, but this is to go too far ahead.

I was going down Westland Row to get the train and go on a Holiday Fellowship walk when I saw an acquaintance on the other footpath. It transpired that she was going for the first time to walk with the Holiday Fellowship. Our acquaintance was limited to having been at some Quaker meetings at the same time. Neither of us realised that this was the start of a close very happy relationship, which still lasts stronger than ever. I am a very lucky man, and have been blessed far beyond my deserving, for which I thank God.

*Cousin Annie Jacob,
of Colwyn Bay.*

A Jacob Family
Tramore in the 1900s

*Back: Marguerite (Jacob) Skelton, Edwin and Jessie Jacob.
Front: Janet, Peter, and Bernard Skelton, late 1940's.*

Chapter 19

Memories of Midvale
Bernard A. Skelton May 2008

I had started to set down memories of Midvale and of Granny and Grandpa a couple of years ago, and had got to the stage of writing out a list of items to include. My brother and sister, Peter and Janet sent me copies of their efforts. Almost every one of their memories coincided with mine. Virtually all the items on my list had been covered. As the youngest, my lack of memories is due to the fact that the entire time that I spent in Tramore was when I was under ten years old. As far as I can determine, the last time that I stayed in Midvale or Summerville was in the summer of 1955, on the way to or from my summer holidays in Kerry with Mum and Dad. I was still only nine that summer.

Like Peter I had distinct memories of long, slow train journeys from Dublin to Waterford. Mum, in her own inimitable way, would try to occupy us when we started to get bored. One of her tricks was to teach us the names of the stations to be passed along the way, and so to this day I can still recite those between Kilkenny and Waterford in order, ending with Ballyhale, Mullinavat, Kilmacow, Waterford. As we passed each, we would shout out the names amid great excitement. Also like Peter, I remember being allowed onto the footplate of various steam locomotives at Kingsbridge, and I too was allowed onto the engine at Tramore station when it ran round the carriages and took on water for the return journey to Waterford.

However my very first memory of the journey to Tramore was not of a train, but of a motor car. It is in fact my very first memory of my life. When I told Mum of it some time later, she reckoned that I must have been just three. She was going down for a short visit to Midvale and was taking me with her. We were getting a lift from some Friend, she suggested a name to me later but I cannot remember who. The arrangement was to meet our driver at 6 Eustace Street, and I distinctly remember, as my very first memory, being carried through the front door of Eustace Street on a winter's evening and through the green baize covered inner doors. I remember nothing of the actual car journey, as a three year old I was presumably asleep on Mum's knee. I do however remember waking up outside the gate at Midvale and seeing the lights of the house on. Legend always had it that I clearly announced "There's Midvale!" but that part of the story is most likely apocryphal.

As regards memories of Midvale itself, I too remember the "ree-kart" and pushing Janet around in it, the pump, all the various parts of the garden. For some reason I also remember a postal weighing scales in the front room that I played with, and also have memories of the kitchen full of sticky, runny honey sections and the pantry where Granny kept the left over cold boiled potatoes. For some reason I used to adore those, and probably ate her entire stock of them for the week every time I came to stay!

The geography of the upstairs of Midvale defeats me, though I slept on a camp bed on the landing return on at least one occasion – probably the "Jacob Jamboree". Of the "Jamboree", I do remember falling in love with my older female cousins, Ann, Lynne and Lesley and being carried round on Lynne's shoulders, to my great delight.

I remember Grandpa from Midvale as a lovely, gentle, very deaf man, seriously old to a youngster like me. I was rather in awe of him, sitting watching him quietly and deliberately working his way through his breakfast. He would drink his tea from what was to me an enormous cup. Unusual as it may seem, he did once get cross, when I tried his patience to the extreme. I was "assisting" him with the gardening. I started to try to push a full wheelbarrow and Grandpa, seeing the obvious dangers, asked me not to. I persisted, as six/seven year olds are wont to do, and the whole wheelbarrow overturned spilling its contents. Grandpa got cross and gave out to me, I cried and ran off. I never offered to "help" him again!

Memories of Granny at that time are almost entirely in the kitchen. I can't recollect much more of her from that period, but I do remember a little more from some years later when she came to live in Dublin. As a young teenager I sometimes visited her in Upper Leeson Street, where she lived with Mrs O'Byrne. She would sit quietly knitting or crocheting or sewing, and she chatted away to me about Halstead in Essex and her family there. I have sadly forgotten almost everything she told me, but she did tell me one thing about herself that has stuck in my mind ever since.

She told me that when she read something, she saw individual letters as different colours. Thus different pieces of writing took on different hues to her, depending on the individual letters and words therein. A passage of print would be predominantly blue or red or "a greenish/yellow colour". I was always fascinated by this trait of hers, so much so that I have never forgotten it.

I have never come across anyone else who claimed to see letters in a similar way, and wonder if anyone else has.

As regards Tramore itself, I too remember the Doneraile Walk. When you went down Love Lane leading to it I seem to remember the old coastguard station on the left. Dad pointed out to me once that you could expect to see the remains of a coastguard station in most seaside towns in Ireland, often burnt out during our country's struggle for independence.

Mum once told me of an incident that occurred presumably during the War of Independence, sometime between 1918 and 1921, though possibly during the Civil War in 1922. As I remember it, she told me that when she was a young girl she was woken up by gunfire in the middle of the night. She told me that it was the IRA attacking the coastguard station. Apparently Grandpa became afraid that stray bullets might reach Midvale and so got everybody to put their mattresses up against the windows as protection.

I did a quick web search through Google and came up with the following entry in that "authoritative" source Wikipedia for January 7th 1921 in their Chronology of the Irish War of Independence:-

> "A feint attack was made at the Tramore RIC barracks to draw out the military from Waterford where they were ambushed at Pickardstown. Participating were 15 men from the West Waterford Brigade (Deise) under the command of O/C Pax Whelan and Flying Column Leader George Lennon. A larger force from East Waterford was under the command of Brigade O/C Paddy Paul. The ambush went awry and East Waterford Volunteers Thomas O'Brien and Michael McGrath were killed."

Maybe it was this attack that Mum was talking about. She would have been 10 at the time. Even if she had by that time gone to school in South Wales, she presumably would have been home for the Christmas holidays in early January. Quite where the RIC barracks was in Tramore, whether it was one and the same as the coastguard station or near it, or whether Mum had got the details mixed up, I am not sure. The ambush at Pickardstown, outside Tramore on the Waterford road seems from this to have been the bigger affair, with tragic consequences. While the attack on the RIC barracks was merely a feint, it could well have involved much noise and shooting from a distance to alarm the RIC. It certainly seemed to alarm Grandpa considerably!

Tramore Coastguard Station, which later became the Garda Barracks.

A Jacob Family
Tramore in the 1900s

Susan Maguire.

Reclining against "Submarine Rock" on "Daisy's" car seats.
Back: Stella Jacob, Dorothy Jacob.
Front: Elizabeth Maguire, Weston Jacob, Susan and Tim Maguire, Philip Jacob, Anne Maguire.

Chapter 20

Our time in Ireland 1940 - 41
Susan (Maguire) Hill
(Tom and Nora Maguire's third daughter - written in 2004)

In May or June 1940 when I was nine years old, I remember quite suddenly being told we were going to Ireland. On a sunny June day I was excited as I said goodbye to school friends. Irene Tubbs came with Mummy to take us to Fishguard to cross by night to Waterford. Anne and Elizabeth were 15 and 13 years old, and I felt reasonably safe with them to look after me. It must have been much more difficult for Anne. How did Mummy manage to apparently calmly say goodbye to all of us? She felt things deeply, and often her eyes watered involuntarily, empathising with a sadness, but somehow on that occasion she didn't cry and so sent us off calmly.

Charles met us at Waterford Quay and took us to his office for us to send a telegram of our arrival to our parents. I think Charles had told Daddy that he would find living arrangements for us all. After a few days he and Stella decided to keep us all in their own home. This was wonderful of them. They had only been married about three and a half years and Weston and Philip were only just adapting to having a stepmother. I believe Stella actually found it a lot easier to firmly tell all of us that it was time to wash our hands for meals, or bed times, or time to get ready for school – there was no question of any of us getting away with being awkward.

The Jacob home was the right size for four people, but crowded with eight of us! I can't remember, but I think Anne and Elizabeth (called Buff), or Weston and Philip, slept up at 'Midvale' looked after by Charles' parents who were just lovely people, gentle, peaceful and loving. Their home 'Midvale' was only about two hundred yards from Summerville and it was lovely to go there. Grampa Jacob kept bees, and I have a good memory of being around in the garden near him in his bee hat!

My general memory of living at Summerville is of feeling well cared for, with a good firm pattern to our lives. Charles and Stella gave us affection, and I felt safe that their guidance was always fair.

The Jacob family's way of life was more active in their enjoyment of the countryside and coast, than our lives in England. Their home Summerville was only about 300 yards up a rough road from Tramore pier, so immediately their surroundings were those of a holiday to us. We spent many happy hours playing on and around the pier. We fished for crabs with a piece of string, bent pin, and a piece of limpet, quickly learning the art of rapidly lifting the string as soon as the crab started to eat, enticing it to hang on to the bait tight. Then we could quickly put them in a bucket. There were beautiful rock pools nearby with wonderful coloured fronds of seaweed and sea anemones, shrimps and sometimes little fish. The sun was always shining!

A Jacob Family
Tramore in the 1900s

The Jacob parents were very good at getting young Quakers to help with taking us on outings. Expeditions to nearby beaches, to swim and picnic – boiling water over a campfire in a double cone-like kettle, that somehow I believe went over the fire. On at least one occasion mackerel drove sprats up onto the beach, probably at high tide. The stranded sprats were easy to gather into bags and buckets for very good meals! Someone had a sailing dinghy, and we were sometimes able to go out in this and fish for mackerel, learning that art and how to deal with the fish.

The Jacobs had found a very simple cottage in the Comeragh Mountains about 24 miles from their home and rented this very cheaply. Going there was a delight. I was certainly proud of myself when, aged ten, I was able to cycle up to the cottage with the older children! The second summer Mummy came over to Ireland and had all six of us children at the cottage in the mountains, probably to give Charles and Stella a much needed holiday.

At the cottage cooking was over an open turf fire which had a blackened kettle, and a big stew pot, to hang on a hook above the flames. Having cycled from Waterford, pigs kidneys bought in Kilmacthomas and fried over that fire, have never tasted so good! We fetched water from a well in a nearby field, we took potatoes to the small stream down the road to scrub, we fetched milk in a can from Mrs Drohan at the farm.

Kind, delightful Mrs Drohan who showed us her way of life. She baked her bread in a tin in a hole under her turf fire. At lunch time she put a clean sack on the table and put the potatoes out onto this. I think there was a bowl of cream or butter to eat with the potatoes, eating these with their hands. Mrs Drohan's husband had died and she had brought up her six (or seven?) children. At that time the boys were aged I think from 14 to 22 years, and the one daughter had gone to be a nun.

Washing was the simple way, a good place for the toilet was the woods a field away – but there was also an "Elsan" that had to be emptied!

The Drohan boys took their milk in churns to the creamery each morning. A good outing was to ask for a ride and sit on the side of the flat donkey cart to go down to the shop by the creamery. A shop that in those days sold everything from rubber boots and mousetraps, to sausages and tea – and probably biscuits! I can't remember there being any shortage of food.

The road ran beside a river, a small one as it was near its source. It tumbled over the boulders, rushing through gaps, and sometimes over waterfalls. One pool was special, only about ten feet by eight, but deeper and good fun, and named "The Pools of Moab". Over that summer of 1941 I collected a great variety of wild flowers with Mummy, and learned to identify them.

In term time we went to Newtown School. I remember Newtown as having an atmosphere of being relaxed and warmly caring, and a feeling of children being appreciated as individuals. The expectations were more free than the girls private schools I had been used to, but with adequate containment and discipline.

Curiously odd mental snapshots remain in my mind of "Transition" classroom, the quadrangle, the workshop and woodwork master, the dining room and having little cubes of cheese in soup. Then particularly of playing with Tim on the tennis court as we waited for Buff to have finished school at the end of the day. And going to spend a penny or two of pocket money at the corner shop (Paddy Kiely's) was special. Buying liquorice allsorts, aniseed balls and oddments in small amounts.

I learned not to steal by the guilt of stealing. Terrible. Two big pennies I believe from the 'Midvale' phone money box. I then went to the shop (Maggy beyont) which I remember as a hovel that was opposite 'Midvale'. I was not found out but felt very bad.

Probably only a few months after our arrival at Summerville, the Jacobs had a room built on their lawn for us four Maguires to have as our bedroom and family room. That was wonderful of them too. I wonder how difficult it was for Anne and Buff to find a quiet corner to do homework or read – I hope they had bedside lights and could read after Tim and I were asleep.

One last memory. In December 1941 it was suddenly possible for us to go back to England. I can vividly remember 'Uncle' Charles coming over to the new room to tell us. An emotional realisation, but not without mixed feelings as to what we would be leaving. Memories of Charles helping us pack, rolling everything up very tight to make suitcases very compact.

The Jacob family did a great deal for us for those eighteen months.

Weston Jacob has a quiet moment in Summerville garden, 1940.

A Jacob Family
Tramore in the 1900s

Sunday afternoon by the sea 1940.
Back: Stella Jacob, Philip Jacob.
Front: Elizabeth Maguire, Robert Jacob, Weston Jacob, Jim Sexton, Tim Maguire, Susan Maguire (front), Anne Maguire (back), Charles Jacob (with hat).

Chapter 21

Ireland 1940 - 41
Timothy Maguire
(Tom and Nora Maguire's son,
the youngest of their four children - written in 2004)

I was six and a half when we were evacuated, and as I was so young some of my memories are now blurred, so many years later. I had a dental problem on the night we left, and I was taken to a friend of our parents who was the King's dentist! I sat where the King sat in Mayfair watching an air raid while my teeth received attention. I recall the searchlights and flashes. The train was dimly lit, and the ferry was carrying cattle on the upper deck. It was a rough crossing and the cattle pens broke. Barrage balloons were rigged fore and aft. A line of jaunting cars on the Quay at Waterford was waiting, and I think we used these to get ourselves and our luggage to the station, or to the office.

I recall the loving smiles of the Jacob family on arrival at Summerville, and Stella, caring and dependable – rocklike. The Summerville garden seemed sunlit and the fuchsias amazed me. I'm afraid I popped some of the buds. I don't remember feeling homesick, which is a huge tribute to Charles and Stella. Weston and Philip were my heroes. It was a happy home, if a bit crowded!

Midvale was also a lovely place for me, and the grandparents were very loving. I was intrigued by their telephone – with a wooden box and a black "daffodil" speaker – and by the bees.

I was sometimes allowed to buy a penny surprise packet at the corner shop, and I remember the awful feeling when one day I threw the contents onto the fire by accident and was left with the wrapping – a feeling that has recurred since whenever I did something silly without thought!

I don't remember much of Newtown School, as I was sent to Miss Darton's kindergarten after a term or so. There was the train – and Christie the guard, the walk from the station along a river to school (and in the river once I think over the mud). A cartload of new school desks arrived, and the children soon discovered coins in the inkwells! At Miss Darton's I must have looked out of the window a lot, as I loved the view of the sea and the strand. It was a good place.

I remember going to Meeting, and being in trouble for failing to change out of my "elastic sided slippers" beforehand. There was the day when Grandpa and Uncle Charles were elders, and I was mortified when Grandpa nodded off, as I thought Meeting would go on for hours! I remember exploring The Cove with Susan, and the little green shop, which was closed and smelled of peppermint.

One dark memory was of the day a cottager on the way down to The Cove was digging a ditch next to a wall. The wall fell on him and killed him. This made me face death for the first time.

The picnics with Jimmy Sexton and others were great, as were the days on the strand. I remember singing "My eyes are dim I cannot see…" and lots of fun and laughter.

Fishing trips were exciting, catching loads of mackerel - until the seals came - and the view of the cliffs and the Metal Man from the sea.

"The Cottage" impressed me deeply. The ladder to the bedroom. The wheel. The gas lights. Fetching water and milk. The gravel road and little stream. The submarine rock. Climbing the hills – Dov Beg. Visits to Mrs Drohan – seeing her pray in front of her picture of the Sacred Heart – baking the bread under a stone under her turf fire. Her remarks; "You're a fine boy, 'tis a pity you're a hathen" "What would I be wanting with a penny a pint for milk when we can live on a ha'penny?". Jolting down to the creamery on the donkey cart with Willie – tousle haired and about 15. (I saw him not many years ago with Elizabeth – still there in his seventies, with a modern milking parlour! He remembered us all by name).

Overall, I felt happy and secure. I must have missed Mummy and Daddy greatly, but it is a huge tribute to Charles and Stella and their family that, despite the underlying anxiety and uncertainty of the war, I didn't feel that cloud unduly, and I don't think that my upheaval at such a tender age had a bad effect on my development. This is also a tribute to my sisters. The responsibility of being the eldest weighed heavily on Anne. I can remember now how tense she looked at times.

The Jacob family's great gift to us was to make us feel like part of their extended family, to be loved and nurtured, and never as evacuees who were a nuisance.

I have read Susan's "memories" and rather than write more myself I would prefer to endorse heartily her vivid impressions, and express my deep gratitude for all that the Jacob family gave a scruffy little boy, by what they did for him, and by what they were.

Chapter 22

Reminiscences of Ireland
Marianne (Fischer) Johannsen
(Written in 2003)

At last World War II came to an end. We were in Thuringia *(about 200 km south-west of Berlin)* when Germany collapsed. The Americans marched in, in May 1945 (I was thirteen) and now many years later I am writing my memories of that period – probably with some inaccuracies.

We heard on the radio for the first time of the appalling Nazi atrocities. There was much pillaging and plundering. The Americans confiscated our house where we lived on the top floor in two tiny rooms. My father's brother, Uncle Hans Fischer, was the bank manager. The bank was on the ground floor, and Uncle Hans, Aunt Ilse and their three children on the first floor. Once the victorious powers had negotiated the partition of our country between them, Thuringia was in the east Zone, under the Russians. Even Berlin was divided among the "Allies". Our own home was in Berlin-Siemensstadt. We were fortunate – after the Russians entered Berlin and made use of our home we found ourselves in the British Zone.

In October 1945 we returned to Berlin. Our house was ruined; wrecked; full of excrement, and many things had disappeared – stolen. Mother had a lot of cleaning to do! We children went back to "school". At first it was all very make-shift in our teacher's little home. There were few school books, and we sat on tables, chairs, pouffes and window sills.

Berlin street devastation 1945.

Civilian refugees receive help amongst the Berlin ruins, 1945.

On 2nd November 1945 Father returned from prison camp. (He had been sent to a prisoner of war camp in Siberia), with a shoulder wound. Emaciated, infested with lice, shaven-headed, with a clean bandage and a loaf of bread under his arm (given to him by some charitable person) – there he was! We all hugged him tightly, and his lice soon found themselves new homes. Mother burnt all his clothes immediately, but too late. Very soon we all had nits, and a little later we were itching and scratching. During the war Father was a policemen in Berlin, and he was also involved in the Last Stand in Berlin.

The years after the war were very hard. Father worked for the British. He exchanged home-grown tomatoes from our tiny garden for other food which we could not get otherwise. Sometimes an English soldier gave him a couple of pieces of bread that he hid inside his shirt as he passed through the control barriers.

We often went on "Hamster Journeys". Sabine and I travelled on the train to Neustadt outside Berlin in the eastern Zone. We worked on an estate, which had been confiscated by the Russians, harvesting the cabbage and making sauerkraut, and in exchange received a bowl of potato soup and a piece of bread. On festive occasions we received a shovel full of potatoes (about ten or fifteen lbs) which unfortunately were often frozen. On our way to the station we often stole some sugar beet and sometimes the Russians at the station barrier would confiscate the whole lot.

Syrup was made from the sugar beet. In the worst times mother turned the beet remains into "vegetables" seasoned with salt and marjoram. Added to this were the frozen potatoes and perhaps the remains of the green tomatoes from our garden. Little Karin (four years old) got something else to eat, Mother and Sabine soon had enough of this, and only father and I (who were always hungry) ate more of it.

For the very first time there were leftovers! Perhaps as a result of these terrible meals Father lost some of his inhibitions and wrote to his friend of long ago and begged for help. Chas Jacob's family began to send us food parcels, but unfortunately few reached us as there were many other hungry people who took them first. So one day Charles Jacob offered to take one of us children for a year or so to restore our health. Sabine, because she was so bloated and puffed out from the potato soup was not a suitable representative of starving Germany to send to Ireland. Karin was too young, but I was tall and skinny with nothing showing in front and nothing behind!

After many formalities my parents brought me to Templehof airport on 8th May 1948. Then to Frankfort and Shannon where I spent the night – my first night in a foreign country.

Now I was in Ireland, and I started a diary. No-one spoke German, but having learned English for four years in school it didn't take long to become used to it and within a week of arriving I was able to understand almost everything. My diary was written in a mixture of English and German, so I have written a shortened version in English only.

A Jacob Family
Tramore in the 1900s

The Fischer Family, 1948.
L to R: Karin, Irmgard, Sabine, Ernst, Marianne.

Marianne's Birthday, May 1948.

But before the diary you may like to read what my Father, Ernst Fischer, wrote on 8th May 1948 about conditions in Berlin:-

"*The city is divided into four sectors. We live in the British Sector. At present there is great anxiety about the fate and the future of the 3¼ million people. It is almost three years ago to the day that the dreadful war ended. We had just had the first news of our East Prussian relatives who came from the former Konigsberg – they were now the poorest of the poor and had to be taken care of and given a new start in our Germany that was so damaged and sick.*

City life is just possible, but very expensive and existence without the Black Market would be impossible. The distribution of any kind of clothing is virtually nil and what there is is of the poorest quality. String replaces shoe laces, we use (twine) if one had any instead of thread.

Mother is "not available for work" (i.e. is a housewife) so she is not entitled to or eligible for anything. She carries the load of anxiety and worry for our well being as much as your Father does. Soon after came the first distribution of one sewing needle for a household of more than three people.

Food is of course strictly rationed. An adult receives the following per day:-

   400 gm rye bread

   400 gm potatoes

    40 gm meat or fish or egg

    20 gm sugar

    40 gm of other foodstuff (if available)

    10 gm fat

     5 gm ersatz coffee"

(All the above has been translated from Marianne's German by Brigid).

(All the diary pages that follow are wholly Marianne's writing. They have been transcribed exactly as written by Marianne. The explanatory notes at the end about some of the people (and other things) mentioned by Marianne were written by PRJ.)

I – Marianne Fischer – was the choosen girl from Germany to live with Family Charles S. Jacob for about eighteen months starting on 9th May 1948. I was almost 16 years old, very thin, quite tall with a very "huge permanent wave"!!!

My father Ernst Fischer spent some time in Ireland working as an engineer in his German firm Siemens, who built up the Shannon-Scheme in Ardnacrusha. He and my mother got married in Limerick with Charles S. Jacob as their witness. They also made some motor-cycle tours through Ireland with their young wives. I think my parents returned to Germany in 1928/9. I don't think there was a great correspondence between them. My father remembered the lovely time in Ireland and tried to get in touch with Charles again after the 2nd. World War. As he told me later he was begging for help.

*River Shannon Hydro - Electric - Scheme at Ardnacrusha,
where Marianne's father Ernst worked during its construction.*

At first Charles and Stella sent parcels with food, but many parcels got lost. So Charles and Stella decided to help us in taking over the most hungry girl of the family. In those days my sister Sabine asked me "do you like to go? You don't show it". Well, I didn't know what to think of my going to Ireland to these strange people. In those days food was very important. Perhaps I was convinced that I will no longer be hungry. In my diary I wrote down what kind of food I got. <u>Milk</u> is underlined! Only my 4-year-old sister Karin got some milkpowder on her rationcard.

I landed in Shannon-Airport in the middle of the night. Two men escorted me to the hotel, where I got a meal with a "big piece of meat". The next day was a Sunday. I had no watch but it was church-time. I saw well-dressed people going to Church. I noticed the red and green-coloured coats. We only had black/grey-coloured-ones.

After a while the two men led me to the breakfast-room and I loved my first ham and eggs! As my English was at the standard of 4 years English at school, I did not understand everything – so I ate quite a number of toasts with butter and jam and when I was "filled up" ham and eggs were served. – hm..hm.. !

Afterwards I was led to the waiting-room. I saw planes coming and going. I was watching the two-wing-door and was looking at all the people who passed through. At last the door opened and Mr. and Mrs. Jacob's and Philip's eyes were looking out for me. We recognised each other – by photos. They were talking slowly to me and seemed to be happy to have me! (So I wrote down in my diary! "They are extremely nice people") . On our three and a half hours drive in the van, Joe I noticed that the word "nice" was often used! After arriving in Summerville I met so many nice people. I met Grandpa, Jenny and the Glas-family.

I only had a small suitcase with very little in it. A small wooden plate and a children's picture book for Jenny. Perhaps I had another slip, socks, a dirndl and a jacket. My mother had to share her clothes with her growing-up daughters. One could not buy anything. In the first few days Stella and I went by car to Waterford to get some clothes for me. Mrs. Darton gave me some of her dresses.

On the 15th of May 1948 Newtown School celebrated their 150th Anniversary. Jennifer and I slept with Grandparents Jacob, while Charles, Stella and Philip were involved in the celebration-affaires. On the last afternoon Stella and I joined the dance-party. I was surprised: I also was asked for a dance by two pupils, friends of the Jacobs and cousin Robert.

After a week I could understand almost everything. Soon I did no longer say Mr. Jacob and Mrs. Jacob. I said Aunty Stella and Uncle Chas. I met Veronica. In those days Stella used to do her "big wash" in her machine. The other washing was done by hand. On Sundays I preferred to go to the meeting and not to church. In this quiet hour I was thinking of my poor family in Germany. I was so happy staying with the Jacobs. – Aunty Stella told me on our way home: "I was thinking what we should eat tomorrow". So I no longer felt guilty not to think of God too much!

Quite often I mentioned that Stella and I bought food for my family to put into a "ten-pound-parcel".

I loved the outings on Sundays. Either we went to one of the small coves for the day including picnics and a swim or went "up to the mountains", where Jacobs had a cottage – soon the turf-fire was lit to get rid of the dampness in the house and beddings.

On some evenings I helped Charles and Philip repairing/polishing the boat (Dunlin). In August was holiday-time. We packed things together. A caravan and a tent were placed in a field in Dunmore. It was a very romantic time – I loved it. On the 17th of August 1948 there was a race in Dunmore. We had very rough weather, our mast broke and a fisherman brought the men home to savety. They were able to lend (sic) a mast from Norman Baker's second boat. My diary: Weston was quite green and yellow.

I did not feel well. But Philip was well-off. Uncle Chas came out of the tent absolutely naked as it was pooring with rain and everything would have been drenched (so A. Stella told me…)

Weston, Philip and I were playing "Halma" and they sang like in an opera higher and higher – we laughed and laughed – and had lots of fun.

My diary: Tuesday 7th July 1948: Stella and I made preparations for Philip's birthday - oh my God!, Philip came in suddenly, was astonished as he has his birthday on the 8th!!. Next time we see each other I want to see Philip's Passport!

On 7th September Weston's birthday was celebrated. He got a lovely sponge-cake with icing on it. It turned out to be as hard as stone, so we had to suck it!

The summer came to its end. I started school. Philip accompanied me to the secretary Mrs Gelesby and she led me to Mrs. Webster. The teachers and the pupils were always very nice to me. My lessons were mainly to learn English. In my form was also Brian Little. I remember the mid-day meals which I had on Thursdays with Family Smith. I think both of them were teachers. Their daughter Hazel was as old as I was. – I made many mistakes in my compositions/essays, so Mrs. Webster told me to write down all my experiences during and after the war. Today I think it was very clever of Mrs. Webster.

November 26th: A few days ago Philip got a nasty rash all over his face. On 6th of December we had a terrific and sudden thunderstorm, shortly afterwards Uncle Chas came home and told us that the flash of lightning was very near. In those days Stella, Philip and I were working on Jennifer's dollshouse. On 23rd December we celebrated her birthday. Winfried and Ortrud Fettke, both German (Strand House) came also. They made a lot of noise! Early next morning Uncle Chas and Philip went up to Dublin to fetch Weston from the boat. In the evening Philip brought Jenny to bed – she was very excited and afraid of Father Christmas! Chas and Stella with Weston went for Carol-singing – three x singing they got 20.07 shillings – a good result!

Christmasday: At about 9 o'clock Uncle Chas came down the stairs, switched on the Aga and came to my door to wish "happy Christmas". He even came into my room and gave me a kiss. After our breakfast we went into the gardenroom, where Weston had his bed – since I used his room. Underneath the Christmastree were all the gifts. I got a lot. From Philip I got a toothbrush and a bar of chocolate! My present for him were hankies! After Meeting and before we had our Christmas turkey/plumpudding Uncle Chas said "let us all think of Marianne's family in Germany". – In the evening grandparents and Dorothy/Kenneth Clay came over (with 1-year-old Rosemary) and they showed us pictures about the Libanon. *(They had just returned from heading up the Quaker Brummana High School there for a couple of years - PRJ.)* At the end of the year I helped Miss Dorothy Darton with the preparations for the New Years Party in Waterford.

People I met during this year – I don't know much about them. Fritz Marckwald, Mrs Hinze. With the Glasens I met Mrs Heinz? Hinrich. – Auntie Maria, Brian, Olof. Miss Herta Gunther? Mr. and Mrs. Frederic Jacob – Helene a German girl. Mr. and Mrs. Armstrong from Dublin. U Billi with brother. U Robin Glass. Mr. Basil, Mr. Wep (Dublin). Philip's room was done with the help of Mr. Darnelen.

"Rabbitholes", Vealstrand, Boatstrand. Mrs Herr and Dirte (Dorte?). Passage, the last point before Dunmore. "Rawlings" with their kids. Tom had a very big sailing boat with motor. Margarete-Anne. Elisabeth Gardener and Jenny must have been of the same age. F. Smelzer, Don Smeltzer and the two babies. Bessy and both Ivenskids. Mirtel, Even, Basil. Mr. Bennis and daughter. Mr Little. Mrs Drawn. Mrs Chapman. Mr & Mrs Campbell. Mrs Pool. Mr Parker (french teacher).

In 1949 Patricia Herbert *(concert pianist)* stayed with us. In February 1949 Family Dorothy/Kenneth with Rosemary left for their new home in England. On that day we got a lorry full of wood to Summerville, but on the road. So Philip through over the hedge, one piece after the other. In these days I had lunch with Cousin Dorothea; Helen Sontken, who stayed with them was soon to leave home to Germany.

9th February Philip left Tramore to go to Dublin to Basil. Hilda Marsh/Roberts stayed for the weekend. Mr and Mrs Da…y with their 2½ year-old daughter made a short visit. After school I went to Dorothy Darton to bake biscuits for my family (4 pounds!).

20th Feb. – Mrs & Mrs Jacob (Southparade) Margy, son Mark and Helene came for lunch. "Carmen" and Stella as Chorus Master was given from 21st – 26th Feb in the Royal Theatre, Waterford. 9th March – Grandpa's 81st birthday! – 17th March St Patric's day we went up to the mountains, there we met Bakers, Littles, and Grubbs. The porch was taken down, dirty and dead tired we returned home. I met Master D Walton. He could speak German very well. 13th April 1949 my schoolfriend Hannelore arrived from Germany to stay with Phillis Baker. 18th April we carried stones all day long – up at the mountains. By the end of April Philip went up to Dublin for the Yearly Meeting.

5th May Philip drove us up to Dublin. I was to stay with the Skeltons for a week. Next morning by 10 o'clock Philip fetched me. He had been staying with Cousin Basil. Basil's flat was extremely clean! We went to an exhibition for 2/6p entry fee. First looking together at everything - after lunch separately and at 4 o'clock we met again and looked at a horse-spring-show. We became quite cold. After tea in the Skelton's home Philip left. I had a nice week with the Skeltons. Stella came to Dublin to take me back home. There was also Frida Little, her mother and Richard, At 6 o'clock we were home and Uncle Chas had new teeth we also saw Philip with Robert in his MG. By the end of May I must have been jealous of Jennifer! Everybody was taking notice of her. "I" was not convinced of the correct bringing-up of Jenny! But on the other hand I loved little Jenny and we played together very well.

3rd June 1949 – Arnold, Hilda and Ethna Marsh came in the afternoon. A day later Mr and Mrs Lamb with their 2 children came also. I do not remember these people. Who was Iven Allen? I was asked whether I would help them in the house. But I didn't want to, I wanted to stay with "my" family.

15th June 1949 – Uncle Chas and Philip went to the pier to bring the small boat "Pram" into the water. 19th June after Meeting almost all things were put into Philip's small boat, which was then brought to "Sand Hills" with the van "Joe". Stella took Jenny on her cycle and I took Philip's cycle with some luggage on the backseat. In the evening we went back the same way. It must have been a lovely day.

In this summer Granny had an operation. Uncle Chas, Grandpa and Philip drove to Dublin to bring Stella and Jenny to Granny. They wanted to stay there for 1 or 2 weeks, until Granny is all right again. I met the German girl Lore Schomburg. She stayed with Bells. Mr Mrs Chapman, and William and Joy - we went with them to Kilfarrasy.

Once Hannelore and I were invited by Mr and Mrs Webster. In August the Storrars arrived with their boys Martin and David. We went for a swim to Brownstown. Mrs Storrar rubbed Jenny after the swim and on the next day – it was Stella's birthday – she said she had lost her engagement ring. In the meantime there was a race in Dunmore. Weston had also arrived from England. So only two days later we again went to Brownstown with rakes, sieves, shovels to look for the lost ring. After 10 minutes the ring was found and we were all very happy. Several times the tide had come in and gone out – it was very good luck to find the ring. After a few days Mr and Mrs Storrar went out by bike and returned quite pale after a while. They have seen an accident: the milkman came round the corner too quickly and fell on its side. The milkboy – about 13 – was severely hurt. Half his brain was seen.

21st August: last day with the Storrars. Philip went to a good place for David to dive in Dunmore. The others were sailing with Dunlin.

In September 1949 Sally and Bernet were in Midvale and on 8th Philip packed up his most needed things, put them on his bike and drove off "as happy as can be" to Shanagarry and Co.

11th September was the day Robert wanted to kiss me and I refused. "Oh no Robert, I am much too young for that, I am only 17!". Today I am laughing about this, but in those days I was a child, although my body did not look like a child. During this time we very often went for plucking blackberries, also with Grandpa. 19th September: the postman brought the news: I have the permission to go to England for a short visit. On Sunday 3rd October we went up to the mountains the very last time, on Monday I said good-bye to so many good friends. I got some presents – from Jim Sexton a small watch – In Midvale I said good-bye. Later on – I was already in bed – Granny came into my room. She hugged and kissed me and said "we will always love you". My last food were chopps. Philip was feeling alright, but I was very upset. On the 4th October we were brought to the boat in Waterford. So many friends said good-bye, I had great difficulties to hold back my tears. On the boat we met Declan Walton and his friend. At 2 o'clock we arrived in England,

We sat in the train with Declan and friend. In the morning we had our breakfast in the train. At 11 o'clock we were in London. Philip brought me to Liverpool Street and waited for my train to Chelmsford. He helped me into the train and said "good-bye". I felt very sad to say good-bye – he was the last member of my beloved family Jacob.

I came to Ireland as a very shy child. And the little English I knew helped me to overcome my shyness. The Jacob family were very kind and understanding people. You never gave me the feeling I am a stranger. I am sure it was not always so easy for Stella to have me around her. Very seldom I got homesick. I think I never made the first step to get home again. I think my parents made it. Perhaps it was a good ting to help Dorothy before going back to Germany. Dorothy and Kenneth were also very friendly and I loved little Rosemary. While Dorothy was in hospital I was staying with Sally and Bernet, of course with Rosemary. I learnt a lot of things about bringing up children which helped me in the school to become a Kindergarten-teacher.

One thing which was very embarrassing; Dorothy went to the baby-Elizabeth-check-up together with me and Rosemary and somebody said something….. that Dorothy is the granny and I am the young mother.

I continued to keep a diary for the 6 months with Dorothy and Kenneth in Chelmsford before I returned to Germany, but I must have lost the pages.

Explanatory notes by PRJ

"the Glas Family" – Billy & Maria Glass and their children Hjordis, Brian and Olaf, recently arrived from England.
"Mrs Gelesby" – Gladys Gillespie, Newtown School Secretary (and much much more!), who later married Liam Glynn.
"the Glasens" – the Glass family as above.
"Miss Herta Gunther" – daughter of Herr Gunter, a German refugee who for a short while taught at Newtown.

"Mr Basil" – Basil Jacob, Charles Jacob's first cousin.
"Mr Wep" – either Leonard or Watson Webb, Quakers from Dublin.
"Mirtel" – Myrtle Allen (nee Hill), Ivan's wife.
"Even" – Ivan Allen, Quaker, later owner of Ballymaloe Hotel & Restaurant.
"Mr Bennis & daughter" – Ernest Bennis a Quaker from Limerick (very elderly, with a fine white beard) who I think was the Marriage Registrar in Limerick when Marianne's parents Ernst and Irmgard were married there in 1928 [?], with Charles and Kathleen Jacob as witnesses. His daughter was Emilie.
"Mrs Drawn" – Mrs Drohan, a farmer's widow near "the Cottage" in the Comeragh Mountains, who was so kind to us children when we stayed at "the Cottage".
"for 2/6p entry fee" – Half a Crown entry fee to the RDS Spring Show, equivalent to 15 cent today.
"with the van Joe" – our Jowett Bradford van with a 2-cylinder horizontally opposed engine, which Stella affectionately christened Joey.
"Sally & Bernet" – Bernard & Sally Jacob (Uncle Bernard was Charles Jacob's brother, and was a teacher at Saffron Walden Friends School).
Miscellaneous – I am not sure who a number of the other people Marianne mentions are.

The Fischer Family, August 1954, Marianne is second from left.

And finally!

Weston Jacob astride his BSA Motorcycle, in the 1950s.